Dissecting the Danchi

"Dissecting the Danchi' takes an unusually in-depth and insightful look behind closed doors of Japanese state-subsidised, suburban housing estates. These buildings were once the pinnacle of modernity and innovation, but the aging structures and their 'unconventional' inhabitants have long since become stigmatised and labelled as undesirable by the mainstream. The book is endlessly rich and unique in that it combines Knoroz' imaginative architectural perspective with the kind of deep ethnography that many anthropologists aspire to. A brilliant bonus lies in her unveiling of "Devicology"; a new methodology to study interior environments more effectively and positively impact on regeneration policies. This is a fascinating and much-needed study of contemporary Japanese homes that will engage readers interested in urban housing issues worldwide as well as those drawn to the complexities and ambiguities of Japanese society."

—Inge Daniels, *Professor of Anthropology, University of Oxford, Author of The Japanese House, Material Culture in the Modern Home*

"Devicology, a word that Tatiana Knoroz coined with reference to Wajiro Kon's notion of Modernology (kō-gen-gaku), might be translated into Japanese as "inventive science" (kō-an-gaku): the study of ingenuous gimmicks responding to a given situation. In this book, Knoroz traces the mixture of hope, irony, and despair in the history of danchi housing complexes, but then takes us inside those buildings to reveal a new style of living—one that may no longer be hopeful, restricted by systems that prohibit self-renovation and refurbishment, but nor is it hopeless, based as it is on flexibility, convenience, temporariness, and low cost. Such lifestyles are filled with the wisdom and universal ingenuity that keeps reappearing throughout human history."

—Kiyoshi Sey Takeyama, *Architect, Professor Emeritus of Kyoto University*

"There is a purist position that architecture is unable to solve social problems. Disproving any such architectural autonomy, Tatiana Knoroz shows in Dissecting the Danchi how Japan's model minimum dwelling, the 2DK apartment—assembled into danchi, the postwar low-rise "new town" developments built around the nation—has been solution, problem, and now a type with an ambiguous status in Japanese society. At a time with a renewed interest in government support of progressive housing, the book thankfully illuminates a key area in the history and present reality of Japanese housing that is unfortunately far overshadowed (at least in English-language sources) by a focus on pristine and extreme private houses. The danchi is dissected indeed, with valuable insights from vernacular responses to climate, the economics of building height, the pathologizing of danchi in Japanese films, to fieldwork with present-day danchi residents. The architect-anthropologist Wajiro Kon, an influence on Knoroz, felt it was critical to listen directly to the people you were designing for. Knoroz's work reveals that even if listened to, it can be difficult to get residents to speak, a challenge provoking her exploration of multiple approaches to engagement, helping us better understand danchi life, and more generally, a challenge of participatory housing design."

—Casey Mack, *Architect, Author of Digesting Metabolism*

Tatiana Knoroz

Dissecting the Danchi

Inside Japan's Largest Postwar Housing Experiment

palgrave
macmillan

Tatiana Knoroz
Kyoto University
Kyoto, Japan

ISBN 978-981-16-8459-3 ISBN 978-981-16-8460-9 (eBook)
https://doi.org/10.1007/978-981-16-8460-9

Cover credit: Created by Tatiana Knoroz

This Palgrave Macmillan imprint is published by the registered company Springer Nature Singapore Pte Ltd.
The registered company address is: 152 Beach Road, #21-01/04 Gateway East, Singapore 189721, Singapore

Acknowledgments

This book would not be possible without the unwavering support of Prof. Thomas Daniell, who in the past three years took my understanding of Japanese architecture to a whole new level and gave countless advices on academic writing. His help with text editing and words of encouragement is truly invaluable. Thank you for generously sharing your time with me and I hope we will be able to work together again in the future.

Many thanks go to Prof. Gaia Caramellino, who introduced me to the topic of Japanese housing back in 2017. As an expert in the history of postwar mass housing, she patiently advised me on the methodology for the initial stages of my research. Although we couldn't meet in person most of the times, our video meetings meant a lot for my work.

I am indebted to Yohei Suzuki and his friends, who were helping me throughout my entire fieldwork process in Ibaraki Prefecture, as well as Ren Naka, who traveled from Tokyo to interpret the interviews and assisted with filming during my second site visit, and Pavel Io, who kindly helped me with translating and transcribing the interview videos and recordings. Conducting fieldwork in a foreign language is an exhausting task and I couldn't have done it without you all. I also would like to thank all the danchi residents who agreed to show their apartments and give interviews, which wasn't easy for many of them. I do not mention their full names anywhere in the text and some names have been changed completely to protect their privacy.

Special thanks go to Kenichi Yoshinaga for agreeing to share his professional insights on danchi, as well as allowing me to reproduce the danchi plan drawings from his *Danchi zukai* book and the photographs of his renovations. Moreover, I would like to thank Mitsuhiro Sakakibara from RAD for connecting me with Mr. Yoshinaga, and for his brainstorming suggestions that guided me during the development of the new interior analysis method. I am also very grateful to Asako Yamamoto for her interview about municipal danchi renovation in Kyoto.

My deepest gratitude goes to Shigeru Matsumoto, the vice manager of Uzō Nishiyama Memorial Library, who passionately shared his knowledge of Nishiyama's research and gave permission to reproduce rare photographs and drawings from the archive to illustrate the book. Similarly, I would like to thank Kōichi Tanohata from UR, Mr. Tanaka from Wajirō Kon Memorial Archive in Kōgakuin University, and Souta Mori from nmstudio architects for the images copyright permissions.

Some sections of this book have grown out of my papers published in Strelka Magazine, Log 51 and Optimistic Suburbia 2 Conference proceedings. I would like to thank all the editors for their insightful comments.

Last but not least, gratitude beyond measure goes to my husband Ian for his continuous help with interpreting, handling image use permissions, copyediting and solving technical issues, as well as emotionally supporting me throughout the entire book writing period. The world pandemic has been a huge challenge with many plans and aspirations shattered, but thanks to you I could always feel I am not alone and succeed in finishing this work.

Introduction

Japan is often portrayed as a country where robots, crazy gadgets, cutting-edge engineering, and million-dollar corporations elegantly coexist with centuries-old cultural heritage and striking achievements in contemporary art, design, and fashion. The consistency of this globally established image is quite recent; in fact, it is an artificially achieved result of the Cool Japan campaign started in the 1990s that attempted to compensate Japan's industrial economic losses with the assertion of soft power through media export and cultural dissemination (Sugimoto, 2014). While you might find all of the promised technological advancements and other "coolness" when visiting the most popular neighborhoods of Tokyo, day-to-day life in other parts of Japan is still full of twentieth-century remnants. Many shops, supermarkets, and fast-food chains only accept cash payments. Opening a bank account without a custom-made personal stamp might turn out to be harder than storing all of your money under a mattress. Receiving any kind of governmental service requires a stack of filled out forms and certificates, and some important correspondence can only happen by fax or postal mail.

Outside of Shibuya's and Shinjuku's skyscraper districts, Japanese urban environments can also be strikingly retro. Leaving the centers of big cities will get you immersed into faceless rows of cookie-cutter townhouses occasionally pierced by dusty shops with outdated electrical appliances, and faded posters featuring smiling candidates of municipal elections from ten years ago.

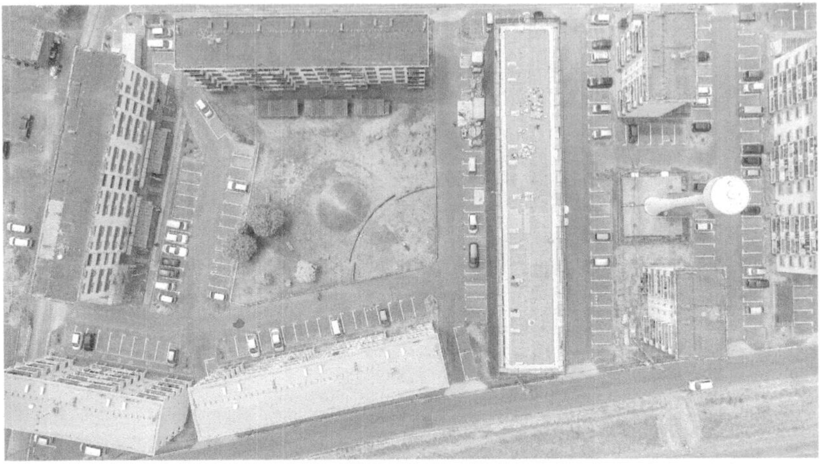

Fig. 1 Wakamiya Danchi, drone footage by Yohei Suzuki, 2017 (*Source* courtesy of Yohei Suzuki)

If you wander around those suburban areas long enough, you will surely stumble upon neighborhoods consisting of uniform gray concrete apartment blocks which may remind of Soviet *khrushchevkas*—one of the most famous postwar housing typologies. Thousands of similar projects were built all over Japan from the 1950s and into the late 1970s to solve the housing crisis which took place in the aftermath of WWII. Originally celebrated by the public as a highly desirable living environment, *danchi* are currently becoming a popular backdrop for contemporary horror movies and a source of various problems for the local governments, just like their prototypes in Europe (Knoroz, 2019).

With monotonous concrete slabs sometimes arranged into enclaves or small satellite cities (Figs. 1–2), these multi-story mass housing estates were designed and constructed by the local municipalities and the semi-private Japan Housing Corporation (JHC) as a partial solution to the

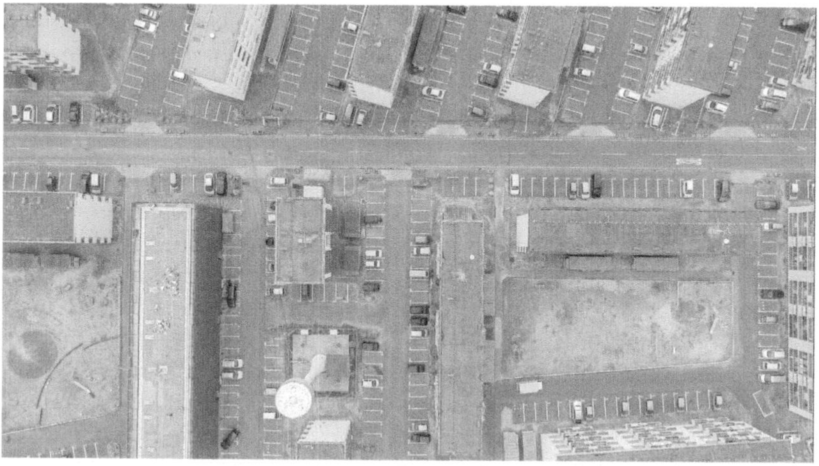

Fig. 2 Wakamiya Danchi, drone footage by Yohei Suzuki, 2017 (*Source* courtesy of Yohei Suzuki)

postwar housing crisis. Despite the small number of completed danchi,[1] clever advertising campaigns and publication in popular media increased their impact on residential design, domestic culture, and the establishment of a Japanese middle class (Nietzel, 2016). Their architecture was directly inspired by European and Soviet[2] modernist housing models, with one significant difference: as they were intended for short-term tenancy, the units had comparatively small floor areas. Every danchi dweller was assumed to be saving to purchase a house, thereby freeing their apartment for the next person to take a step up the "housing ladder" promoted by the Japanese government (ibid.).

[1] 1.13 million units were built between 1955 and 1983 (*A Quick Look at Housing in Japan*. 1985. Tokyo: Ministry of Construction), and as of 2015 there were more than 750,000 rental units managed by the Urban Renaissance Agency alone ("Profile of UR", Urban Renaissance Agency, https://www.ur-net.go.jp/profile/english/pdf/profile_en_all.pdf).

[2] Read more about the Soviet influence in Chapter 2.

Given the short life span of buildings in Japan, nobody expected these homes for young nuclear families (usually a white-collar salaryman, a housewife, and two kids) to survive more than half a century, let alone become permanently occupied by a very different population, as they did after the asset bubble burst in 1991. In the following "Lost Decade"[3] of economic stagnation, full-time employment and the birthrate fell, while the percentage of citizens 65 or older drastically increased. For many financially struggling elderly people, single parent families, and socially excluded groups, such as low-ranking yakuza or former criminals, municipal danchi became the only accessible rental housing in the country because most landlords avoid unemployed or otherwise disadvantaged tenants (Izuhara, 2000; Murakami, 2018; Ōnishi, 2017; Yasuda, 2019).

When I came to Japan in 2018 to start my research, most municipal governments were disinclined to propose regeneration strategies, in the hope that potential economic growth and housing demand will lead to total demolition and new construction. Similar in quality and scale postwar mass housing projects in Russia are normally owner-occupied and in most cases are not considered socially problematic by the public, but the government has the same demolition-oriented attitude toward them. *Khruschevka* demolitions in Moscow got especially intensive from 2017, and were met with active opposition from the apartment-owners and people interested in the protection of the architectural heritage and existing urban environment. The political clash produced a wide media coverage of both the negative and the positive sides of life contained in the standard plans of the postwar mass housing in Russia. Similarly, European modernist heritage of the same period have been getting an increasing public attention since the early 2010s, and are often used as regeneration study projects in architectural universities in Western Europe. Surprisingly, the new wave of state-subsidized danchi residents was still largely ignored by the Japanese-language media in 2018. This lower intensity of coverage compared with the Western cases was what started my initial interest in the topic.

As a person who grew up in a Soviet *khruschevka*, I was overcome with nostalgia when I visited a danchi neighborhood for the first time and encountered intimately familiar architectural elements such as entrances,

[3] Some economists believe that the recession has not ended and use the term "lost 30 years".

stairs, buildings' overall proportions, and the shape of the open spaces between them. According to the plans, however, the interiors look nothing like their Western counterparts and it was hard to imagine how they got adapted to the contemporary life by their new users. Intrigued by the stigmas of poverty and immorality that adhere to state-subsidized (or Publicly Operated) danchi, I began investigating their history, what happens behind these concrete walls and how this postwar apartment model is being inhabited by people who were not the designers' intended occupants (Knoroz, 2021). This book attempts to summarize the results of this research and produce a comprehensive architectural outlook on the origins, the current state and the possible future of danchi with a particular focus on their interiors, that once radically transformed lifestyles of an entire nation and started a revolution in the Japanese housing industry, but now are facing an uncertain future.

Unlike European modernist projects that replaced earlier apartment buildings, danchi didn't have an established precedent typology in Japan and produced a much deeper disjuncture in the course of local architectural history and living patterns. To position the development of danchi designs and the public's reaction to them in appropriate context, Chapter 1 provides an overview of the fundamental architectural traits of traditional Japanese residences and prewar typologies, that became the point of departure for the postwar mass housing.

Combining governmental, architectural, and social perspectives, Chapter 2 traces the history of danchi from the birth of their original standard plans and related housing policies to their present state popular media image and recently finished renovation projects. This chapter uncovers the architectural meanings behind the most recurrent danchi design elements, follows the timeline of the gradual change in their evaluation by the public, and sheds light on their newly re-discovered advantages in the contemporary renovations.

Written in first-person narrative, Chapter 3 shift the focus to the currently inhabited interiors by presenting the results of ethnographic fieldwork carried out in state-subsidized Wakamiya Danchi (Figs. 1–2) from 2018 to 2019. Unexpected gaps in the interviews and peculiar lifestyles of socially disadvantaged current tenants lead me to invent a multidisciplinary methodology for an architectural evaluation of rental postwar mass housing interiors that can make their adaptation to our rapidly changing post-industrial society more effective and assist in a development of better renovation strategies in the future.

Transliteration Note

The book uses the Hepburn system with the long vowels indicated by a macron (e.g., shōji) for Japanese transliteration, except when words are commonly used in English with a different spelling (e.g., Kyoto). All Japanese names are given in the Western order (e.g., Uzō Nishiyama). Common Japanese nouns are written in italic and proper nouns in regular font. English plural endings are not used for Japanese words (e.g., three tatami, two *fusuma*). For the sake of convenience, due to frequent use in this book, the word "danchi" is written in regular font, and since it is defined as "a cluster of high-rise multi-apartment buildings with shared facilities," the plural ending is never added.

References

Izuhara, M. (2000). *Change and housing in post-war Japanese society: The experiences of older women*. Routledge.

Knoroz, T. (2019). The rise and fall of danchi, Japan's largest social housing experiment. *Strelka Magazine*. https://strelkamag.com/en/article/the-rise-and-fall-of-danchi-japan-s-largest-social-housing-experiment.

Knoroz, T. (2021). Devicology. *Log, 51*. Anyone Corporation.

Murakami, S. (2018). Danchi highlight complexity of Japan's interculturalism. *Japan Times*. https://features.japantimes.co.jp/danchi/.

Neitzel, L. L. (2016). *The life we longed for: Danchi housing and the middle class dream in postwar Japan*. MerwinAsia.

Ōnishi, N. (2017). A generation in Japan faces a lonely death. *The New York Times*. https://www.nytimes.com/2017/11/30/world/asia/japan-lonely-deaths-the-end.html.

Sugimoto, Y. (2014). *An introduction to Japanese society* (4th ed.). Cambridge University Press.

Yasuda, K. (2019). *Danchi to imin kadai saisentan "kūkan" no tatakai*. Kadokawa.

Contents

About the Author

Tatiana Knoroz is a scholar with a special interest in Japanese housing, anthropology of lived space and built environment.

List of Figures

CHAPTER 1

Japanese Prewar Housing: Missing Context

Approaching Japanese Architecture from the West

To a reader who grew up inside or in visual proximity to mass housing in Europe or the United States, living in unit plans of apartment buildings appears to be a natural trait of urban life since the beginning of the twentieth century. Seen within this Western continuous architectural context, the fate of danchi estates in Japan and the testimonies of their residents may be labeled as quite an "ordinary" chapter of the modernist housing storyline, and therefore seriously misinterpreted. Unlike other countries with modernist heritage, apart from a few careful experiments in the 1920s, Japan did not implement mass concrete construction for multi-story apartments until the postwar period.

Moreover, pre-existing residential typologies were so poorly adaptable to a high-density solid wall box structure imported from the West that their clash produced a deep rupture in local architectural criticism and traditional domestic culture, which can't be attributed to the postwar situation in Europe or North America because there the paradigm shift of modernization emerged locally and therefore in a more gradual manner before WWII.

To better understand the impact of danchi as the main vehicle of this drastic change, it is important to approach the topic from an overview of the concepts that formed traditional housing designs and the perception

T. Knoroz, *Dissecting the Danchi*,
https://doi.org/10.1007/978-981-16-8460-9_1

of residential spaces in Japan before they were challenged by the postwar reality.

What comes to your mind when you think about traditional Japanese architecture? Most people mention *wabi-sabi*, tea houses, tatami, and wooden temples. "Japanesessness" of paper partitions, wood-bamboo aesthetics, and minimalist interiors inspire architects and artists from all around the world, but these are mere visual manifestations of an underlying logical structure that evolved over the centuries to replicate functional homes, ensuring survival in Japanese environmental and social climate. The de-contextualized "quintessential traits" of Japanese architecture have been mythologized in both academic and popular literature in the West since the beginning of the twentieth century (Daniels, 2010). In order to see the big picture of meanings behind the already familiar yet disconnected architectural elements disseminated in the Western media, we must cast aside all those images first because they are superimposed on our system of values that has very little to do with their origins and purpose.

Frequent interactions through trade, religion, and consumption of popular content made a group of human collectives with shared social structures that we now refer to as the "Western people" operate within a comprehensive set of common values that are almost impossible for its users to synthesize without going outside of the Western context first. It is difficult to become aware of the existence of these values when phrases such as "time is money" and "sleeping in class is inappropriate" sound entirely reasonable in both a major American city and a tiny Italian village. Fundamental assumptions of a certain society at a given period, or "episteme" as defined by Michel Foucault, are usually a result of historical and environmental factors (Foucault, 1988). Of course, Italy and the United States have different climatic conditions even within the confines of one country and drastically different histories and thus possess very diverse cultures. However, zooming out, you'll find that most of the commonsense values are still similar. To give a brief structured outlook on Japanese housing history, I chose to use the term "episteme" instead of a more generic "culture" to focus more on the fundamental logic of architectural thinking, its theoretical skeleton, rather than the entire complexity of its cultural components that will take another book to uncover.[1]

[1] For an anthropological investigation of a Japanese home, refer to Inge Daniel's book "The Japanese House: Material Culture in the Modern Home" (Daniels, 2010).

Let's examine a few everyday life episteme examples outside of architecture. In a Western country, if one person usually finishes his tasks at the office faster and works more efficiently than others, chances are he can get permission to go home earlier with a possible promotion in the future, or at least a good word from his superiors. However, in most Japanese companies, he would probably be given more work with no encouragement and some perplexed looks from his colleagues, who suddenly received unwanted pressure to perform better by his outlying behavior. The practice of *tsukiai zangyō*, translated as "collective overtime work" when employees can't go home on time out of guilt for "letting down" their colleagues and superiors who are still in the office, is very common in Japanese corporate environments, where time is not always money (Ono, 2018). While in Western universities, it is rude to nod off in class, none of my Japanese professors ever scolded anyone sleeping during the lectures, and many students did this in a shamelessly obvious manner right in the front row. Right now, this attitude is undergoing changes as a result of ongoing Westernization in academic institutions, but there is still a persistent belief that sleeping in class can get you a reputation of an especially hard-working student because it implies you had studied until late the night before (Steger, 2003).

These cultural "common sense" inconsistencies illustrate the fact that Japan historically had very few contacts with the Western civilization prior to the Meiji period (1868–1912), and its current episteme is at least partially based on something nurtured independently from the West: native occurrences and Chinese and Korean influences. Japan managed to avoid both Christianity and cultural-economical connections with the West for the major part of its history. Religious differences seem to be a particularly important factor since many Western fundamental a priori beliefs originate from Christian doctrines, whose influence goes far beyond the confines of the religious community. The impact of Christianity on Western civilization extends from our ideas of human rights to what we think of as acceptable behavior in public. Regardless of the actual level of our personal belief in God, biblical parables play a role in what we think of as good and evil. Take the "Good Samaritan," for example, wherein the main moral is that we should help people in distress even if they're complete strangers of inimical beliefs and culture. It does not matter even if a particular person has never heard of the parable itself because its idea is embedded in every Western mind as "basic ethics" thanks to our ancestors. Most would still run to help a heavily wounded person who had got into an accident even if they end up late for work because it is an acceptable excuse for most employers. But in Japan, it is not always the case again. Some victims of the 1995 Tokyo metro gas attack recall that when already seriously poisoned with sarin, they finally managed to get out on the street, most of them crawling or kneeling on the ground, crowds of commuters were rushing to work right beside them as if they were in a parallel disconnected world, as Haruki Murakami describes in *Underground*, one of his few non-fiction books, based on the interviews he conducted with 60 victims of the attack. This seeming indifference is explained by a different cultural code: being late for the start of the working day is an inexcusable transgression in the Japanese corporate environment, especially so in the 1980s and 1990s; and if a person decides to help someone, they feel that they are obliged to do it until the issue is completely resolved, meaning going with the victim in the hospital and staying until his relatives come—a commitment that not everyone can grant to a stranger at the expense of their reputation in the office.

Apart from the logic of social behavior, the difference in episteme can inevitably be seen in architecture and especially housing, a physical product and a stage for this behavior (Fig. 1.1). While it is certainly possible to compare modernist housing models within the context of Europe and America without preparatory studies of local architectural traditions and climate, using the same framework for making assumptions about Japanese case studies may lead to confusion.

The comparative relevance of researching postwar mass housing is itself a good example of the problem. In Europe, modernist architecture is recognized as cultural heritage, so generally, it is easy to find public support for preserving and reusing postwar mass housing, as well as organizing lectures on the subject and writing articles for architectural magazines. At the same time, in Japan, many colleagues questioned the relevance of my danchi research because until recently, there was a prevailing preference for demolishing and rebuilding residential architecture as soon as it was deemed technologically or ideologically outdated. While shrines, temples, and other public monuments are generally accepted as architectural heritage, common people's housing in Japan is regarded as temporary and eventually disposable. Even something as old and culturally valuable as wooden *machiya* townhouses, a defining architectural feature of Kyoto, were widely destroyed or heavily altered for the sake of promoting commercial activities on the streets in the late 1990s and the early 2000s. *Machiya* were finally given some protection and

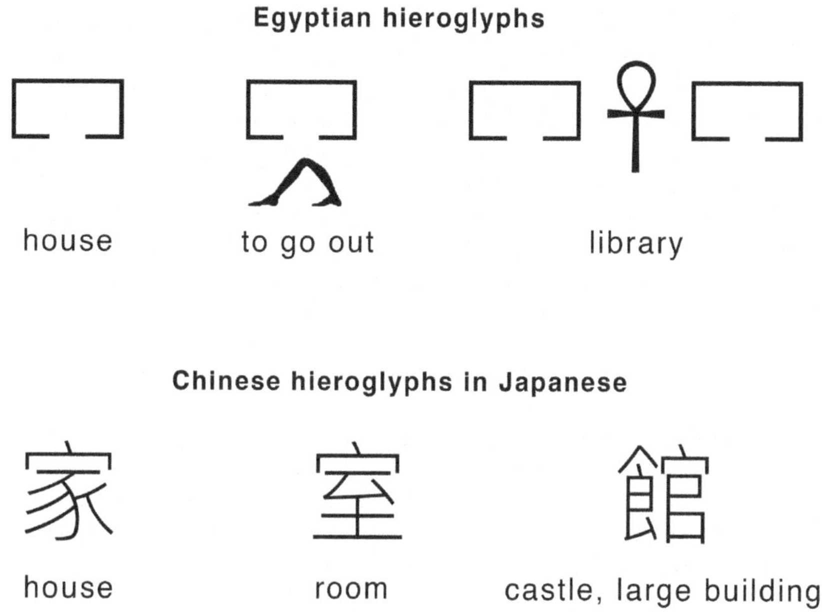

Fig. 1.1 A lingustic example of different architectural epistemes. The Egyptian civilization focused on the walls' enclosure when hieroglyphically depicting a house, while the ancient Chinese envisioned buildings primarily in section, emphasizing the roof

financial support by a private fund only in 2005. Sixteen Dōjunkai Apartments, the first reinforced-concrete public housing complexes from the 1920s and one of the most notable architectural experiments of prewar Japan, having survived the wartime bombing, were all sold to private corporations and torn down for site redevelopments in the period from 1984 until 2013. Postwar modernist projects are even further away from receiving any public protection in this sense. It was hard to understand and accept this urge for constant renewal at the expense of historical values when I just started my research in Japan, but soon I discovered specific environmental reasons behind the local architectural episteme that fully justify such attitudes toward reuse, preservation, and other important ideas concerning the treatment of the built environment.

In European universities, architectural history courses are usually taught based on detailed studies of relevant historical periods and important exchanges with other cultures that a particular country or culture might have had. One rarely starts by analyzing climatic conditions as the primary influence on architectural styles in Europe, as we tend to take for granted generally mild weather and relatively homogeneous continental natural environment. However, teaching the history of prewar Japanese architecture from the perspective of Chinese and Korean influences and religious and cultural tendencies might not be as effective when addressing a foreign audience for the first time, especially in terms of housing history, which didn't rely on Asian mainland prototypes as much as Buddhist architecture. Japanese residential interiors, building materials, and ways of living can be faster understood as a derivative of a different architectural logic, or episteme, influenced by island environment with its geographical isolation from the continent, its extreme weather conditions such as typhoons, rainy seasons, summer humidity, as well as frequent earthquakes and very intensive variations of topography and flora even within small regions.

A Quick Look at Japanese Traditional Housing

Minimalism and Temporality against Humid Heat

Japanese Islands are situated in the middle of the Pacific high-pressure zone, affected by the East Asian monsoon belt. Because of this particular location, there are six seasons: four temperate ones as in continental Europe, plus the rainy and the typhoon seasons. They form a distinct cyclical rhythm that puts people's lifestyles in a much more dependent position with nature than on the continent. The most difficult period to survive through and maintain buildings starts in late May with the rainy season, which is immediately followed by high humidity and scorching heat of summertime that extends until late September, creating ideal conditions for the breeding of bugs and development of mold. In the summer months, the air's mugginess is so heavy that women's long hair can mildew if not properly dried, which is hard to imagine in continental climatic zones of European countries (Kōji, 1981). The growth of various types of micro-fungi is further facilitated by relatively mild winters with above zero temperatures. In such a climate, enclosed structures made from stone or bricks will be gradually destroyed by mold and micro-flora from the inside, rendering the interiors unlivable.

The first settlements of Honshu Island in the early Jōmon period (5000–2500 BC), however, did not need to solve this environmental problem for a couple of thousand years. As Jōmon people had not discovered agriculture at the time, they preferred to settle and forage in the central mountain areas with less humidity and more wind than the plains and the forests on the seashores, where their descendants would relocate later. Jōmon dwellings took the form of pit huts with wooden frameworks of poles fixed in the ground, crossed at the top, and covered with grass, which provided all the necessary protection from the mountain weather (Fig. 1.2). The huts were sunken in the ground and did not allow much freedom for ventilation, but they always had their entrances oriented toward the southeast, from where most of the summer winds came. Heavy grass roofs were changed regularly to prevent deterioration since the material was easily accessible.

Since the Yayoi period (300 BC–300 AD), when the rice cultivation was introduced to western Japan from mainland Asia, the indigenous people came down from the mountains, and their Neolithic pit huts had to adapt to a change of geographical location as well as a global climatic warming trend that happened at that time. The floor was raised to the ground level, and grass roofs were upgraded with an opening at the top for passive cooling, similar to wind towers in the middle east. To protect the grain from small animals and humidity, a raised-floor granary structure was imported from China or Korea for rice storage. The structure's effectiveness against the problem of the mold first repurposed it into a popular residential typology for religious purposes and among the richer

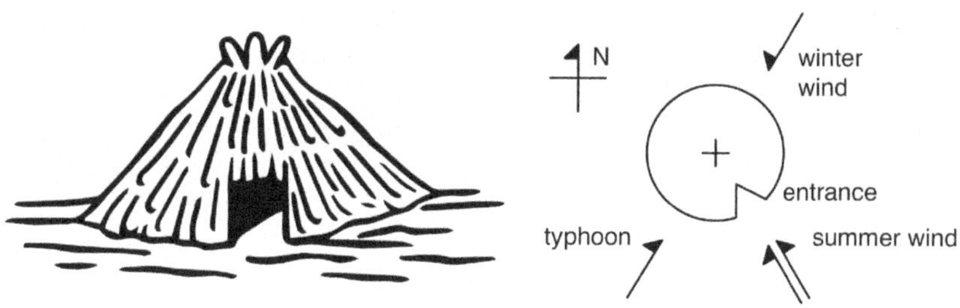

Fig. 1.2 An early Jōmon dwelling, elevation and top view

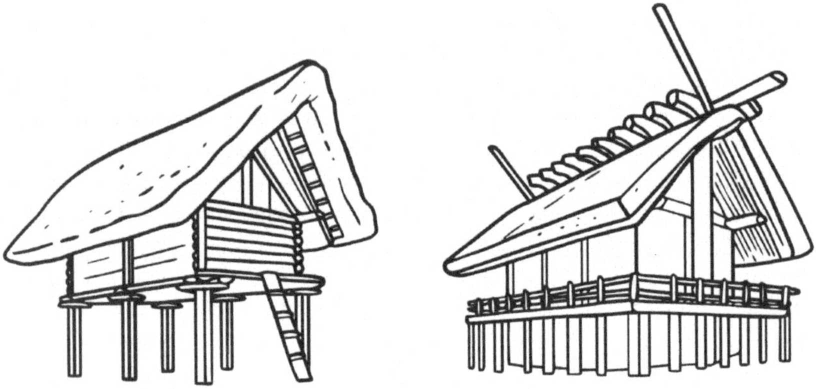

Fig. 1.3 Left: Yayoi Komegura Granary. Right: The main building of Ise Shrine

families, but soon slightly raised floors with a central enclosed plaster-walled room, surrounded by open spaces with movable partitions on the perimeter under one roof, became a widespread religious building and housing template for all strata of early Japanese society (Fig. 1.3).

Essays in Idleness (*Tsurezuregusa*), a document written by a Japanese monk Kenkō Yoshida around 1330 AD, states that "when building a house, it should be designed to suit the summer. In winter one can live anywhere, but in the hot weather an uncomfortable house is indeed trying" (Porter, 1914). The ancient Japanese houses were built with the assumption, that human body can bear the difficulties of cold with the aid of clothing and fireplaces, while rain and humid heat can only be dealt with by proper construction: a massive roof and openable walls allowing full ventilation. Fast rotting of infills and the breeding of fungi also generally discouraged the use of paints, varnishes, and waterproof finishes, leaving all the building's elements open to inspection.[2] Contrary to layered walls common in European architecture, here material deterioration signs of the structure could be easily noticed in early stages and instantly replaced. The designs of postwar danchi buildings followed the

[2] *Shoin-zukuri* architecture in the late sixteenth century challenged this original attitute with painted partitions, coffer ceilings and the use of decorative gold elements, still structural wooden elements in principle would never be treated.

same logic: there was a minimum of finishing on plain concrete exteriors; piping and electrical connections were installed on the wall surfaces.[3]

Strict observance of both in-house and street cleanliness and the obsession with newness in Japanese culture are usually attributed to religious practices, but Shinto philosophy, in fact, can be seen as naturally evolved guidelines to survival in the local environment rather than an organized religion (Hendry, 2019; Nute, 2004). Keeping inhabited interiors free of bulky furniture is a great way to continuously control the condition of all surfaces and corners while rebuilding houses or their parts every 15–20 years was the best solution for accumulating mold and insect damage. The tradition of dismantling and completely rebuilding the Ise Shrine, one of the most important religious sites in Japan, every twenty years on an adjacent site may be well in accordance with Shinto's cyclical understanding of life, but in this short span of time, the shrine's straw roof and untreated wooden posts get visibly decayed, and rebuilding is simply unavoidable. An even costlier religious custom of moving and rebuilding the capital city after the emperor's death up until AD 710 may have similar hidden practical implications.

Timber, Modular Construction and Heavy Roofs Against Nature's Mechanical Forces

Another environmental problem for house maintenance in Japan is typhoons, especially in coastal areas, and frequent earthquakes that pose serious mechanical damage risks to any type of construction. To protect themselves from destructive winds, people in ancient Japan tended to settle around groves or forests, using them both as shields and as construction materials due to convenient proximity. Wood was found to resist earthquakes much better than stone masonry, which fails easily under lateral stresses and is harder to extract. Common Japanese types of wood such as cryptomeria, pine, and cypress (*hinoki*) are highly resistant to insects and mold and can be harvested after just 40 years of growth. Even if eventually rotten, any wooden detail in a house may be replaced with a new one without destroying the entire structure. The choice of wood as the main building material was further supported by its availability: thanks to the generally warm humid climate, even

[3] This trait makes danchi facades visually far more similar to cheaply produced Soviet *khruschevkas*, than the more elaborate Western modernist housing.

now approximately 70% of Japanese islands are covered by dense forests (Forestry Agency, 2019).

At the same time, metal fasteners and nails were not used as much as in medieval Europe and continental Asia since they are loosened by daily and seasonal expansions and contractions of wood and get rapidly rusted in the Japanese climate. Moreover, metal joints restrict wood's adjustment to movement and break easily during earthquakes, so Japanese craftsmen perfected ***kigumi***, all-wood interlocking joints.

The need to avoid metal was not the only motivation for the evolution of extra-complicated systems of timber connections. The constant danger of strong winds and long rainfalls urged the development of heavy cantilevered roofs, impossible without an elaborate supporting structure. Originally imported from China with the Buddhist architecture, ***tokyō*** (also called ***kumimono***) interlocking bracket systems allowed redistribution of the roof's weight into the horizontal directions with the use of ***odaruki*** tail rafters and thereby increased the stability of the entire structure (Fig. 1.4). Japanese carpenters perfected ***tokyō*** by adding more layers and cantilevered members to the system to create even larger overhangs required by the climate (Sakamoto, 2018a).

Contrary to the principles of Western masonry, which assume that all the walls are built first and covered with the roof at the very end, traditional Japanese timber construction requires raising the roof as the

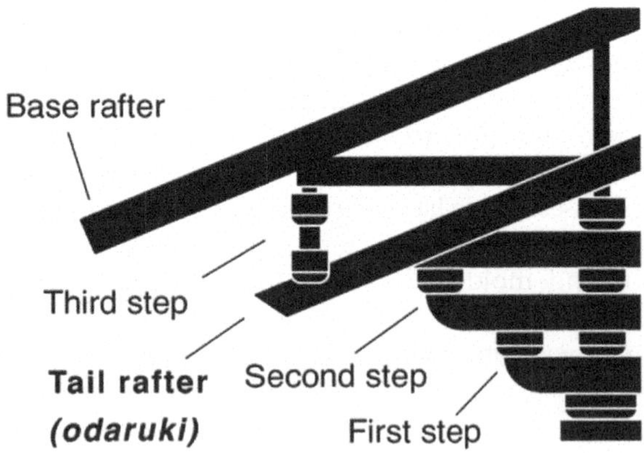

Fig. 1.4 *Mitesaki tokyō*—three-step bracket system (Redrawn from an original by Urashimataro, CC licence)

most important element for weather protection of the initial post-and-beam framework on the ground. Such building order results in a greater conceptual unity of interior space under the roof, which could be divided later but is always perceived as initially whole.

For the convenience of the building process and ease of eventual additions or replacements, spatial intervals between the posts, called *ma*, were kept equal by the carpenters throughout an entire village and even regions. Since large roofs supported by posts with equal distances between them provided enough protection from the rain, there was no need for fixed solid walls anymore, and instead, a variety of flexible partitions made from light materials such as paper and bamboo could be used to achieve better air circulation during the summer season. In winter and during strong winds, the exterior layer of partitions could be replaced with sturdier wooden shutters of the same sizes.

The techniques gained such an astonishing complexity over time that it became impossible for an ordinary villager to replicate some of the details. During the Heian period (794–1185), carpenter guilds started reproducing the nuances of woodwork in secret technical scrolls that were passed down for generations of professionals (Sakamoto, 2018b). These craftsmen were the main source of the entire country's housing production up until WWII. According to the Japanese National Census, in 1930, there was one professional carpenter for every 140 people living in Japan (Matsumura, 2019). After the war, with the development of concrete construction industry, their number significantly dropped; however, the "unified" perception of interior space, the use of standardized construction modules, and shared proportion systems has continued to be a persistent characteristic of postwar Japanese architecture, including danchi designs.

The visual and constructive "uniqueness" of traditional Japanese architecture is, therefore, strongly influenced by environmental concerns, and consequently, the strong reliance on timber. Western visitors often wonder why prewar Japanese cities used to be continuously rebuilt in wood even though they were regularly destroyed by terrible fires. The above discussed climatic issues that point in favor of timber construction seem to have outweighed the risk of frequent fires in the past when reinforced-concrete and steel beams weren't an option. Constant rebuilding was moreover required to get rid of the accumulating humidity damage. However, even after modern construction techniques were introduced to Japan in the twentieth century, the life expectancy of buildings did not increase significantly due to solidified cultural assumption that a complete renewal is the only means for purification, which is conveniently strengthened by Shinto and Buddhist beliefs. Nowadays, most Japanese residential units experience a sharp drop of value in just 15–30 years after their construction, depending on whether the building material is wood, steel, or concrete. In the same way, danchi districts were only meant to serve for 30–40 years, unlike Western modernist housing and *khruschevkas* that were aiming at 100–150 years of lifespan. With danchi's originally intended demolition time long overdue for all remaining districts now, it's not surprising that they are perceived as undesirable living environment by many Japanese—such opinion is justified by the prevailing characteristics of the local architectural episteme.

Flexible Interior Planning and Portable Partitions for the Cyclical Lifestyle

The idea of a dwelling's transience and temporality, reliance on wood, and the development of standardized modules deeply influenced the interior planning and lifestyles, making them very distinct from the ordinary spectrum of living patterns we are used to seeing in the West.

Japanese traditional domestic architecture can be roughly divided into commoner and aristocratic residences. While the former varied greatly depending on the region and family's occupation, the latter had a more consistent style throughout the country and also exerted a delayed top-down cultural influence on commoner's housing, establishing preferred proportions, spatial organization systems, and creating the image of an "essentially Japanese" lifestyle, that was in early twentieth century selectively exported to the Western media and forged a persistent stereotype about Japanese architecture in Europe and America (Yoshioka, 1958). It is important to understand the most persistent concepts of aristocratic residential interiors since, throughout history, their main features ended up being repeatedly replicated in one way or another by other social classes in their own homes.

Until the Heian period, aristocratic houses did not have partitioning walls in the open space under the roof around *moya*, the core plaster enclosure. *Moya*, together with the open wooden floorboard platform, limited by structural posts, between which *shitomi-do* (wooden half-doors) were hanged, represented a building typology called *shinden-zukuri* (Fig. 1.5). Since the interior space had to remain free of bulky fixed objects for humidity damage prevention, appropriate movable accessories and partitions were used for daily life, replaced, and relocated

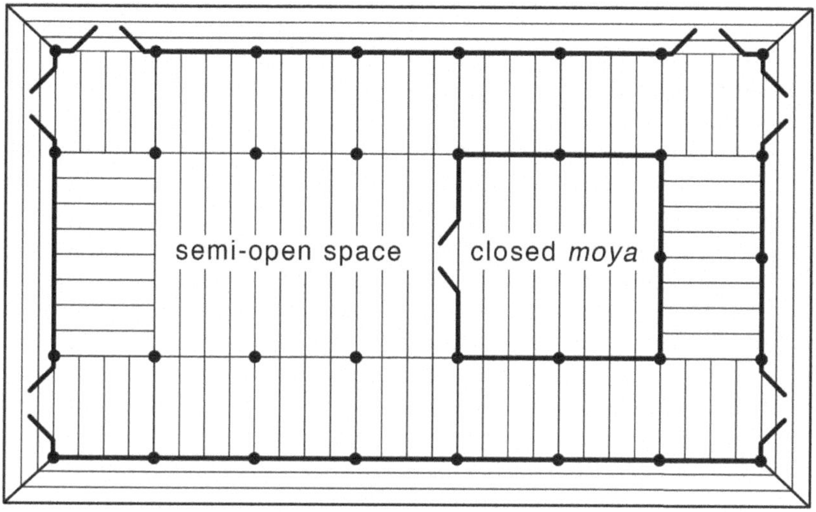

Fig. 1.5 *Shinden*-style residence plan

depending on the time of the day and the season, as well as the grade of formality during guest receptions. In bigger residences, there could be a special servant called *kuroudo* in charge of this daily and seasonal accessory flow and interior transformation (Kōji, 1981). The perceived size and decoration of living space could be significantly altered in several minutes, reinforcing the scale of temporality and cyclicality of domestic life that characterized traditional Japanese housing up until WWII.

There were three main categories of house accessories in the early Heian period that remained in use long after: floor furnishings, vertical partitions, and small utensils. The floor furnishings included cushions, thin reed mats, and tatami, which at first were used as individual mobile devices to equip hard wooden floors for accommodating guests, sleeping or sitting where they were needed, but by Muromachi period (1336–1573), when the guest-welcoming practices became central to the aristocratic families' social standing, with frequent use they became fully integrated into the floor as a top layer from wall to wall first in the reception rooms, and later in the entire living quarters.

To divide space and improve building's adaptability to the weather, light partitions such as rope or cloth curtains called *noren* and hanging bamboo screens called *sudare* as well as mosquito nets could be fixed to the main post-and-beam structures. Additionally, single-standing panels and folding screens could be placed anywhere in the rooms to improve privacy whenever needed.

Finally, various smaller freestanding practical and decorative items such as lamps, chairs, shelves, and ornamental scrolls were chosen and placed individually depending on the time of the day and the occasion. By the sixteenth century, aristocratic residences would be upgraded with a separate storage house in the depth of the garden called *kura*. Made of inflammable materials such as stone blocks, *kura* were used to protect the ever-growing number of valuable family heirlooms from fires and thieves, as well as assist in keeping seasonal items out of the way and ensuring smooth accessory circulation (Sand, 2003). The reliance on *kura* and garden storages as a necessary backstage for maintaining tatami rooms free of clutter didn't align well with the introduction of collective housing typologies in the twentieth century: the strive to preserve traditional tatami lifestyles with the minimum of storage furniture combined with the limitations of floor surfaces led toward inevitable accumulation of personal belongings in apartments (Daniels, 2010).

As the military class rose to power during the Kamakura (1185–1333) and Muromachi periods (1336–1573), the houses of aristocracy grew in size, but the amount of open space between previously separate buildings diminished with defensive intentions, and residential complexes became more compact and denser. The adjacent buildings would get attached to the main *shinden*, so the number of rooms with different functions surrounding the central *moya* multiplied, and a new spatial organization model had to be developed in order to manage and separate all the activities.

The introduction of Zen Buddhism from China in Kamakura period was favored by the rulers of military regime, since it somewhat coincided with their main doctrines based on self-discipline and strict hierarchy. During the Momoyama period (1568–1600) the resulting ideology was reflected in aristocratic houses: *shinden-zukuri* architecture was replaced by a style known as *shoin-zukuri*, that can be translated as "study hall building style." It incorporated some typical elements from Zen monastery buildings to decorate *moya* that became reception rooms—*tokonoma* (alcove), *shoin* (study desk), and *tana* (bookshelf). *Tokonoma* was an evolved form of a priest's individual altar on a low table that became a built-in secular alcove devoted to display of decorative items in the reception room. Over time the decorative items put in *tokonoma* obtained fixed meanings: flowers, scrolls, and paintings were connected with specific seasons and while reflecting the status of the household, they also sometimes corresponded to the contents of the garden, usually visible from the inside of the room. *Shoin*, a study desk built as a window sill overlooking the wooden terrace of a priest's house, and *tana*, case for religious scrolls, together with *tokonoma* became symbols of scholarly and spiritual refinement. The fixed locations of these objects, along with the configuration of tatami mats, dictated the choreography of room use and guests' positions according to their social status, creating a space loaded with hierarchical meaning. Reception rooms would have lavishly painted *fusuma* and occupy the south-facing end of the building, the most well-lit and well-ventilated space in the house, and were meant for the exclusive use of the head of the family, who could sleep, spend his free time, and entertain his distinguished guests there. In the meantime, women and children were expected to occupy deeper recesses of the house containing simpler generic tatami rooms and the kitchen. Before the mass introduction of new living standards by danchi in the 1950s, kitchens in Japan had a long history of being associated with unclean activities such as raw food processing and dishwashing, which made them a rather marginal space in the house and therefore an off-limits area to the visitors.[4]

With the spread of *shoin-zukuri* and condensation of formerly disconnected buildings into one main residence, a single entrance hall called *genkan* was developed to welcome the guests and control the flows of people. Moreover, the use of sliding solid wooden partitions such as *maira-do* and *sugi-do*, or lighter timber-framed doors covered with paper called *fusuma*, became common, so structural posts had to be transformed from circular into square shape in order to accommodate permanent partition fixtures—*kamoi* head jambs attached to *nageshi* horizontal tie beams and *shikii* grooved floor thresholds that contained tracks for sliding. *Fusuma* and *shōji* paper screens had the same length of one *ken* as one tatami mat, so *kamoi* and *shikii* together with vertical posts were used to frame all human-height partitions into the entire height of the living space, creating a distinct visual rhythm for the interior (Fig. 1.11).

[4] Even in the early 2000s this attitude persisted to an extent in the inhabitants of some older detached houses as evidenced by the fieldwork described in the book *The Japanese House* by Daniels (2010).

Rectangular openings between *kamoi* and the ceiling, *ranma*, could be adorned with wooden latticework or equipped with smaller sliding *shōji* screens to allow light and air to pass through even when all the main partitions are closed. The grade of privacy and openness varied between the rooms with both the choice of the sliding partitions, and the type of *ranma* installed above them.

Most of the interior furnishings were made in consideration of the basic unit measurement for *ma*, the space between two posts, measured in *ken*, that since the Heian period has been fixed as equal to the length of a tatami mat, which had to be long enough for one person to lie on. Though the actual tatami measurements varied throughout geographical areas, being 1910 × 955 mm in Kansai (Kyōma or Kansaima tatami) and 1769 × 880 mm in Kanto (Edoma or Kantōma tatami), they were a stable point of reference to calculate and communicate room and house sizes within one region. This system, however, was challenged in 1955 with the emergence of 1700 × 850 mm Danchima or Kōdan tatami that were implemented to fit the metrically designed concrete danchi apartments.

The resulting combination of regular column spacing and modular accessories gave freedom to the modification of openings and room sizes that could be changed according to the number of guests and therefore tatami needed for every occasion. In the hottest summer days, *shōji* separating interiors from *engawa*, the roofed veranda running by the perimeter of the house, could be completely removed. If the internal *fusuma* were also to be removed for better ventilation, most of the building except for the plastered part of the reception room and wooden enclosures of *to-bukuro*, containers for outside wooden shutters, could be left as a completely open skeleton, sheltered only by the roof with wide overhangs.

By the end of the Momoyama period, luxurious tastes of *shoin-zukuri* were defeated by the popularity of simpler austere aesthetics of tea-ceremony rooms. Tea ceremonies, introduced by Zen masters from China, gained popularity among Japanese aristocracy, so building tea halls, *chaseki*, and tea pavilions, *chashitsu*, became a regular practice in wealthy residences by the end of the sixteenth century. The main features of tea house architecture that were originally propagated by tea master Sen no Rikyū were the use of bare, undecorated materials: unpainted plaster showing sand and straw, unpolished wood, non-squared tree-trunk posts, and irregular bamboo details. Contrary to the *shoin* reception rooms, tea rooms were meant to put less hierarchical restrictions on people, objects, and spaces.

Tea room architecture gradually blended with the highly versatile interior organization with different degrees of visual separation of *shoin-zukuri* buildings that gradually lost the excessive decorations such as *ranma* carvings and *fusuma* paintings, culminating in the less formal *sukiya-zukuri* style. The idea of quiet simplicity and closeness to nature appealed both to the samurai elites that were exhausted by constant wars at the time and to commoners that could finally partake of the new aristocratic fashion that aligned well with their limited budgets and native Shinto practices. With diminished spatial and material manifestations of status, by the end of Edo period, *sukiya-zukuri* has spread to all aristocratic villas and most townspeople residences all over Japan.

Behavior Patterns Inside the House

The abovementioned absence of fixed solid boundaries between the parts of the traditional houses and the outside created a stronger psychological emphasis on the separating meaning of the floor levels, that differentiate between the living and less private quarters of the building, stressing the contrast between the dirt of the street or earthen floor of the entrance, *genkan*, and perfect cleanliness of the wooden floorboards and tatami (Sand, 2003); *Genkan*, which became an integral part of every Japanese house since the Meiji period (1868–1912), is located under the roof inside the perimeter of the house, nevertheless is never considered to be fully "inside" and acts as a liminal space (Daniels, 2010). Similar to a Western front porch, in the *genkan* neighbors and guests can enter freely[5] and interact with the owners without intruding on the privacy of the living quarters. Urban townhouses and farmhouses usually had *genkan* continue into a dirt-floored kitchen called *doma*, that shared its liminal space qualities. The tradition of always removing the shoes in the *genkan*, walking barefoot and sitting and sleeping directly on the floor inside, helps to mentally reinforce the special qualities of living spaces and the invisible

[5] Before WWII most people would leave the front sliding door unlocked during the day, so that casual visitors could come in uninvited and call out for the owner in *genkan*. Although this practice is still common in detached houses in rural areas of Japan (Daniels, 2010), with the introduction of metal pivoting doors in danchi, the social function of the *genkan* in postwar apartments was lost.

boundaries of home. The texture of tatami and the wooden floor becomes as important as walls and ceilings; carpenters would give careful attention to its grain and polishing.

With such architectural ambiguity, the physical traits of the inside developed distinct cultural connotations, being associated with purity, warmth, and intimacy, while the outside remains unclean, dangerous, and strange (Ozaki & Rees Lewis, 2006). The process of entering the Japanese house therefore became a ritual of recognizing and reinforcing the special feeling of being inside as opposed to the outside; it consists of a sequence of shifts in a person's sightline. When entering a Euro-American dwelling, the visitor's sightline usually remains unchanged. In a Japanese traditional house, however, one must turn around at the *genkan* to remove the shoes, then turn back, step up, and proceed inside. Next, when people are about to sit on the floor, they adjust their position to face the garden either frontally or laterally, aligning themselves according to tatami directions, and so the sightline turns again until it lowers down at the end of the process (Fig. 1.6).

Inside, people are to view all surfaces and openings frontally. First adopted with the tatami-based hierarchy of guest receptions during the military regimes, this tendency is also supported by the simple fact that all wall sections and panels are perpendicular to each other, identical in size and transient in nature, so they don't provide any kind of individual visual focal points. Moreover, spaces usually lack any freestanding objects of interest such as furniture, apart from items displayed in the *tokonoma* wall recess and the view of the garden, which became especially important in *sukiya-zukuri* architecture. The habit of frontal perception is especially notable when comparing works of Western and Japanese architecture photographers: the former tend to portray spaces by emphasizing perspective to show volumes, while the latter usually take photographs frontally to reflect surfaces (Ferreras, 1981).

The framing of the garden views by the openings and sliding partitions is controlled for the best appreciation in the formal sitting position called *seiza*, which was another result of formal military attitudes of the Muromachi period. In the same way, decorations in *tokonoma*, that in *shoin-zukuri* were oriented toward the host and in *sukiya* style faced the guests, are put to be best visible while in *seiza*. Together with the cycles of daily movements of furniture, accessories, and partitions, the strictly calculated choreography of human positions in accordance with the preferred views produces a sequential procedure of movements in the

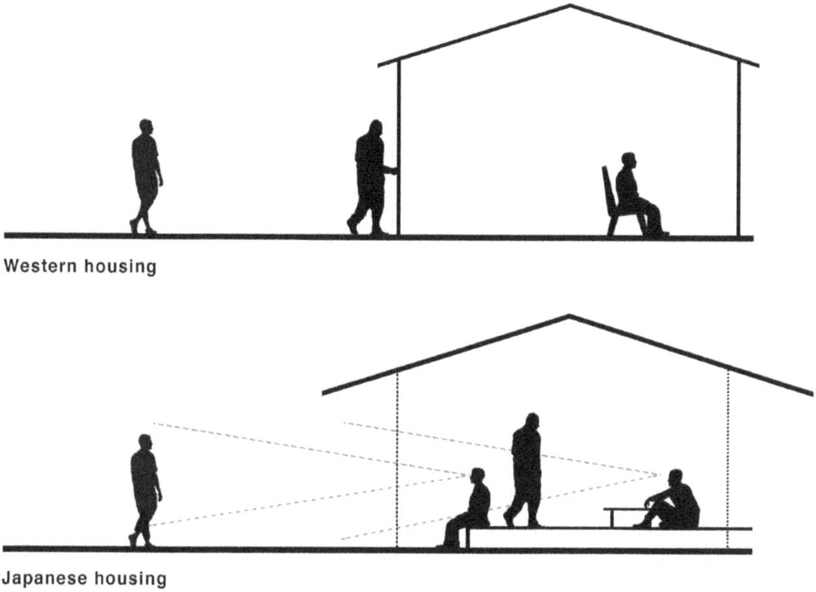

Fig. 1.6 The difference between entering a Western and a Japanese house in the shift of sightlines

house. "If Shinto and Zen Buddhism are to be called religions, then a man's house in Japan was not his castle; it represented rather his church" (Alex, 1963). Living in a traditional Japanese house, indeed, recalls a ritual that is unconsciously but flawlessly performed by its inhabitants every day.

Diffused Boundaries with the Outside

As we discussed above, wooden frame structures, as opposed to masonry, do not necessarily require any enclosure between the posts, so the relationship of the house with the outside can be regulated by manipulating the sliding screens. In the West, such a fluid relationship with the outside is almost impossible because of the cultural requirements for safety and privacy—buildings are expected to firmly protect the interiors from the outside, which is usually perceived as highly hostile. In Japan, however, the vagueness of house boundaries, much needed because of the climate, is more feasible due to a higher degree of cultural homogeneity and social trust that could be achieved in the isolated environment of the islands, relatively remote from the continent. People were united in a clear social hierarchy by rice cultivating practices and tended to have a certain degree of common understanding within their regions, with rare instances of foreign visitors, so an indication of boundaries could be fixed without stating them explicitly, through "reading the air" and temporary partition placement rather than building thick house walls. Despite the past popularity of defensive fences in aristocratic residences during the frequent wars in Kamakura period, one can rarely find high property barriers or house security devices in contemporary Japanese cities, where burglary and trespassing is uncommon.

While in masonry construction, every room is similar in terms of privacy gradation, with *shōji* and *fusuma*, the amount of separation increases with the number and the thickness of the sliding partitions used, creating a gradation of privacy levels for interior spaces. From the plaster room enclosing the most important space of the house, going toward the exterior, the degree of openness increases with sequence of more flexible tatami rooms that culminates with *shōji* screens opening into the wide wooden terrace—*engawa*, guarded by the deep overhanging eaves of the roof, at times closed by heavier wooden storm shutters. This multilayered yet flexible complex of vertical screens creates a gradual blending of the interior to exterior, and this relationship could be altered by adjusting the partitions (Fig. 1.7). Sometimes, various additional structures such as moon-viewing platforms could be built with the same module far beyond the eaves of the house, extending one of the rooms into the outside world.

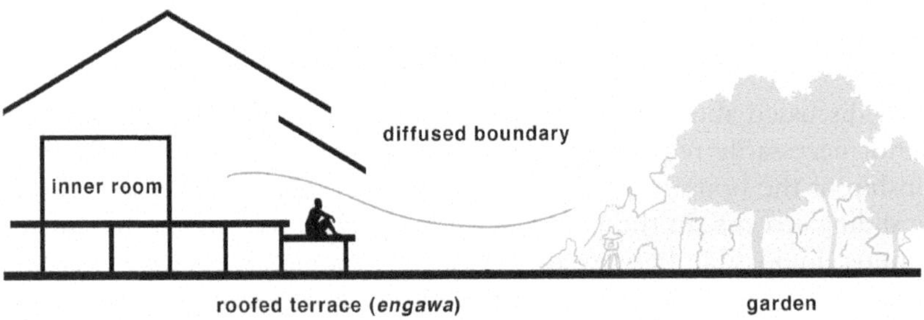

Fig. 1.7 Absence of solid exterior walls creates ambiguity of boundaries

Another manifestation of the ambiguous connection between the inside and the outside is the Japanese garden. In contrast with the Western idea that gardens are made to be admired together with the building from the outside, Japanese gardens are often designed specifically to adhere to various sightlines from the interior of the house, as already discussed before. Static framed views were controlled and perfected by interior details, thus integrating the room with the landscape design. For example, the Bōsen Tea Room built in 1612 by Kobori Enshū is divided from the garden by an unusual suspended *shōji*, shielding the interior viewer from sun glare but also constricting his sightline to the lower part of the garden, creating an interesting framed view as a decoration of the room, best appreciated while sitting in *seiza* (Nomura, 2018) (Fig. 1.8).

A similar technique of creating relationships between the building, the garden and a distant outside landscape trait in traditional Chinese and Japanese landscape architecture is called *shakkei* or "borrowed scenery." The view of the adjacent garden is blocked by a low hedge or a fence, hiding the immediate "undesirable" surroundings and allowing

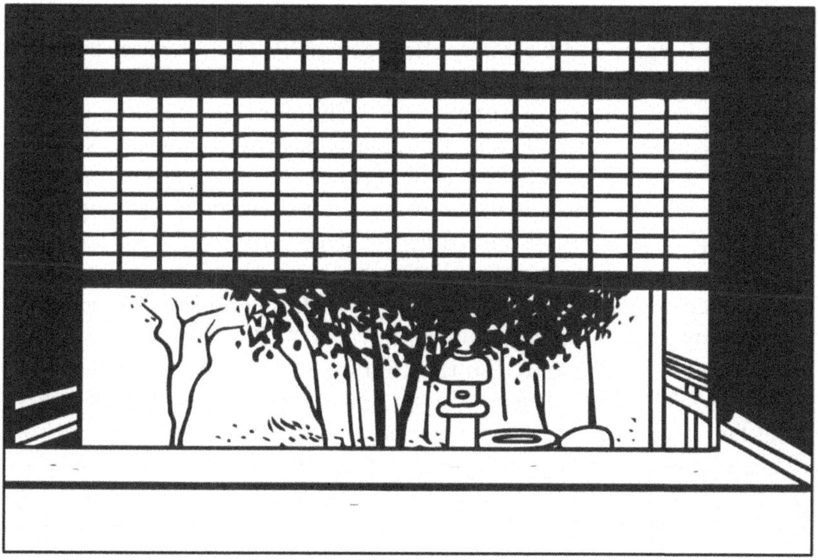

Fig. 1.8 Garden framed by *shōji* sitting above a raised veranda sill, Bōsen Tea Room

the sightline to extend to a framed view of a mountain or trees in the distance, visually incorporating it into the garden and consequently into the interiors.

To summarize, choices and treatments of materials, unique structural systems, greater attention to nature and orientation, flexible interior space organizations, and a fluid understanding of boundaries and building life expectancy in Japanese residential architecture are results of complex influences of local climate, natural environment, location in a seismically active zone, imports of mainland culture, and secluded island conditions. Some architectural concepts, such as raised floors, modular construction, and flexibility of interiors may appear identical to the ideas of the twentieth-century European Modern movement in architecture that aimed at rationalizing built spaces, but in the Japanese context, they have always had completely different meanings and reasons for existence.

Prewar Urban Housing in Japan

The Prewar Family Structure

Historians often highlight certain similarities in the miraculous economic recoveries of Japan and Germany after losing WWII. Liberated from the costs of keeping their own military forces, both countries sent most available resources to heavy industries and technology production, gaining constant economic growth and rebuilding destroyed housing stock in the course of roughly fifteen years (Izuhara, 2000). However, there are significant differences if we consider the governments' strategies for the housing recovery. Contradicting the deeply rooted European belief in individual rights to social welfare, in Japan, there has always been an unspoken assumption that welfare, including housing, is the direct responsibility of one's own family (Hirayama & Ronald, 2006; Izuhara, 2000; Ronald, 2004), rooted in the country's prewar history.

Before WWII, Japan was a homogenous patriarchal society with very strong family bonds. Traditional extended family with a male household head functioned as a basic self-regulated social unit and was called "*ie*" Japanese *Ie* family system was similar to the Confucian model of feudal household organization based on the idea of filial piety in China. In military class, male family leaders would hold all the family property as well as rights over other members in exchange for taking full responsibility for their relatives' actions and life. This system was legally defined, intensively supported, and extended into all strata of Japanese society by the Imperial government during the Meiji period (1868–1912) as it liberated the state from certain types of law enforcement that could be carried out by the father of the family, who acted as a ruler of a miniature country himself. However, patrilineal stem families and inheritance by the eldest son were not especially common for pre-Meiji feudal Japan; they were practiced by not more than 10% of the population—the Samurai classes (Ronald & Alexy, 2011). The Meiji Civil Code of 1898 and the Family Registry System of 1871 legislated patrilineal family organization as a tool of efficient taxation, land ownership regulation, as well as delegation of individual welfare issues to household heads with an intergenerational continuity. With the establishment of the new system, women lost all social responsibilities and rights that they could hold at least de facto prior to 1868 (ibid.).

The Meiji government interpreted Confucian filial piety as inseparable from feudalistic loyalty, which helped extend the obligations and rights attributed to household heads to the emperor, positioning him at the top of all Japanese families as the ultimate "father of the nation." The "pseudo-family state ideology," as Ito (1982, cited in Ueno, 2009, 65) defines the *ie* system, transformed diverse and fluid pre-Meiji families with complex organizations and loose household-community-village boundaries into more easily controllable units with strict gender labor division and a clearer distinction between the private and the public.

Although the laws concerned with the *ie* system were not abolished until 1947, fast industrialization at the turn of the century made masses of young workers move into the cities, and the state shifted their attention toward the regularization of nuclear-family units. With many Japanese scholars that went to study abroad participating in the public discourse, Western family ideals centered around the intimacy of married couple and home as a core of the family collectivity and shelter for child-rearing became increasingly popular as a notion of a successful modernized society that Japan should strive to develop. Lawmakers and politicians realized that home itself can become an important tool in shaping the moral values of a growing number of nuclear households. The hierarchy of extended family estates was far too complex to influence and control, but urban dwellings of nuclear families became a subject of political and popular media discussions in late the Meiji period. The role of housewife and educator of children among with the benefits of such labor division started to be promoted by women-oriented magazines in the 1920s (Daniels, 2010; Satō, 2003). Word *katei* (literally home) was adopted into everyday language to be used in parallel to *ie* (family system), denoting more intimate and modern family relations as opposed to lineage and extended family. Still, Westernized *katei* and Meiji-legislated *ie* were not mutually exclusive, as nuclear families were just considered a smaller integral part of *ie* and could still function effectively according to the Civil Code of 1898.

Despite the heightened ideological interest toward the influence of the physical characteristics of dwellings on the family values, up until WWII, the Japanese government had never engaged in any kind of centralized housing regulation or provision program that could significantly influence national housing standards and supply, leaving the responsibility for those fully in the hands of private landlords. The intensive promotion of the Western housing models and incorporation of chair-based lifestyles thus only affected a small minority of wealthy urban homeowners that had the money to afford heavily furnished houses with functionally diversified rooms that were meant to harmonize family relationships (Uchida, 2002). In the meantime, the rest of the Japanese population still led a floor-based lifestyle in multifunctional tatami rooms; in case of urban environment, those were usually rented in densely built timber tenement blocks. There is a lack of official statistics for the period before the first nationwide housing census was undertaken in 1941, but anecdotal and other evidence suggests that in the late nineteenth and the first half of the twentieth century, most inhabitants of Japanese cities had to rent their dwellings (Waswo, 2002).

Nagaya: The Only Role Model

Unlike Europe, prewar Japan didn't have many examples of multi-story mass housing; slower rates of industrialization and the abovementioned climatic concerns made low-rise timber detached and row houses a more reasonable choice for city life. There used to be three main types of urban dwellings in prewar Japan: *ikken-ya*, *machiya*, and *nagaya*. *Ikken-ya* were freestanding houses of different shapes depending on the region and family occupation, usually belonging to wealthier lineages. They shared many similarities to *minka* rural housing, significantly differing from the other two typologies that could only be found in cities. *Machiya* is a two-story townhouse usually built on a long strip of land with a narrow street façade (Fig. 1.9). The land taxation system in urban areas of medieval Japan, mostly applicable to Kyoto and Nara, relied not on the square meters of the plot but on the width of the street-facing facade, so most *machiya* tended to have extremely narrow fronts and didn't have openings on the elongated sides (Fig. 1.10). *Machiya* houses often belonged to merchant families that had a shop in the room facing the street on the ground floor. This room could be freely accessed from the street and formed a semi-public area that replaced *genkan*, where the family welcomed customers and business partners. As one proceeds inside, the level of privacy rises with every layer of *fusuma* (Fig. 1.11). In the deeper parts of the house, one could usually find one or more *tsuboniwa*, internal gardens with an open roof, that allowed more light and air to reach all living quarters since the townhouse had a limited number of openings (Izumida, 2011). The dirt-floor kitchen was located in the narrow space

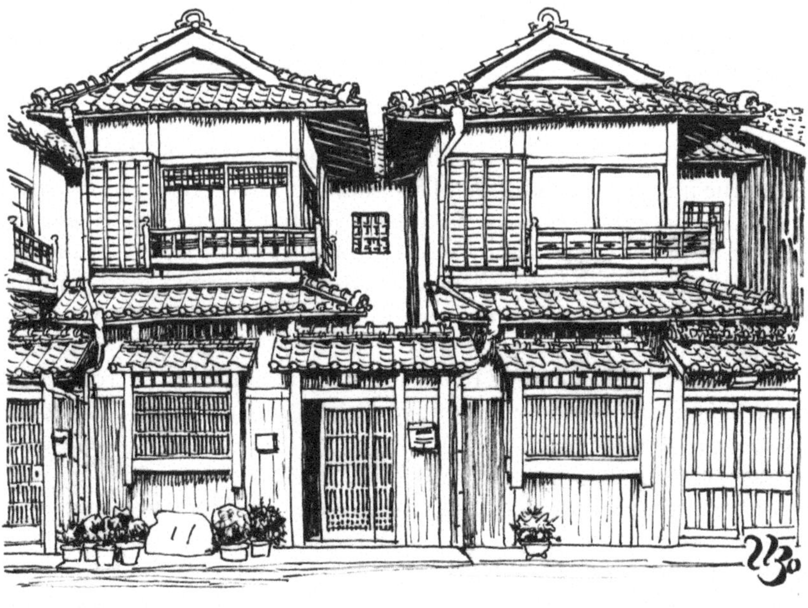

Fig. 1.9 *Machiya*. Sketch by Uzō Nishiyama (*Source* Courtesy of the Uzō Nishiyama Memorial Library)

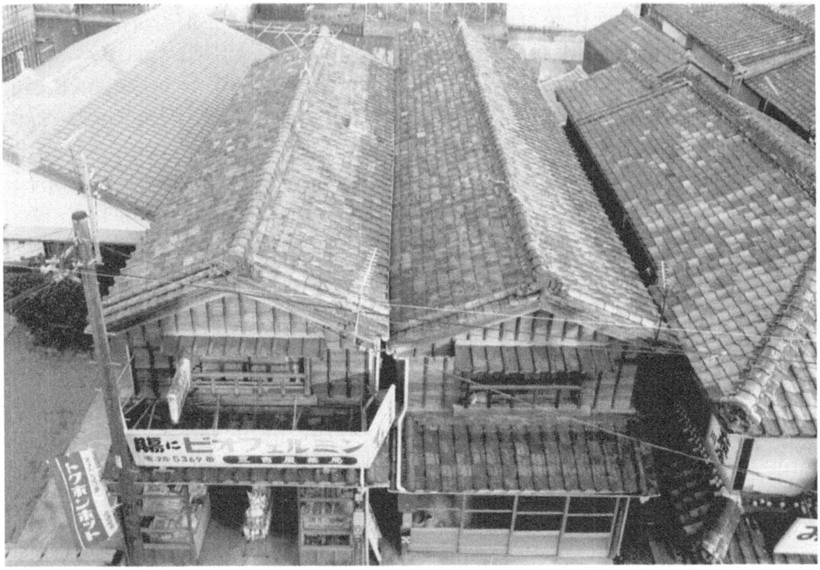

Fig. 1.10 *Machiya* in Ise, Mie Prefecture, 1979, taken by Uzō Nishiyama (*Source* As for Fig. 1.9)

behind the entrance by the side wall, with a double ceiling for better ventilation. The internal organization of the rooms normally reflected the main features of traditional Japanese housing discussed before. While *machiya* could be found in great quantities in central districts of Japanese cities up until WWII, they couldn't be well adapted for multi-family arrangements or partial renting, and therefore were usually associated with the wealthier parts of the urban population.

The most popular type of rental units for commoners in Tokyo and Osaka of the early twentieth century was rooms in *nagaya*, elongated wooden row houses with an either inside or outside corridor along on one side of the building that provided access to every room, which were the only existing traditional prototype for the development of Japanese postwar mass housing (Figs. 1.12 and 1.13). Sometimes *nagaya* could visually resemble a row of *machiya* sharing lateral walls, but the main difference was that *machiya* were inhabited by families that owned the house and the land, whereas *nagaya* were built by companies to house their employees and rich landowners to secure a source of additional

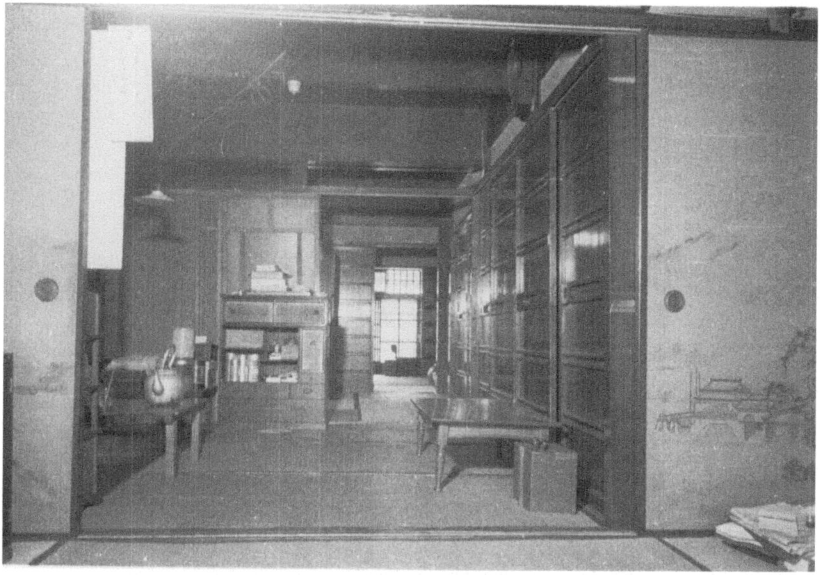

Fig. 1.11 *Fusuma* framed by *kamoi* (head jambs), *ranma* (openings over *kamoi*) and *shikii* (bottom tracks). Interior of a *machiya* in Gojo district of Kyoto, 1966 (*Source and author* As for Fig. 1.9)

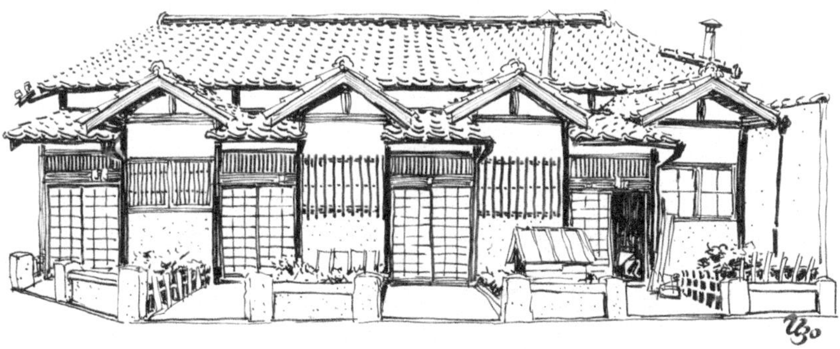

Fig. 1.12 Exterior of a *nagaya* with individual entrances for units. Sketch by Uzō Nishiyama (*Source* As for Fig. 1.9)

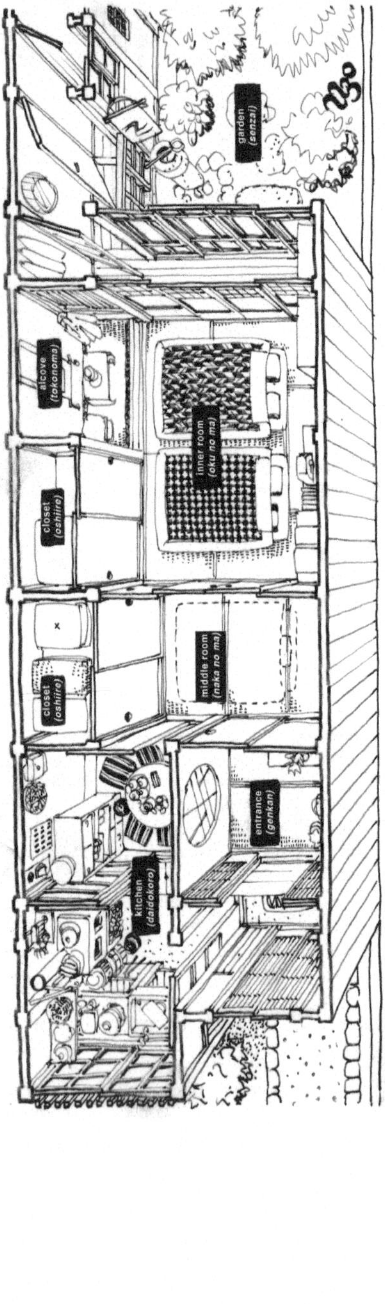

Fig. 1.13 Internal organization of a *nagaya* with an individual entrance. Sketch by Uzō Nishiyama (*Source* As for Fig. 1.9)

income from their unused estates in urban centers. During fast industrialization in the Taishō period (1912–1926), even the farmers from suburban areas started to repurpose parts of their agricultural fields into *nagaya* sites (Fig. 1.14).

Typical *nagaya* were built from cheap wood, consisted of one or two floors, and could fit about a dozen households, which sometimes had to share one kitchen and toilet. Landlords rarely provided *nagaya* with bathrooms since *sentō* (public baths) were still a very common way for maintaining individual hygiene. *Nagaya* rental units normally featured one or two tatami rooms opening onto the veranda or a window opposite the corridor entrance. Even in low-budget housing in Japan, a veranda or balcony is an indispensable element that functions as a laundry and *futon* drying space, essential during highly humid summers and mild winters that facilitate mold growth. The traditional *genkan* entrance was also kept as an important psychological division between outside and inside, so the entrance area of each room was lower than the main tatami living

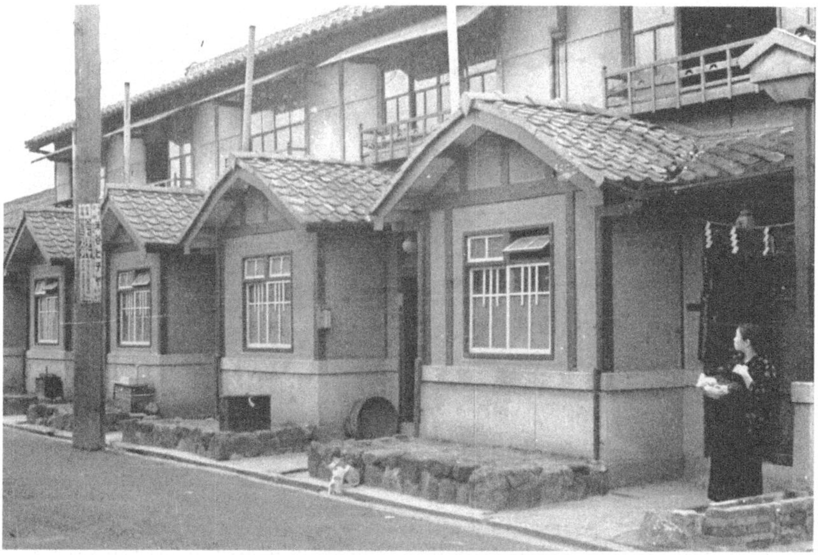

Fig. 1.14 Two-story *nagaya* with "Western" fronts in Kagaya, Osaka Prefecture, 1935 (*Source and author* As for Fig. 1.9)

area, had either dirt or wooden plank floor and sometimes contained a tiny kitchen. Often, however, the functions of both the kitchen and the veranda would be performed in the narrow alley between rows of two adjacent *nagaya* (Fig. 1.15), that became open-air "living rooms" that accommodated a range of activities from play area for children to communal laundry (Nishiyama, 1989). In the latter half of the Taishō period, higher quality *nagaya* featuring Westernized exteriors with white walls, glass windows, and slate roofs as well as toilets in every unit became popular among residents and were given the nickname *bunka jūtaku*, which can be loosely translated as "modern dwelling" or "culture house" (Ishikawa, 2007; Fig. 1.14).

Although *nagaya* plans incorporated many of the traditional architectural elements that aim at solving climatic concerns (standardized timber structures, movable partitions, and flexible relationship with the outside), due to spatial constrictions the densely built units couldn't have as much natural light and ventilation as freestanding houses or even *machiya*.

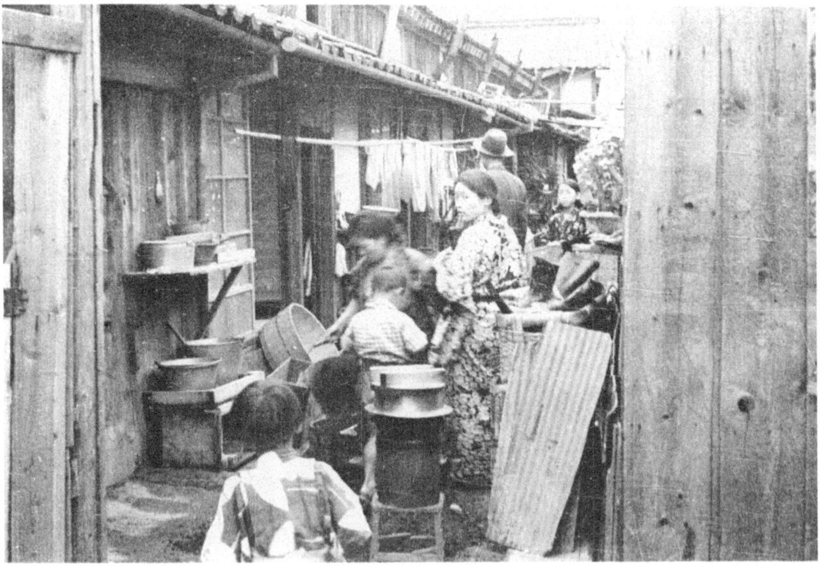

Fig. 1.15 Outside area between two *nagaya* in Sumiyoshi district, Osaka, 1935 (*Source and author* As for Fig. 1.9)

Living conditions in most urban *nagaya* were far from adequate, especially for families with children. Residents complained about minimal dwelling sizes, poor soundproofing, neighbor quarrels over the shared facility use, and sudden changes of rental fees (Waswo, 2002), but *nagaya* remained in high demand as the only affordable rental option for the urban working class up until the postwar period.

Dōjunkai Apartments: A Western Skin for the Japanese Bones

The Japanese government was little concerned with the rental housing control and didn't intervene up until the 1920s, when the influx of population into major cities provoked a sharp rise in the price of land and building materials, leading to a serious housing shortage in urban areas. Self-regulation of the private housing market met unprecedented difficulties, so in order to prevent potential social uprisings, the Japanese Home Ministry enacted the Public Housing Law in 1919, providing loans for public housing construction by municipalities (Shapira et al., 1994). This idea wasn't as successful as expected because the municipalities were reported to either raise the rental fees too high or sell off newly constructed housing to local companies due to the lack of capital return (Waswo, 2002). The state soon produced another initiative, the Housing Association Law of 1922, which provided loans that encouraged construction for owner-occupied units, trying to boost house ownership (Teasley, 2001). This intervention still largely relied on the power of the private housing market and never made a big impact.

The housing shortage was further aggravated in the Tokyo region by the 1923 Great Kanto Earthquake and the resulting fires. To deal with the consequences, the government launched an organization called Dōjunkai (literally, "Association for Equal Profit") Foundation, which was supposed to use about 20% of disaster relief domestic and overseas donations to construct new housing in affected areas. Sixteen Dōjunkai apartment complexes were built in Tokyo between 1924 and 1934 by a group of Japanese architects, who were ideologically inspired by Western urban planning models such as Garden City, Siedlungen, Le Corbusier's megastructures, and socio-rationalist approach propagated by Japanese architect Bunzo Yamaguchi, who briefly worked for Walter Gropius. Moreover, the facade style of Dōjunkai Apartments could be traced to the "restrained horizontality" of Frank Lloyd Wright, who lived in Japan between 1915 and 1923 and exerted a considerable impact on the local architectural community (Pompili, 2014; Fig. 1.18).

Dōjunkai was an unprecedented event in the architectural history of Japan both as a cooperation between the public and private sectors in housing provision and as a first big experiment in merging progressive housing models from the West with the traditional Japanese *nagaya* typology (Figs. 1.16 and 1.17). They managed to satisfy the updated requirements of better sanitation as well as the new earthquake and fire resistance standards for residential buildings and the demand for a new urban housing typology. Dōjunkai's head architect, Yoshizō Uchida, was also a president of the Architectural Institute of Japan (Kenchiku Gakkai) that researched the existing housing situation and actively promoted housing reform at the time, and a professor at Tokyo Imperial University, with his student laboratory directly engaged in Dōjunkai Apartments design. Under Uchida's influence, Dōjunkai's intervention became an important architectural experiment that emphasized the need to design spaces for community activities that were normally neglected in the Japanese cityscape and gave new importance to the voids and courtyard spaces. Each complex was designed individually according to topography and other characteristics of the plot. The overall result could be described as "Japanese bones beneath a Western skin" since Western concrete forms and technology were effectively merged with traditional Japanese interiors (Pompili, 2014).[6] Apart from *nagaya*-like floor plans with one room per unit and common toilets and kitchens, many Dōjunkai buildings also provided self-sufficient standard plans that featured two multifunctional tatami rooms that allowed to save space otherwise required by the fixed furniture, complete with built-in *oshiire* storages keeping *futon* and other bedding out of sight during the day. The rooms could be opened into each other by moving the *fusuma* partitions, fixed to the wooden framework of *kamoi*, that removed the need to build solid partitioning walls. Still, as shown in Fig. 1.17, with the *chabudai* low dining table, armchairs, and additional freestanding storage, an inhabited apartment had very little free livable space, a regrettable tendency that will continue haunting postwar Japanese apartment housing.

[6] The construction technology was so advanced that all Dōjunkai complexes survived the war bombings and all major earthquakes before they were sold to developer companies and torn down in recent years.

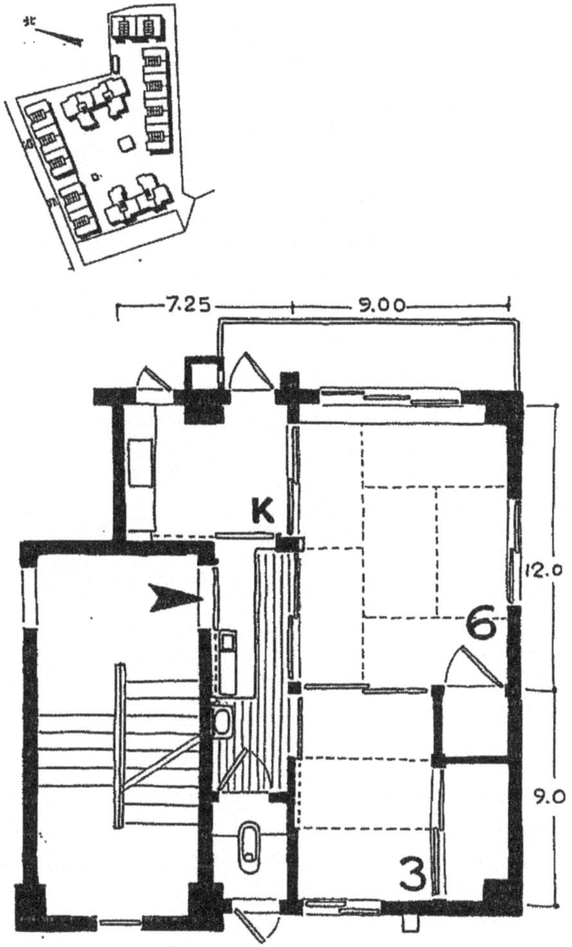

Fig. 1.16 Apartment plan in Dōjunkai Daikanyama complex (*Source* Uzō Nishiyama (1989). *Sumai no kōkongaku: gendai Nihon jūtakushi*. Tokyo: Shōkokusha, p. 222. Courtesy of Uzō Nishiyama Memorial Library)

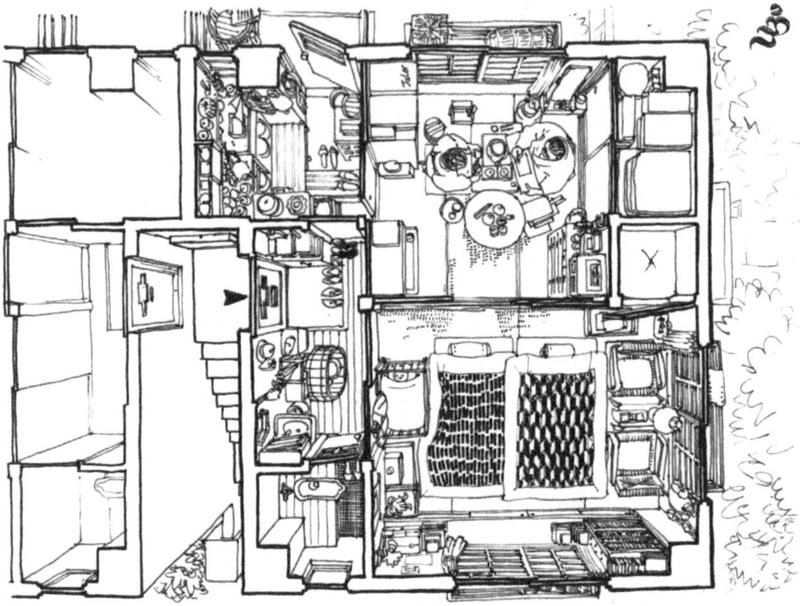

Fig. 1.17 Sectioned perspective of an apartment in Dōjunkai Daikanyama where Uzō Nishiyama lived (*Source* Courtesy of the Uzō Nishiyama Memorial Library. *Author* Uzō Nishiyama)

Genkan was integrated into a small corridor and had its traditional step height reduced due to limitations dictated by multi-story concrete construction. The central corridor connecting the pivoting entrance door and the living rooms was a concept alien to traditional Japanese house, borrowed from Western apartment models. In case of Dōjunkai it also contained a *senmenjo*, small washroom space equipped with a small sink and acted as a psychologically necessary buffer zone between the "unclean" areas of kitchen, *genkan* and toilet and the "clean" tatami rooms that ideally are not meant to be directly adjacent (Ozaki & Rees Lewis, 2006) but because of the new typology and its spatial limitations had to be squeezed close together. As in *nagayas*, there were no bathrooms provided, and the kitchen was tiny but had a door opening into a

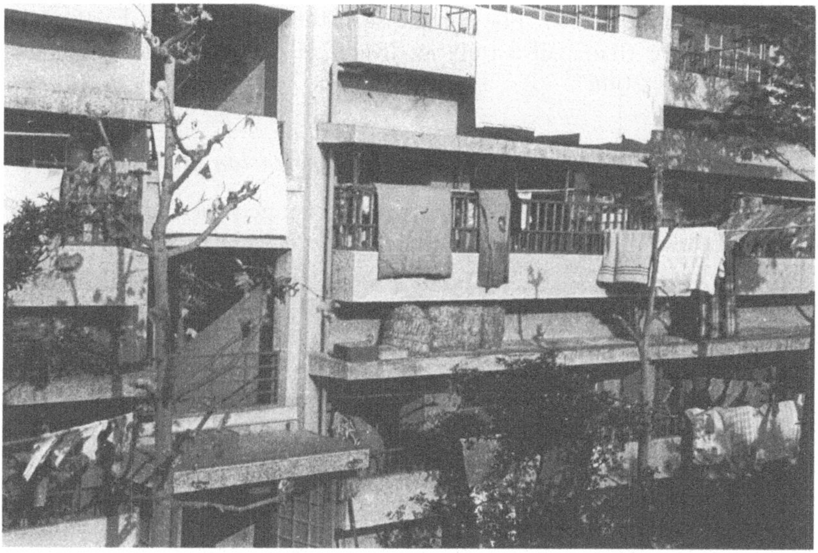

Fig. 1.18 Dōjunkai Daikanyama, the view from the Uzō Nishiyama's apartment, 1942 (*Source and author* As for Fig. 1.17)

long balcony equipped with high rails for laundry and *futon* drying. The glass windows imitated the configuration and sizes of their Western prototypes, but retained the traditional timber structure and sliding frames of *shoji* (Fig. 1.18).

Unlike Europe, where housing typologies were developing more gradually, for Japan this was rather an abrupt turn in residential design history. Even though sixteen Dōjunkai complexes built in Tokyo and Yokohama never set the trend for a nationwide housing program due to high construction costs, the references to spatial organization of the plans and some of their distinct exterior features, such as window shapes and railings, could be found later in postwar mass housing projects and particularly in danchi all over the country.

In 1927 another housing law was implemented to assist the clearance of slum areas in major cities caused by economic decline in the late 20s, but even if put together with all the previous initiatives, it did little to affect the national housing situation. Only 63,000 dwelling units were constructed under the 1919 and 1922 housing laws prior to

1932 (Nishiyama, 1989). For comparison, the Great Kanto Earthquake destroyed more than half a million dwellings in Tokyo and Yokohama alone (Clancey, 2006).

The Housing Corporation: The First Prefabrication During the War

The scale of the Japanese housing policies changed for the first time at the end of the 1930s: the military mobilization for the Second Sino-Japanese War provoked an increased housing demand. Large amounts of people moved to cities to work for war-related industries; cases of people renting single tatami mats hourly or in day and night shifts at lodgin inns in the same shared room became increasingly common (Nishiyama, 1989). The Housing Section of Welfare Ministry was established in 1938 as an emergency measure, and thus an unprecedented specialized office for the provision of national housing policies finally appeared. The range of its activities was mostly limited to war-related affairs, such as support of *nagaya*-type municipal housing construction for military industry workers in major cities, but it also issued some regulations on private rent prices across the country and limitation of access of private landowners to building materials which were in extreme scarcity since the beginning of the war (Ōmoto, 1985).

These restrictions led to an even greater housing crisis: local authorities had to face the consequences of the private sector being unable to provide enough housing for the population, as it used to before. In the face of the problem, Housing Section established Jūtaku Eidan or Housing Corporation, with the goal of constructing 300,000 housing units by 1945 throughout the country's industrial zones, which was only half reached due to the aggravating war situation and Japan's subsequent surrender. The new units were assigned exclusively to war-industry workers, a fraction of the struggling Japanese population. With most carpenters sent off to the colonies and the army, there was a serious shortage not only of building materials but also of capable hands to construct the shelters. Before the war, the entire country relied on carpenter guilds for housing production, so common people had little to no knowledge of timber structural systems. To make it possible for unqualified workers to put together durable buildings, in 1945, the Housing Corporation attempted production of standardized wooden panels in factories that were then transported and assembled on top of simple concrete block foundations on-site—a construction method not requiring any specialized skills (Fig. 1.19). The resulting temporary minimal wooden shelters were a simplified version of a traditional *nagaya* layout: 4,5 tatami units with a small terrace arranged in a row under one roof with common toilets at the end of the building. Although the houses were of very low quality and the initiative was soon shut down due to destruction caused by American air raids, this experiment in mass production of building parts became an important precedent for the postwar housing industry (Matsumoto, 2017).

Only a third of the units built by Housing Corporation were rental, and the average size of units had diminished from 42 square meters in 1941 to 30 square meters by the end of the war (Nishiyama, 1989; Ōmoto, 1985). On top of such inadequate supply levels before and during the war, Japanese urban housing experienced massive destruction by the bombings and fires, leaving postwar policymakers and architects with an unimaginably difficult task to solve.

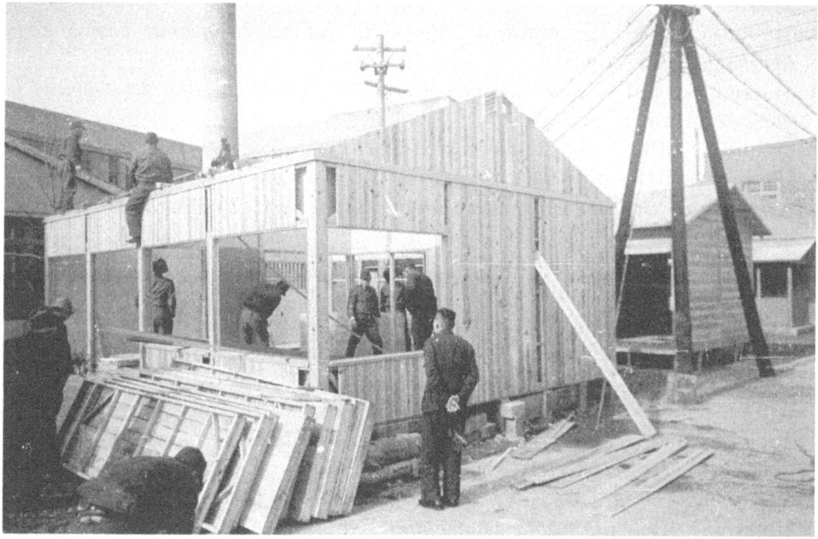

Fig. 1.19 Panel-type prototype housing of the Housing Corporation, at the front yard of the Ministry of Health and Welfare, 1941 (*Source and author* As for Fig. 1.17)

References

Alex, W. (1963). *Japanese architecture*. George Braziller.
Clancey, G. K. (2006). *Earthquake nation: The cultural politics of Japanese seismicity, 1868–1930*. University of California Press.
Daniels, I. (2010). *The Japanese house: Material culture in the modern home*. Berg.
Ferreras, J. (1981). Frontal perception in architectural space. *Process Architecture, 25*, 61–65.
Foucault, M. (1988). *Power knowledge*. Random House.
Hendry, J. (2019). *Understanding Japanese society*. Routledge.
Hirayama, Y., & Ronald, R. (Eds.). (2006). *Housing and social transition in Japan* (1st ed.). Routledge.
Ishikawa, S. (2007). *Seeking the self: Individualism and popular culture in Japan*. Peter Lang.
Izuhara, M. (2000). *Change and housing in post-war Japanese society: The experiences of older women*. Routledge.
Izumida, H. (2011). Machiya: A typology of Japanese townhouses. In *1st TTCL Annual Symposium* (pp. 44–49).
Kōji, Y. (1981). Climate and the Japanese way of life. *Process Architecture, 25*, 25–35.
Matsumoto, S. (2017). *Shōwa no Nihon no Sumai: Nishiyama Uzō Shashin Akaibuzu Kara*. Sogensha.
Matsumura, S. (2019). *Open architecture for the people: Housing development in post-war Japan*. Routledge.
Nishiyama, U. (1989). *Sumai Kokongaku: Gendai Nihon Jūtakushi*. Shōkokusha.
Nomura, S. (2018). Kohō-an Bōsen. In T. Tsuchiya et al. (Eds.), *Japan in architecture: Genealogies of its transformation* (p. 72). Shimoda Yasunari, Echelle-1.
Nute, K. (2004). *Place, time, and being in Japanese architecture*. Routledge.
Ono, H. (2018). Why do the Japanese work long hours? Sociological perspectives on long working hours in Japan. *Japan Labor Issues, 2*(5), 35–49.
Ōmoto, K. (1985). Fukushi Kokka to Wagakuni Jūtaku Seisaku no Tenkai. *Fukushi Kokka, 6*, 397–452.
Ozaki, R., & Rees Lewis, J. (2006). Boundaries and the meaning of space: A study of Japanese house plans. *Environment and Planning D, 24*(1), 91–104.
Pompili, M. (2014). Modern multi-unit housing in Japan and the Dōjunkai Apartments (1924–34). *Fabrications: The Journal of the Society of Architectural Historians, Australia and New Zealand, 24*(1), 26–47.
Porter, W. N. (1914). *The miscellany of a Japanese priest, being a translation of Tsure-Zure Gusa*. Humphrey Milford.

Ronald, R. (2004). Home ownership, ideology and diversity: Re-evaluating concepts of housing ideology in the case of Japan. *Housing, Theory and Society, 21*, 49–64.

Ronald, R., & Alexy, A. (Eds.). (2011). *Home and family in Japan: Continuity and transformation*. Routledge.

Sakamoto, T. (2018a). Kumimono of Byōdō-in Hō-ō-dō. In T. Tsuchiya et al. (Eds.), *Japan in architecture: Genealogies of its transformation* (p. 40). Shimoda Yasunari, Echelle-1.

Sakamoto, T. (2018b). Secret books of carpentry techniques. In T. Tsuchiya et al. (Eds.), *Japan in architecture: Genealogies of its transformation* (p. 45). Shimoda Yasunari, Echelle-1.

Sand, J. (2003). *House and home in modern Japan*. Harvard University Press.

Satō, B. (2003). *The new Japanese woman: Modernity, media, and women in interwar Japan*. Duke University Press.

Shapira, P., Masser, I., & Edgington, D. (Eds.). (1994). *Planning for cities and regions in Japan*. Liverpool University Press.

Steger, B. (2003). Getting away with sleep: Social and cultural aspects of dozing in parliament. *Social Science Japan Journal, 6*(2), 181–197.

Teasley, S. (2001). Nation, modernity and interior decoration: Uncanny designs in the 1922 peace commemoration Tokyo exposition culture village houses. *Japanstudien, 13*(1), 49–87.

Uchida, S. (2002). *Kieta modan tōkyō*. Kawade shobō shinsha.

Ueno, C. (2009). *The modern family in Japan: Its rise and fall*. Trans Pacific Press.

Waswo, A. (2002). *Housing in postwar Japan—A social history*. Routledge.

Yoshioka, Y. (1958). Japanese. *Shinkenchiku: New Architecture of Japan, 33*(9), 2.

No Author

(2019). *Annual Report on Forest and Forestry for Fiscal Year 2019*. Ministry of Agriculture, Forestry, and Fisheries.

CHAPTER 2

The Short History of Danchi

The Birth of Danchi

Catching Up to the West

In the previous chapter, we discovered that most buildings in Japan, even those in urban districts, were built of wood by the time WWII started. This greatly escalated the damage caused by the American air raids. By August 1945, more than one-sixth of the housing stock had been destroyed, and homelessness became a pressing issue. It was estimated that Japan needed to construct around 4.2 million dwellings to solve the postwar housing problem, the situation being more critical than in France and England at the end of the war (Fig. 2.1). Moreover, following Japan's surrender, around 6.6 million civilians and soldiers had to be repatriated, abandoning all colonies in Asia (Itoh, 1950).

There was an unprecedented need for the government to intervene in housing provision nationwide, yet in the immediate postwar years, all the measures were superficial and non-systematic. The government approved the construction of 300,000 housing units for aerial bombing victims. However, only 83,000 units were completed: around 40,000 units set up in pre-existing non-residential buildings and 43,000 minimum-size wooden emergency shelters made by means of the Housing Corporation and the local authorities (Nishiyama, 1989).

T. Knoroz, *Dissecting the Danchi*,
https://doi.org/10.1007/978-981-16-8460-9_2

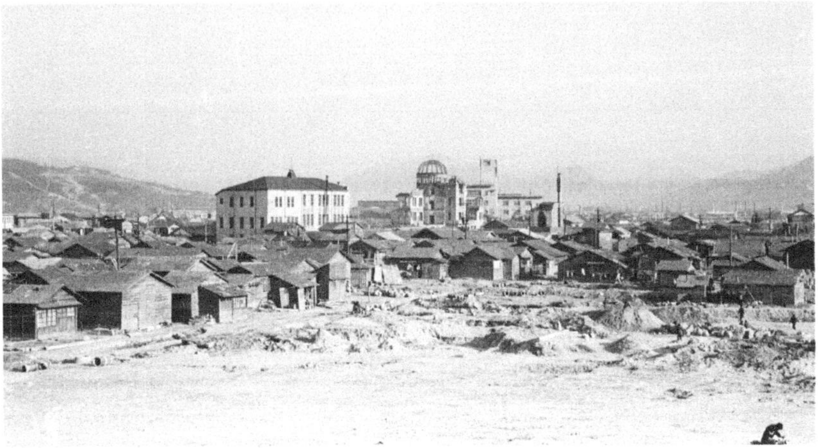

Fig. 2.1 Central Hiroshima, 1952, taken by Uzō Nishiyama (*Source* Courtesy of Uzō Nishiyama Memorial Library)

In March 1946, this program and other "non-urgent" construction was suppressed: the government pushed for another 250,000 units to be built exclusively for workers in prioritized industries, considered essential for the economic recovery of the nation (ibid.). Ordinary people had to survive on their own: anything that had some walls and a roof was then judged adequate for a new home. There are numerous records of people repurposing buses, trams, boats, former bomb shelters, and spaces under bridges into dwellings (Figs. 2.2, 2.3, and 2.4) up until the late 1950s (Matsumoto, 2017). In 1947 the Housing Corporation, which had been producing cheap rowhouses for the government that looked much like army barracks, was disbanded by the American Occupation Headquarters, which deemed it an "instrument of militarism," and all the dwellings it owned at the time were sold, leaving the question of further construction unresolved (Waswo, 2002).

For the United States' Occupation Government, SCAP, the main goal was to democratize and demilitarize Japan, which previously refused to capitulate, despite a slim chance of victory before the bombing of Hiroshima and Nagasaki in August 1945. Despite the horrible aftermaths of the atomic bombings, the surviving Japanese population did not oppose the occupation; in fact, after a short period of fear, most

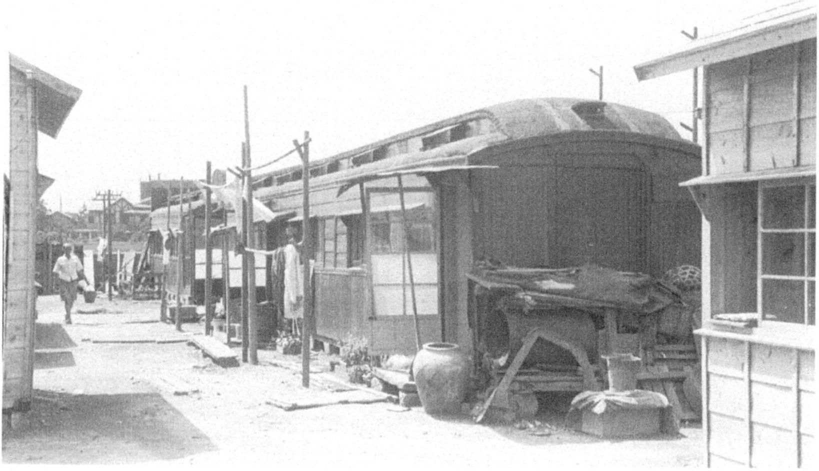

Fig. 2.2 A train carriage repurposed as a dwelling, around Sumida, Tokyo, 1952 (*Source and author* Same as Fig. 2.1)

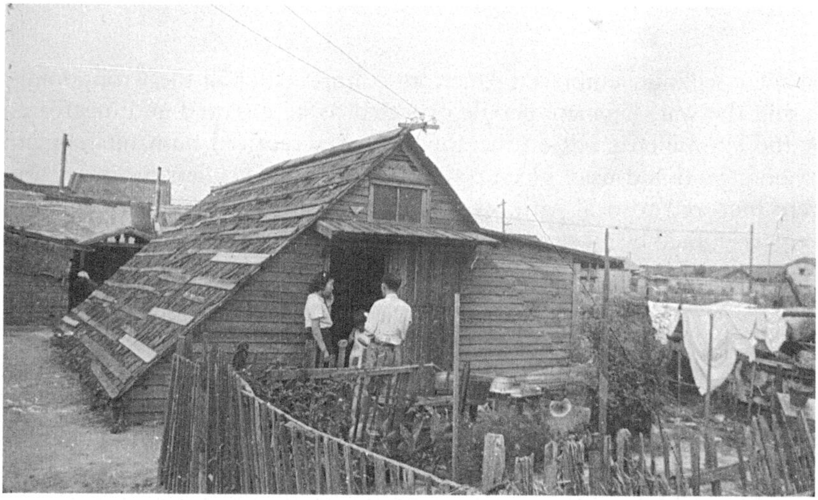

Fig. 2.3 An army firewood warehouse repurposed as a house for two families, Amagasaki, Hyōgo, 1952 (*Source and author* Same as Fig. 2.1)

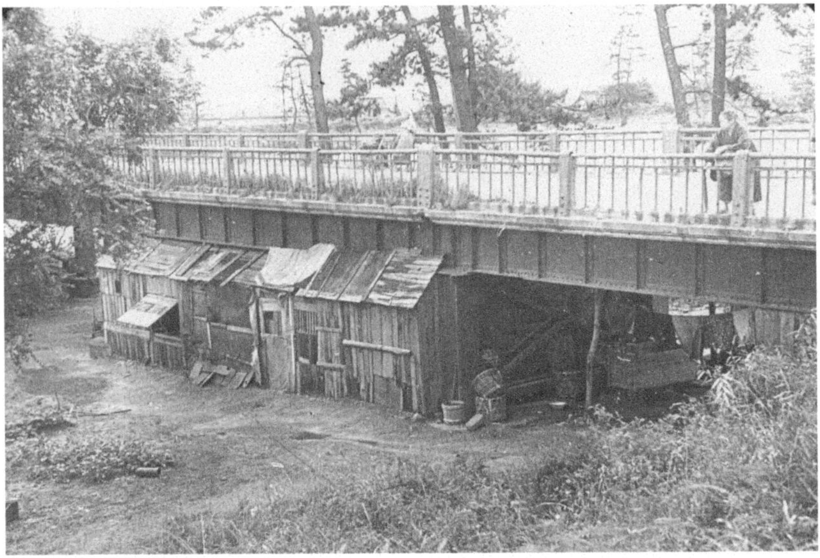

Fig. 2.4 Houses under Mukogawa Bridge, Hyōgo, 1952 (*Source and author* Same as Fig. 2.1)

Japanese willingly embraced American culture. After all the wrongdoings during the war, Japanese people expected to be enslaved and mistreated by the US military, but on the contrary, they received humanitarian and economic aid and were given protection. The US soldiers, in their turn, were prepared to deal with revolts and indoctrinated aggressiveness but were welcomed by most civilians with smiles and gratitude (Atkins, 2017). The reason for such a docile reaction might be psychological effects of the *ie*-system, wherein the most legally powerful member of the family (father) and of the nation (Emperor) is respected and obeyed without any possibility of questioning his authority. When the entire nation witnessed extreme superiority of military forces of the enemy and the surrender of their Emperor, the role of the all-powerful leader was subconsciously passed on to the American government.

From 1945 until 1952, SCAP closely monitored the work of the newly appointed Japanese government. American officials believed that *ie* traditions heavily contributed to the radical nationalism of Japanese soldiers, who during the war were seen to irrationally self-sacrifice and engage in highly immoral military crimes in the name of the Emperor. Consequently, SCAP directed efforts to de-feudalize Japanese families by promoting closer relationships between family members, devoid of extended relatives influence, with equal rights given to women. Film-making studios were banned from producing samurai movies, which had been highly popular in the prewar era, and were encouraged to film love stories with kissing scenes, which had not been previously permitted in Japanese cinematography (ibid.).

Many authors (Hara, 2012; Neitzel, 2016; Waswo, 2002) assert that the "modernization" aspect of the government agenda concerning the multi-story mass housing construction in the 1950s, and an important influence on interior plans and advertisement methods, in most cases meant "Americanization." The American occupation government was confident that exposing Japanese people to American culture would help them become a truly democratic nation. Since most Americans did not know exactly what democracy is in a de-Americanized context and how it could be integrated into a country that had never fully embraced it before, they tended to believe that their entire culture was an integral part of the concept and that exporting it was the only solution. For instance, some SCAP officials believed that if baseball became a national sport in Japan, it could actually make lead to a more democratic nation (Guthrie-Shimizu, 2012). This way of thinking led them to close the main sumo arena in Tokyo in December 1945, and open several baseball stadiums instead. "It was no accident that democratization meant Americanization. Few if any Japanese thought otherwise, and Americans were unapologetic about it" (Atkins, 2017). Japanese people started to admire American culture in almost all possible ways: music, food, clothing, housing, and lifestyle in general. The Japanese Ministry of Construction yearly reports would regularly compare the amount and the quality of completed housing units first and foremost with the numbers in the United States, in a constant effort to "catch up." This drive to "catch up" with the West in general, and in housing conditions in particular, was present even before WWII, when living in *bunka* dwellings with their rationalized kitchen spaces inspired by housing culture from England was a synonym of "living modern." In the 1950s, the meaning of "living modern" shifted toward having a dining kitchen equipped with the latest consumer electronics, right from the covers of American magazines for 1950s housewives (Neitzel, 2016).

One specific event may have initiated the "catching up" paradigm in the Japanese architecture community. In 1946, while most Japanese cities were still in ruins, the Occupation Headquarters imported some construction materials and furniture, and contacted several Japanese contractors to construct 20,000 units of housing for the families of the US military all over the country. The most famous settlement, Lincoln Center, was built right in front of the Parliament Building and Imperial Palace in central Tokyo (Fig. 2.5). Very little was known to the general public about these gleaming white townhouses behind high fences, but the few Japanese workers building them had an opportunity to learn cutting-edge construction techniques.

After they and some lucky architects, such as Uzō Nishiyama, witnessed and documented much more advanced interior furnishings, plumbing, kitchens, and bathroom equipment, as compared to what was available in Japan at the time, the process of striving to achieve the same kind of comfort and modernity could no longer be stopped (Matsumoto, 2017).

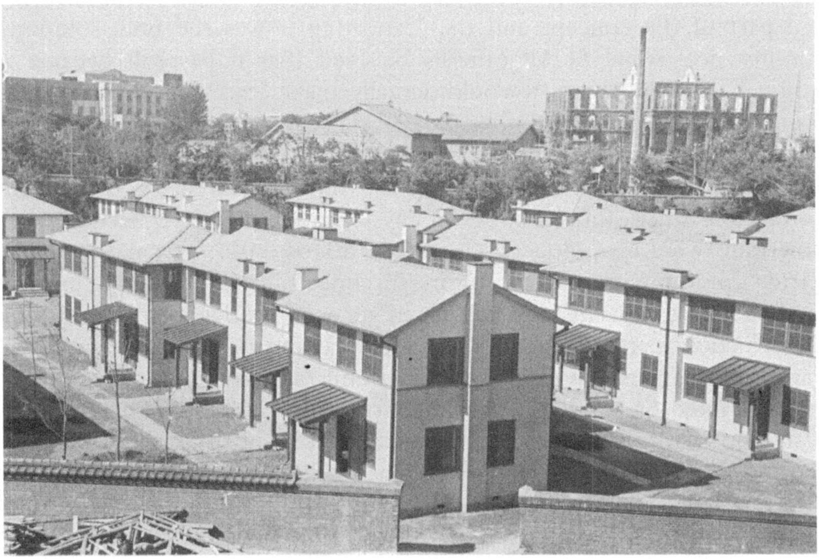

Fig. 2.5 Lincoln Center, Tokyo, 1946 (*Source and author* Same as Fig. 2.1)

However, replicating American housing standards took much longer than catching up with the popular media and consumption markets. In the immediate postwar period, the central government decided to focus on rebuilding the national economy by supporting industry rather than housing recovery, choosing a completely different approach from the European countries that decided to prioritize social welfare (Hirayama & Ronald, 2006; Izuhara, 2000; Uchida, 2002). It is impossible to say whether this strategy was the most sustainable way to recover the country, but the prewar industrial production level was already regained by 1953. Soon after the end of the war, the government introduced Keisha Seisan Hōshiki, a priority production program that defined the "priority sectors" of industrial development such as coal, steel, and electric power that promised the fastest returns in a condition of scarce resources.

Toei Takanawa Apartments: The First Reinforced-Concrete Public Housing Complex

In the meantime, the main source of new housing in the immediate postwar period in Japan were private companies providing company dormitories as well as cheap loans for their employees and the individual efforts of private landlords. By 1950 the housing shortage became impossible for the private market to address, even with the occasional financial assistance from the local municipalities. In addition to the housing scarcity caused directly and indirectly by the consequences of the war, the problems of rapid population increase made the situation even direr.

> Through the bombing and the dispersal, we have lost 18.9 % of the total units of housings in whole Japan, while 44 % of total units in cities were lost. And these are 7 cities where 80 % of the population became homeless and afflicted, and the cities with more than 60 % of the inhabitants having deprived of housings number 16.
> —Goroh Itoh, Director of Housing Bureau of Ministry of Construction, in Housing Situation in Japan Report, 1950

It was estimated that to solve the housing crisis, more than 400,000 units of new housing had to be constructed every year to supply the demand (Itoh, 1950). The same report shows that the proportion of rental versus owner-occupied housing flipped after the war: 71.8% of units built since the end of the war was occupied by the owners, 15% was rented, and 9.2% was state-supplied, while in prewar times, approximately 30% of housing in urban areas had been owner-occupied with 70% to-let and supplied. The existing private rental housing market came into decline due to prolonged rent controls and material shortages, and these numbers suggest that the shortage was especially harsh for the families that were unable to afford their own land.

After the disbandment of Housing Corporation in 1947, following directions from SCAP, the newly founded Construction Ministry subsidized the construction of Publicly Operated housing units for the most financially struggling groups, first in wooden *nagaya*-type buildings and later in low-rise reinforced-concrete buildings (Waswo, 2002). To improve urban fire and earthquake resistance and better control construction costs, Mikishi Abe, the president of the Construction Ministry, who studied construction technology in the United States, pushed for collaboration with university researchers in designing standard plans for the first reinforced-concrete apartments after the war (Nishiyama, 1989). Low-rise wooden *nagaya* housing was a relatively ordinary typology, reproducible with only minor checks of dimensions and materials, so timber construction started right away, but deciding on standard plans for concrete buildings with few local precedents took much longer. The main point of departure for designers was the layouts of the prewar Dōjunkai Apartments (discussed in Chapter 1) as the only existing example of reinforced-concrete minimal housing in Japan. In the postwar reality, however, Dōjunkai's high construction budget was impossible to secure, so the goal was to minimize costs, and therefore, the floor areas of the apartments, but also to come up with efficient, modern living spaces that would be in tune with the democratization strategy of postwar Japan.

The first result of this research was the four-story reinforced-concrete neighborhood built in Takanawa Nishidaicho in 1948, comprising 48 buildings with 180 units. Continuing the legacy of Dōjunkai apartments' interiors, the 40-square-meter plans had two multifunctional six- and eight-tatami rooms that could be used for sleeping, dining, and living depending on the time of the day just like those in traditional prewar housing, a tiny separate kitchen and a toilet, all connected by the core corridor with the entrance efficiently squeezed into the concrete shell (Fig. 2.6). Compared to the Dōjunkai, the corridor was enlarged and now

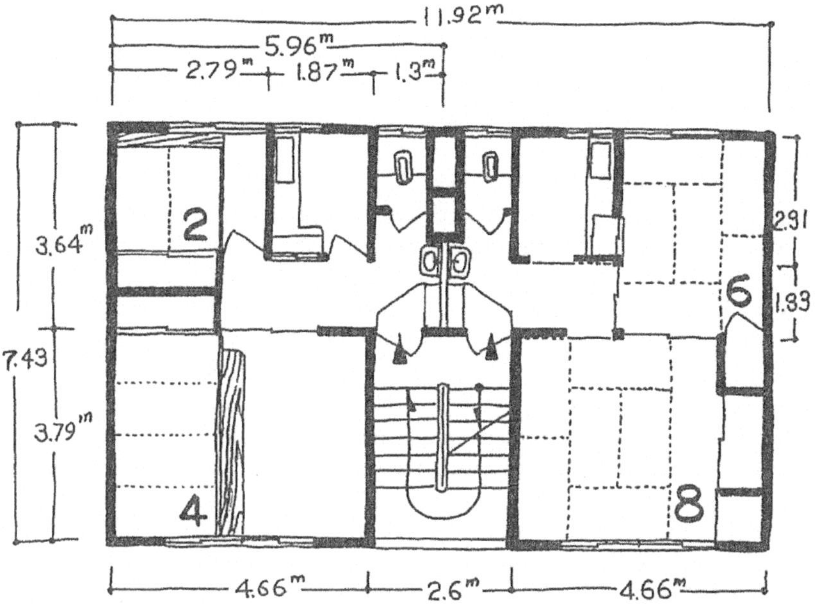

Fig. 2.6 Toei Takanawa Apartments. Right side: standard plan, left side: experimental unit (*Source* Uzō Nishiyama [1989]. Sumai no kōkongaku: gendai Nihon jūtakushi. Tokyo: Shōkokusha, p. 331. Courtesy of Uzō Nishiyama Memorial Library)

opened into all the rooms for better circulation. The designers made a point to continue challenging the prewar custom of the husband sleeping separately from his wife and children, who usually shared one smaller room, and intended the couple to sleep together in the bigger room that was already tested in Dōjunkai Apartments. Aside from the tatami mats, another feature of traditional Japanese housing remained: as in prewar *nagaya* and Dōjunkai, there were no bathrooms included in the buildings. *Sentō* (public baths) were still the most common way to maintain personal hygiene and an important socializing venue in every neighborhood.

The construction method employed for Takanawa was innovative for Japanese housing industry at the time. Unlike European modernist-inspired Dōjunkai, in which massive structural pillars supported the weight of the floors, Toei Takanawa Apartments had entirely load-bearing concrete walls. These minimize the budget and avoid uneven perimeters in the rooms that were considered an issue in Dōjunkai plans (Fig. 1.17, Chapter 1), because they obstructed the fitting of furniture in the limited space. The neighborhood was designated as experimental, so only young government-related workers such as policemen and university professors were allowed to move in.

Two units out of 180 had alternative layouts: the eight-tatami multifunctional room was enlarged at the expense of storage spaces that were relocated to another room, making it only three-tatami in area. The big room was then divided with a wooden stepping board into the "sleeping" area with four tatami mats and the floored "living-dining" area that was supposed to have western-style furniture, which was still a rarity in residential contexts. The idea of a dining table had no precedent in traditional Japanese housing, where people would either eat from individual trays, sitting on tatami or cushions in hierarchal order, or, in case of the poorer parts of the population, eat from bowls or from a shared pot, grouped around the stove or outside the house. In the late Meiji period (1868–1912), housing reformers invented and popularized the use of *chabudai*, a low table with collapsible legs, among educated urban families. It allowed the family members to be closer together, avoiding the hierarchy, and took less space than an ordinary dining table, since one could still sit on cushions instead of chairs (Koizumi, 1979). The experimental layouts in Takanawa, however, were meant to take the westernization one step toward the fully chaired lifestyle.

The design of these two units was most likely influenced by Uzō Nishiyama's "Eating and Sleeping Separation Theory," which a few years later would be adopted for all multi-story mass housing in Japan. Nishiyama argued that all-purpose tatami rooms, despite saving the much-needed square meters with their versatility and superficially resembling the ideas of modernist architecture, required daily effort to adapt to different functions and were one of the reasons why traditional Japanese housing lagged behind Western modernist architecture and its functionally segregated interiors. However, the idea of sleeping on beds was still questionable even in experimental settings, hence the partial living room solution. Although the alternative layouts proved to be no more popular than the standard plans, Takanawa apartments attracted the architectural community's attention:

> ...With the experience gained in the construction of municipal housing after the first postwar four-story apartment house of reinforced-concrete was put up in Takanawa in 1948, it became increasingly obvious that apartment houses of even greater height were both possible and necessary in the larger cities of Japan.
> —Yujiro Kaneko (1958). Multi-story Housing in a City Growing Upward. *Shinkenchiku: New Architecture of Japan*, 33(12), 18

Although the Construction Ministry's subsidies were non-systematic and only a few municipalities received them, the work on standard plan optimization continued in the hopes that municipally built timber *nagaya* barracks could be gradually replaced with safe, reinforced-concrete buildings.

Lifestyle Revolution: The DK and the "51C"

Despite the architectural success of Takanawa, the inflation and inaccessibility of construction materials made it increasingly difficult to build dwellings for rent. The central government once again turned its attention toward encouraging the development of the private housing market: in 1950, all previous rent controls on newly constructed units were removed, and the Housing Loan Corporation was established with the government money and U.S. Counterpart Aid Funds. The main purpose of the company was to provide long-term loans at very low interest for the construction of individual houses by eligible private citizens and collective rental housing by companies. Loans did not include the cost of land and were only given for houses of less than 100 square meters in total floor area, with the maximum cost set by the Ministry of Construction. Any parts exceeding the 60-square-meter area would not be included in the loan. The loan period depended on the material of construction, from 15 years for timber to 30 years for reinforced-concrete or fireproof construction. The Corporation also established higher building standards such as minimum floor surface per person and fireproofing requirements to enhance the quality of the urban fabric.

Only a few middle-class families, who either inherited land or were affluent enough to purchase it, could afford a loan from Housing Loan Corporation for construction, while the others still rented units in old and overcrowded timber buildings or lived in illegally built slums or temporary emergency barracks. To balance out the policies, the government implemented the Public Housing Act in June 1951, a measure that allocated systematic subsidies to all municipalities for roughly half the standard construction costs of low-rent Publicly Operated units (social mass housing) all over the country. The development of this law was a result of political tension between the Ministry of Construction that was eager to assert its power in provision of all housing policies, and the Ministry of Welfare, responsible for providing housing assistance to the most disadvantaged and poorly housed families and the homeless, who couldn't afford the existing municipal rental units even if they were available (Waswo, 2002). Ministry of Construction won the race by submitting their draft of the Public Housing Act approved to the diet faster, thus establishing their state-profit-oriented agenda of limiting social housing access to tenants with steady employment, who could supposedly contribute to the rebuilding of Japanese economy much more, than the disadvantaged and the homeless who couldn't secure jobs. Ministry of Welfare could only succeed on pushing for an additional Type 2 of Publicly Operated units in the final draft of the law, that offered cheaper rents than Type 1 yet also had considerably smaller floor plans that were meant to accommodate the lower margin of the employed applicants (ibid.).

When the law was passed, the Ministry of Construction returned its attention to the ongoing process of designing and upgrading standard plans for reinforced-concrete public housing,[1] with the Japanese Architects' Association taking part in the race. In the same year, Yasumi Yoshitake's laboratory from the University of Tokyo's architecture department significantly improved the plans from Takanawa and presented a series of "51" plans with "A," "B," and "C" subtypes, of which "C" was considered the most "perfected" and started to be constructed on a wide scale (Shinozawa & Yoshinaga, 2017).

The 35-square-meter "51C" plan had two Japanese-style rooms—an ongoing concession to traditional lifestyles, as most people were still opposed to sleeping in Western-style beds (Fig. 2.7, left). The six-tatami master bedroom faced north, and the four-and-a-half tatami child

[1] Throughout the book, the term "public housing" is used to address all fully or partially government-funded mass-housing projects. Those projects that were built specifically to house disadvantaged low-income families will be referred to as "Publicly Operated" or "social housing" units.

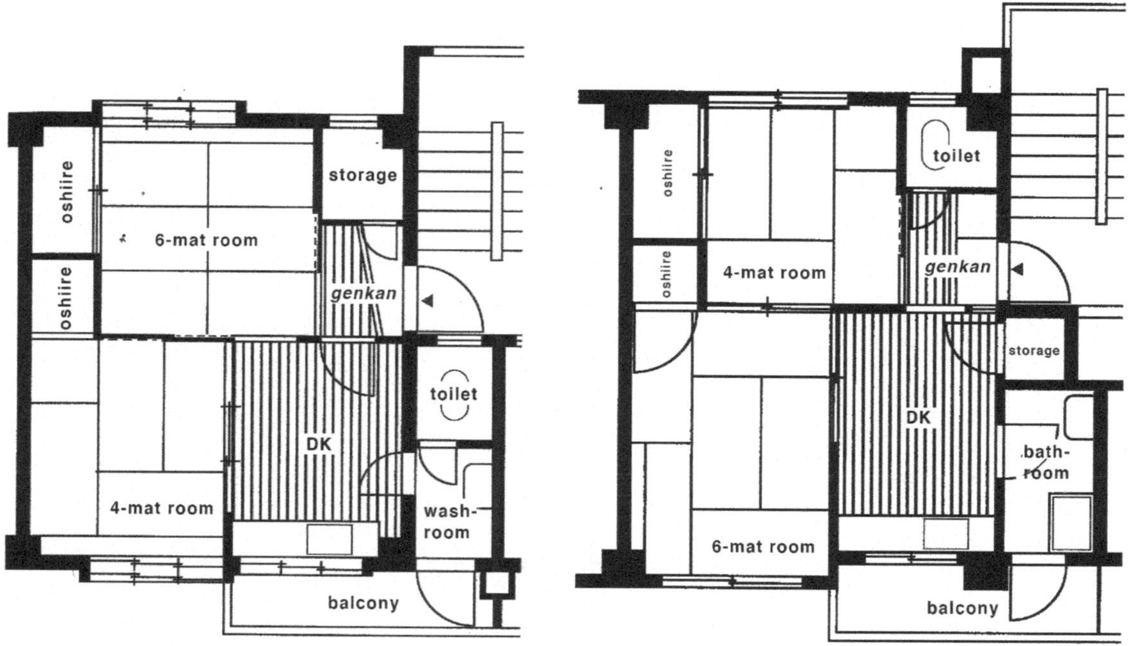

Fig. 2.7 Left: Plan "51C" by Yoshitake Laboratory, right: plan "55-4N-2K-2" by JHC (*Source* Shinozawa, K., & Yoshinaga, K. (2017). *Danchi zukai chikei zōsei randosukēpu jū-tō madori kara yomitoku sekkei shikō*. Kyoto: Gakugei shuppansha, p. 41)

bedroom was oriented toward the south. Instead of movable *fusuma* partitions like in Takanawa, they were divided by a fixed wall, solidly defining spaces for parents and children with individual entrances. This solved the lack of privacy in the preceding *nagaya*-inspired plans, that were thought to limit individual freedom, and therefore, the much-desired democratization of Japanese families by the Occupation Headquarters and Japanese government and architects alike.

Compared to Takanawa plans, the width of the building was reduced by one meter to save more money on construction, while the kitchen area was enlarged, so one of the rooms had to become 3.5 tatami mats smaller. However, the sacrifice was necessary for a greater cause: the introduction of the dining-kitchen, a game-changing domestic innovation, from that moment on abbreviated as DK—a kitchen coupled with additional space for a dining table and four chairs, an invention attributed to Shigebumi Suzuki, who worked at Yoshitake's Laboratory (Fig. 2.8). Despite the floor surface reduction, the architects also included a proper *senmenjo* washroom with a balcony access and a sink in front of the toilet, a luxury improving hand washing laundry process that was absent from previous public housing where the sink had to be squeezed close by the entrance.

The architects believed that, together with individual rooms for parents and children, DK could become the main tool for shaping the "ideal" democratic middle-class nuclear family, as it could rationally separate eating and sleeping and bring all family members together for meals, including the housewife. Before the war, Japanese working-class women rarely stayed in the main living areas during the day since the dirt-floor traditional kitchens were usually located in the furthest and darkest recesses—the least enjoyable parts of the house. Takanawa Apartments didn't fully change that pattern, with their kitchens located in narrow rooms on the northern sides of the buildings, but "51C" made a breakthrough in elevating the position of women in the house. The DK was moved to the southern wall, separated from the four-and-a-half tatami room by four *fusuma* panels that could be opened to unify the spaces. This way, the users were given a choice: to open up the *fusuma* and consume meals on the tatami (creating a makeshift living-dining-kitchen), or to sit at the table, all in the same room. Given the limited supply of affordable Western furniture at the time, this versatile solution allowed families to start from the first pattern and purchase a dining set in the future (ibid.).

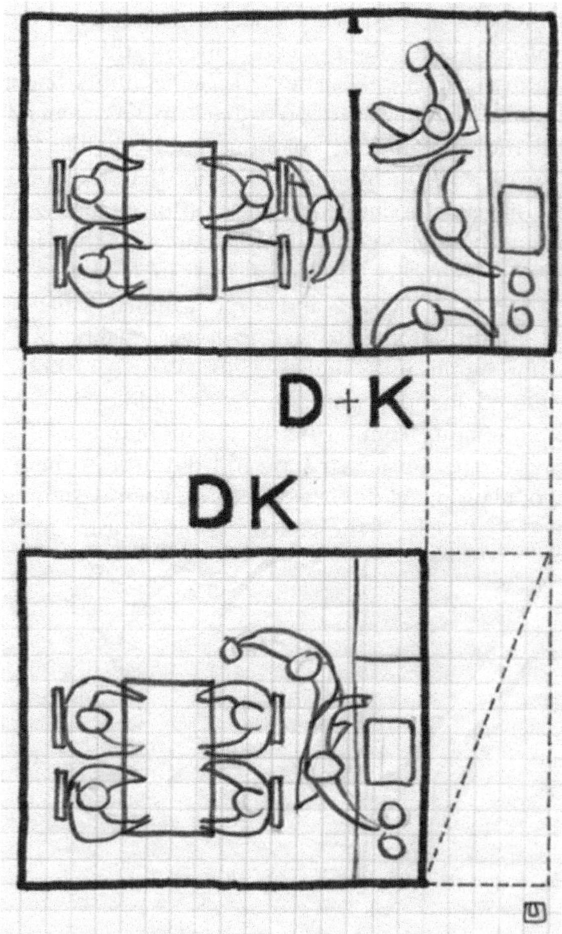

Fig. 2.8 A DK diagram by Uzō Nishiyama (*Source* Courtesy of Uzō Nishiyama Memorial Library)

Soon after the presentation of the plan, it was implemented in Publicly Operated reinforced-concrete projects: one of the first was Toyama Mights in Shinjuku (Fig. 2.9). The "51" series units had the smallest possible floor area (from 33 to 46 square meters depending on the type), but still the total number of households eligible for these low-rent housing exceeded the number of units that the local authorities were able to construct because of their non-profitability. As only low-income applicants (yet who could demonstrate that they had a full-time job) could win a raffle to live there until their income surpassed a certain maximum cap for both Type 1 and Type 2 units, while others in the same financial conditions had to live in lower quality, privately rented dwellings paying significantly higher rents (Waswo, 2002). The initiative thus promoted inequality in the lower middle class, hindered the already approved tenants from trying to earn more in fear of being evicted and not finding a better place to stay, and did little to help the poorest parts of the population. As discussed before, when designing the Public Housing Act, the officials of the Construction Ministry made a decision

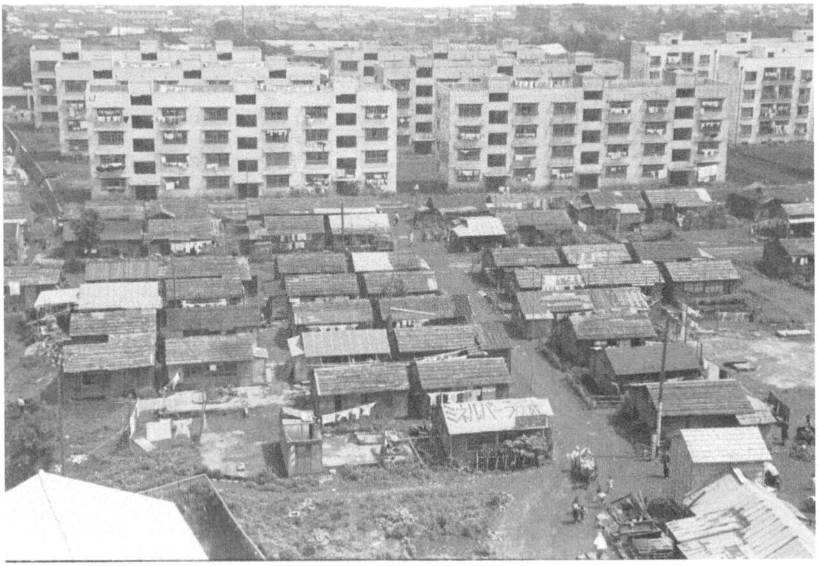

Fig. 2.9 Publicly Operated Toyama Mights reinforced-concrete complex in front of air raid barracks, Shinjuku, Tokyo, 1951 (*Source* Same as Fig. 2.8)

to sacrifice the unemployed for the sake of future prosperity. Interestingly enough, not many things have changed since the postwar period: the Public Housing Act is still in place as of 2020, and even if the conditions of full-time employment were abolished for certain disadvantaged groups such as the elderly and single parents, the current social housing system still retains many of its original shortcomings.[2]

The Japan Housing Corporation and Its First Experiments

The top management of the Construction Ministry in 1951 was expecting the postwar housing shortage to be solved in the next five years. Some thought that the private rental market would be recovered. Others believed that mass homeownership could be achieved by the Housing Loan Corporation initiative alone if the development of the national economy raises the salaries and thus people's eligibility for the construction loans (Waswo, 2002).

The industrial recovery and nationwide improvement in living conditions were indeed remarkable because, by 1955, food and clothing supplies per family had already surpassed the prewar levels. The housing situation, however, was still far from the prewar level and the forecasts of the Construction Ministry were not met. The delay of housing recovery provoked serious discussions in the cabinet as it declared an "Expansion and Enrichment of Housing Measures" that made the housing policy a priority job for the government from that point on (Ministry of Construction, 1965). It was recognized that higher-income households than those eligible for Publicly Operated Houses found it difficult to obtain rental housing in the major cities. As a solution, the Japan Housing Corporation (JHC) was established in February 1955 with a bold initial goal: completing 400,000 dwellings for middle-class families by the end of the year (ibid.). The Corporation's main purpose was to construct fire- and quake-proof residential buildings on an unprecedentedly large scale around large cities, where the housing shortage was most significant because of the mass urbanization that started in the 1950s with the rise of

[2] During my fieldwork in Publicly Operated Wakamiya Danchi in 2018, two tenants admitted that they deliberately avoided of shifting from their part-time jobs to being fully employed in fear of slightly surpassing the maximum income cap and not being able to find an affordable accommodation without the state subsidies.

the national economy. In addition to securing government-owned enterprise subsidies and low-interest loans, various large private companies were asked to invest in the JHC. With such funding, JHC could afford to improve the size and quality of the "51C" standard plans and buy new land for construction, overcoming the financial limitations of the Public Housing Act.

Prompted by the soaring land prices in the cities, JHC initially focused on maximizing the apartment density and thus the floor count of the buildings. In 1956, they began construction of two high-rise reinforced-concrete experiments—a ten-story Building No. 1 in Harumi Apartment Complex on reclaimed land in Tokyo Bay, and an eleven-story Nishinagabori Apartment House in Osaka on a site donated by Osaka City. The purpose of erecting these two very different projects was to compare "a fairly traditional" Nishinagabori with long access corridors with "deliberately experimental" skip-floor Harumi (Shō, 1958). The choice of the building heights was influenced by a study that started back in 1953 when the Housing Bureau of the Construction Ministry commissioned the Japan Architects Association to research the possibilities of constructing high-rise apartments affordable on public housing budgets. The study concluded that if floor areas and the structure were properly calculated, reinforced-concrete apartment blocks up to eleven stories in height could be built with minimal use of expensive steel frame (which was considered necessary for buildings of this type before) and therefore finally implemented in public housing projects (Kaneko, 1958).

Unlike Takanawa apartments, with one standard plan per project, Nishinagabori featured a variety of residential layouts on different floors, all featuring a DK, with 50 out of 263 units designed for a single-person occupancy, prior to this a largely neglected typology in public housing. Already during the drafting process and budget planning, it was decided that Nishinagabori would target affluent residents, unlike the initially middle-class-oriented Harumi, so the interiors were well-furnished and technologically advanced: counters with built in stainless sinks replaced the less hygienic artificial stone dishwashing basins common in preceding concrete public housing, and fridges and gas cookers—a novelty and a surprising luxury at the time—installed in their proper place in the kitchen ensemble.

Another innovation was a dual-function system with shops and offices on the ground level and the floor above, with apartments occupying the remaining higher floors—an idea imported from the modern movement in Europe. However, the configuration of the residential floors was still based on long, lateral corridor access, with the same circulation logic as in prewar *nagaya*. This design, despite its intuitive simplicity for Japanese users, and cost efficiency, has several weaknesses, such as the unattractive look of the access corridors on the façade, the lack of visual privacy for the apartment entrances from the street, and lack of natural light and privacy for the entrance side of every apartment, since some windows have to open into the public corridor. While the last shortcoming is unavoidable in this building typology, the first two issues were solved by a simple yet elegant exterior design: the northern façade of Nishinagabori Apartments was covered by a wall striped with narrow openings running all the way from the bottom to the top.

The building No. 1 of Harumi Apartment Complex, on the other hand, was far from elegant and simple, its structure unadorned, sturdy, lacking color and ornamentation—all to save funds for a massive reinforced-concrete structure and the concomitant amount of steel reinforcing. It had a very monumental quality with its many ins and outs and frames and fixtures exposed to view, yet was designed in careful consideration of the existing surroundings and the adjacent four-story buildings in the same complex.

One of the most innovative ideas of Harumi Apartments was the skip-floor system, meaning that there were corridors only on every third floor, with access to others by stairs shared by apartments in pairs. The advantage of that was that, on the corridor-less floors, the units had two opposite walls in direct contact with the outer air, thus attaining better ventilation and access to natural light. Ideally, if the size of a single apartment could be bigger, it would be possible to join two of them vertically like Le Corbusier did in his Unite d'Habitations, the main reference for Harumi Building No. 1 designed by architect Kunio Maekawa, one of Le Corbusier's former apprentices. However, the budget didn't allow it, and the apartments on the corridor floor with no double exposure had dark and poorly ventilated kitchens and bathrooms.

The size of the tatami bedrooms in Harumi Apartments was unusual and had no precedents in Japanese traditions. Because of the metrification in concrete construction, each tatami had to be made smaller than usual (850 × 1700 mm instead of 1769 × 880 mm for Kanto and 1910 × 955 mm for Kansai) and laid side by side, without the usual short measure parts. Tatami in Harumi established a new tatami size category for public housing that would later be humorously called "Kōdan-tatami" or “Danchima.” When the building was completed, some architects criticized the designers for assuming that people would not care too much about the mat sizes because they were too narrow to even set out two sets of bedding side by side (Otake, 1958).

As soon as Nishinagabori and Harumi were completed, it became clear that the construction budgets entailed setting higher rents than initially expected, making the units available to the upper-middle class only. The quality of constructions sites in both cases wasn’t optimal for tall buildings, so some thought the extra expenses could be avoided in the future. But it wasn’t the only issue: necessary communication systems such as telephone and television lines as well as elevators were significantly more expensive in Japan than in Europe at the time, due to low demand, further increasing the cost of high-rise buildings (Shō, 1958). In the case of Harumi, with its expensive megastructure, the interiors of the units had to be left so plain that some of the first occupants thought that the building was still incomplete (Fig. 2.10).

Despite all their problems, in 1958 it was considered a great luxury to live in such apartments. As discussed in the article dedicated to Harumi Apartments in *Shinkenchiku* (New Architecture) magazine, multi-story apartment housing already had strong emotional connotations in the minds of Japanese people.

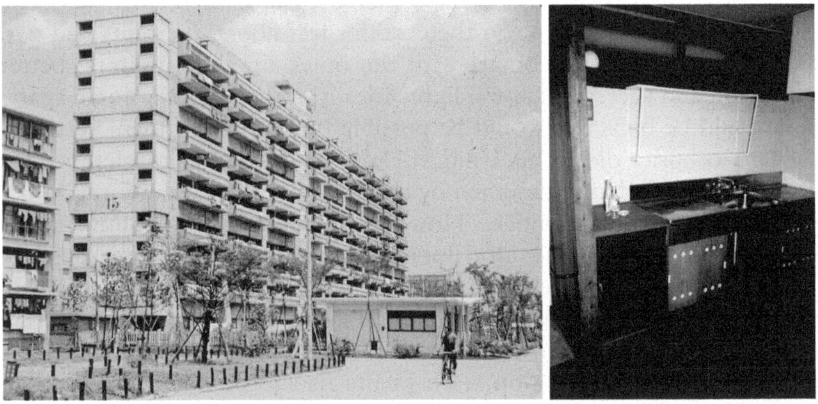

Fig. 2.10 Left: Building No. 1, Harumi Apartments. Right: kitchen of a unit in Building No. 1, Harumi Apartments. Photograph by Uzō Nishiyama, 1959 (*Source* Courtesy of Uzō Nishiyama Memorial Library)

> It brings to mind the picture of a gleaming new building rising up above the flimsy old-style houses around it. Furthermore, it hints of something luxurious and Western, something rather remote from the lives of most Japanese... A multi-story apartment building in Japan is a de luxe apartment building – a flower high in the mountains, as the Japanese saying goes.
> —Akira Shō (1958). High-rise Apartment Houses Today. *Shinkenchiku: New Architecture of Japan*, 33(12), 22

Indeed, up until the 1970s, Harumi Apartments remained a habitat of people with a certain social status, evidenced by high-end black cars lining up every morning in front of the building's entrance.[3]

The Spread of Danchi

Securing the "Group Land"

The architectural community was mostly positive about continuing the tests with high-rise housing, but the immediate results of the first steps by the JHC provoked a lot of discontent in the media at the government financing such costly experiments (Kaneko, 1958).

In the light of the public pressure, the middle-class-oriented JHC had to temporarily suspend high-rise housing projects because of the associated costs and the abovementioned emotional connotations. They turned back to the already well-received and widely tested public housing four-story slab buildings, but for their minimal plans to appeal to the new expected wave of middle-class residents, the interiors had to be improved. Moreover, the architectural community's criticisms of the declining community ties in public housing complexes were multiplying: the new projects had to be upgraded with shared facilities and infrastructure.

The high land prices in the overcrowded city centers left the Corporation with such large-scale building ambitions no choice to buy off patches of cheaper land around railways and in the agricultural suburbs.

[3] Nishinagabori Apartments is still standing; it was recently renovated and available as rental property from the UR, the successor of the Japan Housing Corporation as of 2021, but Harumi Apartment Complex gradually lost its original appearance due to concrete discoloration, and was abandoned by its first-wave residents in the early 1970s, when the first graffiti started to appear on the walls. Soon after, Harumi became a problematic neighborhood, repeating the fate of many European brutalist mass-housing projects, and was fully demolished in 1997.

From 1955 the JHC started to construct four- and five-story ferroconcrete apartment blocks typically arranged in districts around a community hall—a building pattern that received the generic name "danchi," literally meaning "group land." The origin of the word goes back to 1941 when Housing Corporation used it for one of its collective housing projects for war-industry workers. It described an urban typology built anew, where owners of several buildings evenly share land and public facilities, a situation unusual for land-owning Japanese society of the time. The word was reused in 1958 in one of the JHC report pamphlets and gained its final definition with the spread and normalization of JHC-designed housing in the country, and now it describes clusters of mid- to high-rise apartment buildings with shared infrastructure,[4] both rented and owner-occupied.

For the Japanese government, Japan Housing Corporation became a milestone of national modernization. Advised by the Occupation Headquarters, it strived to convey American values to the young Japanese by promoting loving conjugal relationships and the necessity of moving out of the hierarchical multi-generational houses—thankfully, now the JHC apartments could welcome the young couples until they saved up enough money to buy their own house. With working nuclear families encouraged to have at least two children, the demographic growth and the economic recovery of the country were assured. These family units were to become the majority of the Japanese population, forming the "universal middle class," with all men securely employed and working long hours while their wives sustained their undisturbed physical recovery at home with daily cleaning, cooking, and singlehandedly taking care of children who would eventually take over their parents' grand task.[5]

DK as the Engine of Modernity and Danchi as the Origin of the "New Middle Class"

Although the JHC was created with the stated purpose of accommodating the middle class, previously neglected by public housing, it was not precisely true (Neitzel, 2016). Before the war, the majority of the

[4] Company housing included, since the land use, masterplans and exteriors were mostly identical to the JHC projects and the Publicly Operated Housing.

[5] Unfortunately, the second wave feminist movement that reformed American society in the 1960s didn't spur any serious parallel activism in Japan: the gender inequality in family roles and employment possibilities is still a huge problem even today.

middle class in Japan was constituted by small business owners. However, there was also a group called "the new middle class" in the media of the Meiji and Taishō periods, distinguished by the aspect that such families did not own any property and earned their living through employment as white-collar workers, as well as having a certain established "cultural" lifestyle. Even after the war, this "new middle class" remained a statistical minority and did not need to be catered to by such a large-scale housing program. In fact, the postwar "new middle class" might have been forcefully created by the Japanese government to pursue its goals of economic recovery. "A careful reading of the debates that led to the establishment of the JHC, however, suggest that this 'middle class' was less forgotten than found for the purpose of creating the institution." (ibid.)[6] This is evidenced by the fact that soon after the establishment of the Japan Housing Corporation, the income eligibility requirements for the Housing Loan Corporation program were raised, and those for Public Housing applications were lowered, thus creating a wide gap for the JHC's potential target residents (ibid.).

The rental fees of the JHC danchi apartments amounted to twice as much as those of Publicly Operated units of the same size, while the incomes of the prospective tenants had to be at least 5.5 times higher than the monthly fee. It was "an insurmountable barrier to most of the employed population" (Waswo, 2002). At the same time, people who could actually afford to live in JHC-built danchi would prefer private housing opportunities with larger floor areas, so JHC had to decide on a clever marketing strategy to keep the steady demand even after the severe housing shortage would be solved. They chose to promote the prestige of the "middle classness" and the idea that their danchi was its exclusive supplier. In the ten-year history booklet of Japan Housing Corporation, this is best summarized in the phrase that attributed "modern consciousness of how to live" to all "new middle-class" families, therefore they needed a correspondingly new modern living environment equipped with the latest amenities (Jū Nenshi Kankō Iinkai, 1965).

Departing from the tested efficiency of the "51C," the JHC researchers committed to mass producing the new living standards that could overshadow the affordability of the Publicly Operated housing and reform

[6] For a more detailed history of the JHC-built danchi and the new middle class of Japan, see Neitzel, L.L. (2016). *The Life We Longed For: Danchi Housing and the Middle Class Dream in Postwar Japan*. Chicago: MerwinAsia.

Japanese families from the inside. In 1955 the JHC presented a 40-square-meter standard plan with the complicated name 55-4N-2K-2 (Fig. 2.7, right) and its more popular variant 55-4N-2DK (Fig. 2.11), later nicknamed "Housing Corporation's 2DK," implemented for the first time in Hasune Housing Complex, built in 1957 in Tokyo. From that point, all apartment sizes in the country started to be described

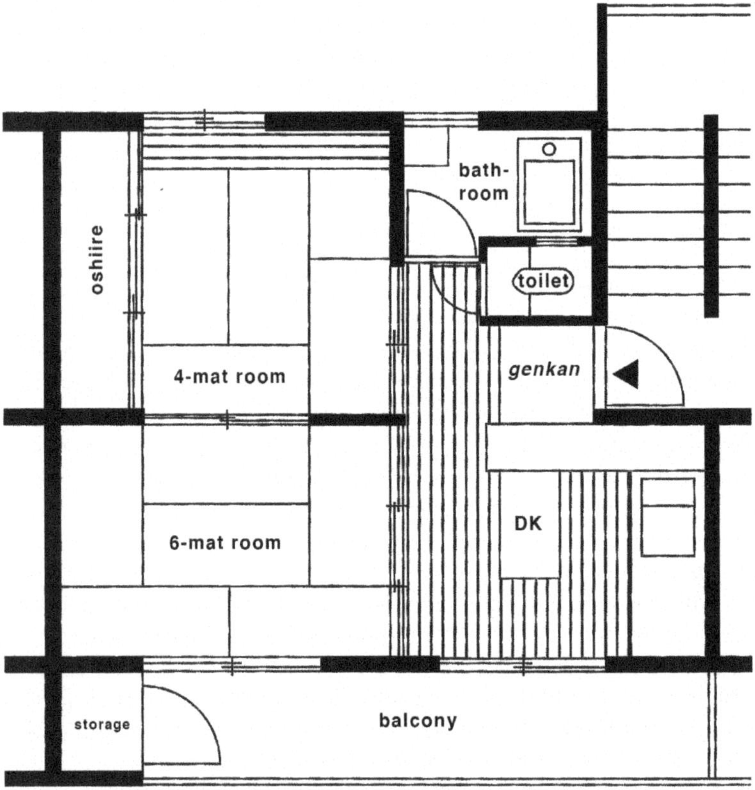

Fig. 2.11 Plan "55-4N-2DK" by JHC (*Source* Shinozawa, K., & Yoshinaga, K. [2017]. *Source Danchi zukai chikei zōsei randosukēpu jū-tō madori kara yomitoku sekkei shikō*. Kyoto: Gakugei shuppansha, p. 46)

using the code "number of rooms" plus "K," "DK" or "LDK."[7] At first glance, all the main features of "51C" stayed in place: the tatami rooms maintained their six- and four-and-a-half-mat sizes, the DK's configuration still guaranteed smooth movement between cooking, washing, and drying, and all the rooms had windows. However, the JHC chose to replace the solid wall between the tatami rooms with movable *fusuma*, sacrificing the privacy concept for more natural light and ventilation to reach every corner of the apartment and allowing the spaces to be used more flexibly. In earlier public housing, it was found out that concrete walls produced very humid environments inside, so the step back to the traditional Japanese housing patterns was necessary to make the climate adjustments in the new material context.

However, one step back was countered by two steps forward: the biggest achievement of public housing, DK, got technologically upgraded and became the main engine of the JHC's housing revolution. In the first 55-4N-2DK variations, the kitchen stone sink and gas cooker got integrated into a single counter with bottom storage cabinets, similar to kitchens in Harumi Apartments (Fig. 2.10), aligned along the wall, this time with top cabinets added. More storage solutions were provided: another wall contained a built in ceiling-height storage cabinet, with an open shelf that was supposed to become a continuation of a freestanding dining table (Fig. 2.11).

Later, architect Miho Hamaguchi, who acted as a kitchen design advisor for the JHC, invented a stainless-steel sink and gas cooker module to complete this ensemble—an easily cleanable alternative to the previous hodgepodge of poorly coordinated kitchen storage solutions with an artificial stone sink in public housing (Figs. 2.12, 2.13, and 2.14). The stainless-steel sinks were already included in the interiors of both Harumi and Nishinagabori, but this time the kitchen was conceived as a prefabricated inseparable whole, simplifying production and installation. Coupled with an electric extractor fan to get rid of the fumes, the new design

[7] The nDK naming patterns were popularized by the Japan Housing Corporation's pamphlets from 1955 and are used for all housing in the country even now, but there is no precise date when the LDK (living, dining, kitchen) was invented, because it was a natural continuation of the DK concept. The word was first used in the standard plan naming patterns of the JHC pamphlets in 1964 and for the first time implemented in Shiba Shirokane danchi in the same year.

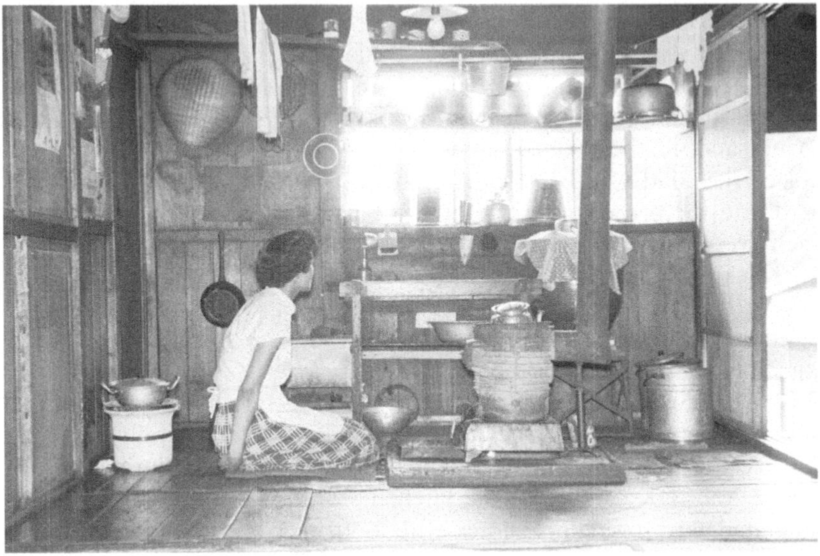

Fig. 2.12 Hokutan Horonai Coal Mine low-rise timber Publicly Operated housing, kitchen with no water supply, Hokkaido, 1957. Photograph by Uzō Nishiyama (*Source* Courtesy of Uzō Nishiyama Memorial Library)

allowed for family members to gather in the enjoyable environment of the DK even while the housewife cooked (Fig. 2.15).

Another important change was the introduction of a bathroom with a bathtub and a specifically designed small gas-powered water heater, replacing the washroom in plan "51C." This serious addition that ate away the ever scarce square meters was dictated by the remoteness of most new danchi from urban infrastructure that included public baths, but then became the proof of JHC units' superiority to the Publicly Operated housing, which would not include individual bathrooms into their plans until the late 1960s.[8]

[8] Although at the time having an individual bathroom seemed like a naturally desirable lifestyle, *sentō* always have been an important facility for neighborhood socialization. Currently, for elderly people, they remain the only place where they can meet and talk to their neighbors in a controlled and comfortable environment During fieldwork in Wakamiya Danchi in 2018, many elderly interviewees expressed regret that there are no *sentō* in vicinity.

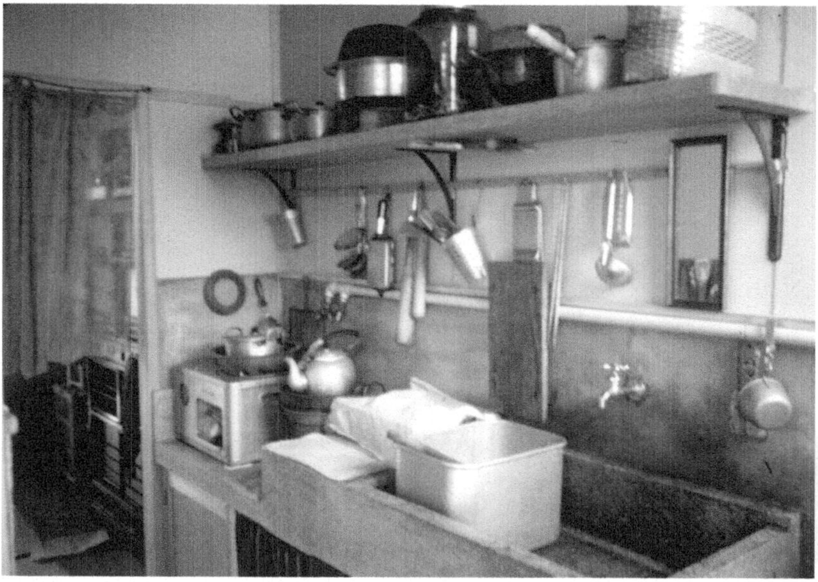

Fig. 2.13 A stone sink kitchen in reinforced-concrete Publicly Operated housing, Kyoto, 1957 (*Author and source* Same as Fig. 2.12)

Other highly publicized JHC amenities were not exactly new; concrete walls, flush toilets, metal entrance doors with locks, individual rooms for family members, and DKs could be found in earlier public and private housing, but only the JHC danchi guaranteed the full "modern lifestyle" in a branded package.

The Connection to the Soviet Housing

It is important to note, that while the insides of JHC-built and later Publicly Operated danchi were mainly associated with the adoption of the American values, these living standards were replicated from the freestanding suburban houses and townhouses. However, some Japanese housing researchers argue that austerity of danchi exterior designs, the proportions of buildings' volumes and the patterns of district master-plans compositions, coincided more with the direction in which the Soviet *khrushchevkas* mass housing was headed at the time (Hara, 2012). The

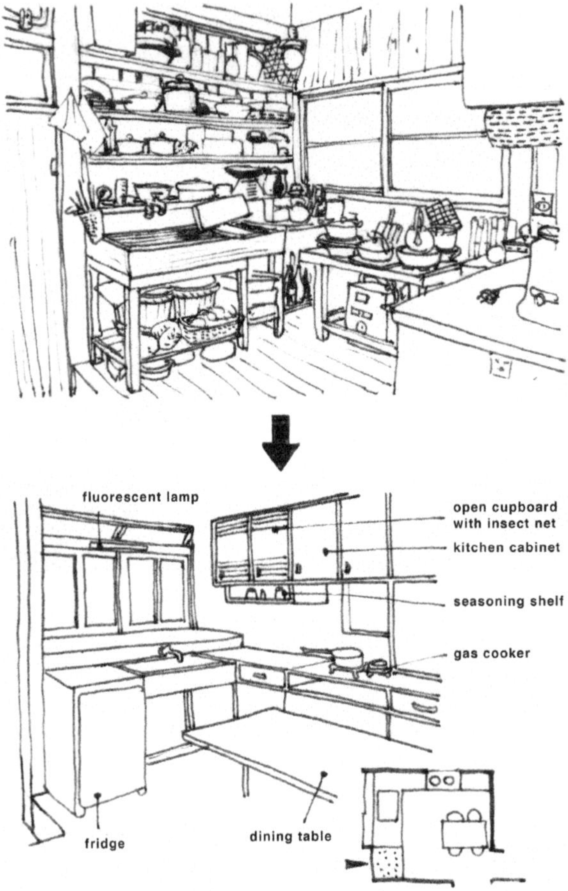

Fig. 2.14 The modernization of kitchen. Sketch by Uzō Nishiyama (*Source* Same as in Fig. 2.12)

scale and the spread of housing and economic crisis in the Soviet Union was similar to that of Japan, and therefore the enthusiasm toward the nationwide implementation of minimal yet efficient standard plans that could reform and modernize nuclear families was well justified in both cases, setting them apart from the American and even European mass housing situations.

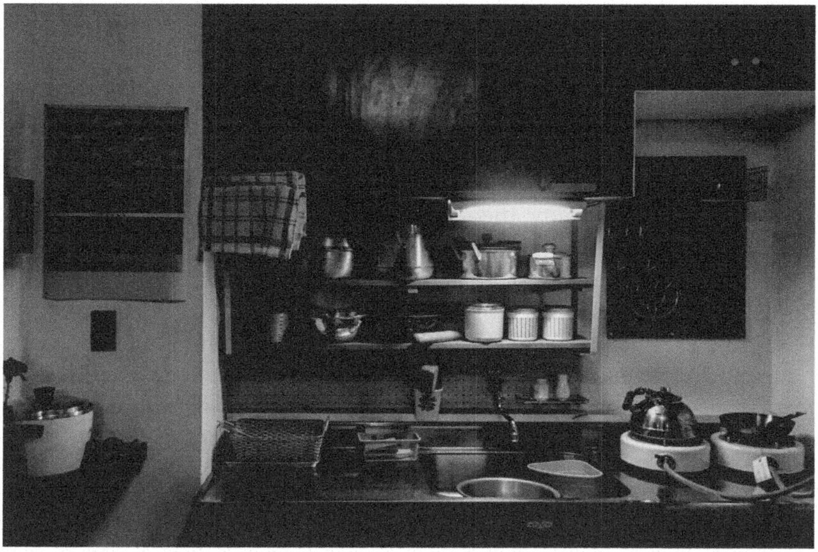

Fig. 2.15 A stainless-steel kitchen module. A replica of an original interior of Tokiwadaira Danchi built around 1960, Matsudo Museum, Chiba Prefecture

Since the Taishō period, many Japanese intellectuals, including architects, were involved in socialist discourses,[9] so danchi and their communal lifestyles regulated by bottom-up neighborhood associations (*jichikai*) naturally got to be at the center of their interest in the late 1950s and the 1960s. At the same time, the previous positivity of public opinion toward America started to decline as the Security Treaty legislating the presence of US military bases in Japan was signed in January of 1960, while the attitude toward the relationship with Soviet Union improved (Hara, 2012). According to the results of a poll questioning political preferences of more than 2000 danchi residents conducted by Yomiuri Shimbun in January of 1960, an overwhelming majority (55%) of the respondents

[9] For example, Uzō Nishiyama, a prominent architect and planner who was involved in many government projects, was famous for his socialist views; during his university years he was a member of a club formed by architecture students at Kyoto University that procured and studied Soviet architecture magazines (Personal interview with Matsumoto his former student 2021).

reported that they supported the Japan Socialist Party (Nihon Shakai Tō) (ibid.).[10]

Since the establishment of diplomatic relations between Japan and the Soviet Union in 1956, several Japanese delegations including employees of Ministry of Construction visited Moscow and brought back detailed information on the designs of *khrushchevkas*. There are few written sources available to study the architectural implications of these visits; Takeshi Hara in his *Danchi no kūkan seiji-gaku* book gives an example of a report on Soviet panel prefabrication system in an interview with Shunichi Yamada, the general secretary of Japan's Labor Union, printed in the August issue of Ienami Magazine in 1960. Although the large panel prefabrication attempts were discarded in Japan due to low earthquake-proofing possibilities, some features of danchi such as unadorned exterior walls, concrete access stairs designs and shapes and density of the buildings and spaces between them turned out to be uncannily similar to that of *khrushchevkas*.

It's hard to say whether there was an actual influence or co-influence between Soviet mass housing and danchi, or the exterior resemblance is a result of the analogous design goals and financial and technological constraints. One fundamental difference, however, was that danchi, unlike *khrushchevkas*, were never envisioned as permanent housing, and were conceived expecting the tenants to come and go with smaller floor areas allocated to individual units.

Moreover, the interiors were conceptually and technically drastically different due to danchi's integration of flexible traditional Japanese models. Instead of solid internal partition walls common in Western and Soviet housing, a wooden frame of *kamoi* jambs and *shikii* floor tracks supported sliding *fusuma* partitions, with the only exception of the solidly enclosed toilet, a continuing legacy of Dōjunkai Apartments. While *khrushchevkas* had four apartments per landing, danchi had only two, that allowed all apartments to have a see-through double exposure (typically

[10] Japan Socialist Party was founded in 1945, was in power from 1947 to 1948, and represented a major opposition force to the conservatives that formed Liberal Democratic Party (LDP) and have been holding a majority government since 1955. JSP successfully prevented LDP from revising the Constitution in the late 1950s, but lost its popularity during the 1970s and was disbanded in 1996.

facing north and south) and therefore better opportunities for natural ventilation, necessary for Japanese humid summers and the problem of stronger solar radiation on the southern and western walls. Since air conditioners were not widely available until the early 1970s, double exposure was the only way to adapt danchi to the climate, although costly for the construction budgets: since only two units per landing could be designed, there had to be a significantly higher number of access stairs per buildings, than in the Western mass housing projects. With such a small number of apartments per landing, too many elevators would be necessary to service the buildings, making construction unreasonably expensive, so after the financial failure of Harumi Apartments, danchi up until the early 1970s were constructed with a maximum height of five stories which didn't require elevators, just like the early *khrushchevkas*.

The interiors' humidity in winter, that wasn't a problem in timber buildings, became another unprecedented concern for Japanese housing industry: all the vapor produced by human activities that involved using water inside the apartments would not fully leave the rooms through the procured ventilation holes, but condense at the contact with the cold concrete surfaces of the walls and the windows. Danchi didn't have insulation or water-powered central heating systems, normally installed in public housing in the West, leaving the residents to warm themselves up with portable gas or oil heaters. As discussed in Chapter 1, Japanese architectural episteme requires houses to be adapted first and foremost to hot weather, while during relatively mild winters people can get by with heating the body directly by taking baths and sitting in front of a hearth, instead of trying to hopelessly warm up the drafty house made of wood and paper. This attitude could, of course, be challenged by danchi designers, but since all the plumbing had to be installed outside of the walls for better inspections in case of earthquake damages, insulating and including central heating, on top of serious financial expenses, would create too many risks for the future maintenance.

To compensate the heat losses, danchi introduced air-tight sliding aluminum sash windows to the masses, but since they were single glazed, together with uninsulated concrete walls they created thermal bridges and did only slightly better than timber windows to keep the warmth inside. Just like in any Japanese freestanding wooden buildings, danchi residents spent winters by constantly shifting between utilizing gas heaters, taking hot baths every evening, sitting around *kotatsu* (a low table with an electrical heater attached under the counter, covered with a thick blanket invented in 1959) and later using the air conditioners on heat mode, electric blankets, and carpets—devices that heat up the body rather than spaces (Daniels, 2015).

In any case, the intensive promotion on governmental and popular media levels succeeded in shifting the initial public perception from seeing the apartment life as foreign and inaccessible to something more common and desirable. In March 1959, the news section of *The Japan Architect* magazine announced the opening of an "apartment corner" in one of the biggest department stores in Tokyo. The editor notes that in prewar days all Japanese dreamed of their own house with a little garden, but now average newlywed couples aim to live in a high-rise building, where women, unlike in a detached dwelling, could easily go out without leaving someone else to look after the house. Life in the apartments formed new habits and entailed buying new types of furnishings, the best-selling item being a floor-to-ceiling wall cabinet that perhaps replaced the traditional *tokonoma* as a symbolic alcove in the new urban home (News & Comment, 1959).

The Suburban Expansion

In the late 1950s, the economic growth pushed urban land prices to rise due to the demand for new factory sites and workers' housing, and it became problematic for the JHC or Publicly Operated housing initiatives to secure land for the new constructions. In the search for new sites, the Corporation started to move further away from already developed urban infrastructure to purchase cheaper land, attracting prospective inhabitants with the promises of future facilities and new public transport connections, thereby contributing to vast urban sprawl in Tokyo and Osaka (Fig. 2.15). Very often, there was little what the JHC could actually do, apart from asking the local government to make buses stop at their danchi more often. These densely populated districts remained isolated from the urban infrastructure for years to come, with the main train lines overcrowded in rush hours and commuting times lengthening for more people every year. In the early 1960s the disillusionment of the new residents who discovered this sudden lack of facilities and impossible commute times was overridden by the positive publicity of JHC (Hara, 2012) (Fig. 2.16).

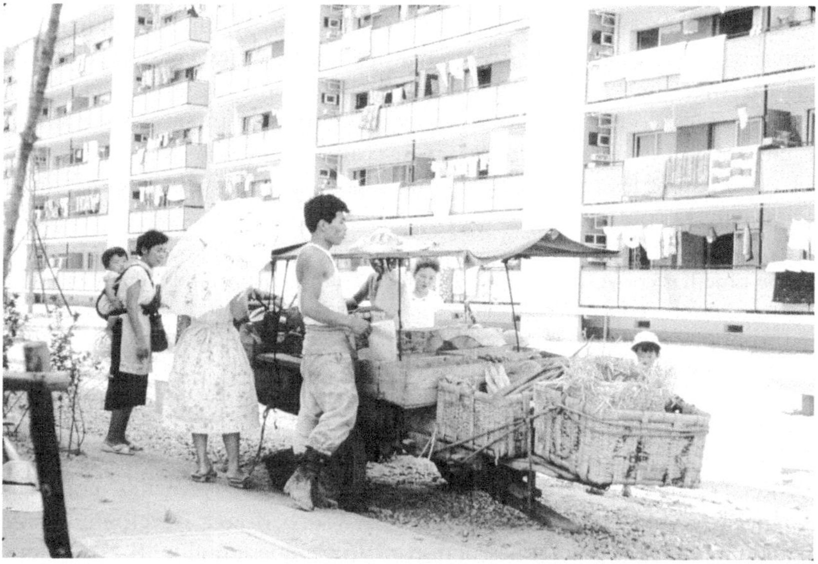

Fig. 2.16 A danchi in Osaka, photographed by Uzō Nishiyama, circa 1970. In the absence of local shopping facilities, street vendors with carts would service entire danchi districts. In 2021, *idōtempo*, mobile grocery trucks, are still a regular occurrence in some remote danchi, such as Wakamiya, discussed in Chapter 3 (*Source* Courtesy of Uzō Nishiyama Memorial Library)

In professional communities, however, discussions on the inefficiency of urban planning in Tokyo and overcrowding started earlier in 1959, as evidenced by a spur of articles on the topic in *The Japan Architect*, the most influential architectural magazine of the time. It was clear that this phenomenon had to be regulated to ensure that the urban structure of Japan could function healthily in the future.

> The national population increase seems to be leveling off at about 1,000,000 per year, but the population of Tokyo is growing at a rate of almost 300,000 annually, or roughly three times as fast... The destruction of Japanese cities during the war presented the best possible opportunity for a sane rebuilding program, but the chance was lost for lack of capital and concerted effort.
> —(1959). News and Comment. *The Japan Architect: The International Edition of Shinkenchiku*, 34(4), 3

Looking through the issues of *The Japan Architect*, which was primarily focused on discussing individual architectural masterpieces, it's peculiar that the "News and Comment" section of almost every issue in 1959 started criticizing the government for not intervening enough in city planning. The October issue came out with four long articles on possibilities for urban redevelopment in Tokyo, highlighting the accumulated problems.

> The time has come for Japanese architects to turn their minds to city planning and for city planners to turn their minds to architecture... We propose to continue prodding Japanese architects to consider the vital problems of urban reconstruction...
> —(1959). To Our Reader. *The Japan Architect: The International Edition of Shinkenchiku*, 34(9), 2

The Japanese government's response to these growing concerns became a formula to implement "the new urban area development for housing" (Ministry of Construction, 1965), encouraging the development of satellite cities as one of the possible solutions to overcrowding. As a result, The New Residential Town Development Act was signed in 1961. It required the JHC to construct danchi with more self-sufficient masterplans that had to include roads, parks, and public facilities such as kindergartens, shopping areas, community centers, and improved transport connections to the city centers. Later these independent urban developments would be called "New Towns," borrowing the name for similar projects from Britain. The JHC was also asked to construct the missing public facilities for the private low-rise suburban housing that was now required to adhere to the regulated masterplans provided by the government. Moreover, to reduce the population flow into big cities, the New Residential Town Development Act urged for relocation of most factories outside of the city centers.

By 1963, the government started reclaiming land around Tokyo Bay that would be sold at controlled prices for redevelopment and made plans for doubling the length of the subway system. This seemed like a careful preparation of the ground for building satellite towns around Tokyo. However, the construction of the first New Town in Japan had already started in Senri Hills in the outskirts of Osaka already in 1961. The need to prepare the city with alarming levels of industrial pollution and housing shortages for the upcoming World's Fair in 1970 accelerated the planning, making the Senri New Town a pioneer of large-scale housing development in Japan and a testing ground for the future satellite towns planned in the suburbs of Tokyo (Fig. 2.17).

The project aimed to create a fully self-sufficient residential city from scratch with the use of public and private funds, housing approximately 150,000 people of 30,000 households on an area of 1150 hectares ("A Complete Look at Senri New Town", 1965). The Osaka Prefectural government collaborated with the JHC, local public housing agencies, architects, and researchers, such as Uzō Nishiyama, to design a well-balanced, varied, and desirable living environment. The resulting planning policy was to mix high-density danchi with low-density private wooden homes and create three districts with their centers providing different functions to enhance the "cultural personality" of the residential zones (ibid.). In addition, the closest train line was extended into the central area of the project, and internal bus transportation was arranged to take under thirty minutes to reach the business center of Osaka from any corner of the New Town. Defining one community of 2000–2800

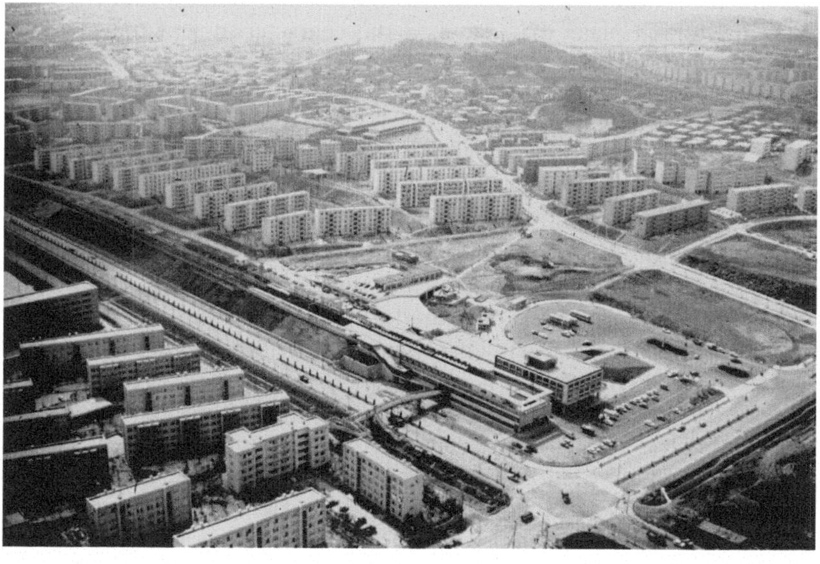

Fig. 2.17 Aerial view of Senri New Town, 1968 (*Source and author* Same as Fig. 2.16)

dwellings as a self-sufficient unit, centered around a primary school, a community hall, and a park, the designers, unified several such units into a district, with three districts making up the entire town ("The Senri New Town Neighborhood Center", 1964). This hierarchy was supposed to reflect the lifestyle patterns of an average middle-class family.

Senri New Town contained both the JHC and the Publicly Operated rental danchi clusters and company dormitories, low-rise condominiums, and townhouses for sale. Immersed into the greenery of the surrounding hills, Senri New Town provided very photogenic first results. The phases of its construction were closely followed by the media, and its successful completion helped to establish the basic elements of large-scale danchi planning in postwar Japan—the green infrastructure, the neighborhood unit, and a district center, that would be replicated and enhanced in the Tama New Town in Tokyo Prefecture (Fig. 2.18) and dozens of others to follow.

With the continuing publicity, increasing budgets, and construction expanding in every region of Japan, the JHC became the main apartment housing standards setter in the country (Fig. 2.19). In every new development, the Corporation tried to test various new iterations of the nDK units, developing plans that matched the characteristics of the sites and geographical areas.

Every year the apartment floor areas and number of rooms gradually increased, with more versatile 3K and 3DK becoming common from the mid-1960s (Figs. 2.20 and 2.21). By 1965, 134 types of floor plans were published in the Corporation's pamphlets. In total, including minor changes, more than 300 plans were developed throughout the JHC's history, accommodating the technological advancements and the ever-growing material demands of postwar society. One demand, however, was purposefully never met: compared to the postwar mass housing standards in Europe, these apartments were not spacious enough for a family with two older children. Just like the Publicly Operated units, JHC-built danchi were never meant to be a permanent housing option, and the tenants were expected to eventually save up enough money for the Housing Loan Corporation's initiative and move into their own detached houses. As already discussed in Chapter 1, the main strategy of the Japanese government in housing policy was achieving mass homeownership, thus liberating itself from the welfare-procuring obligations in the

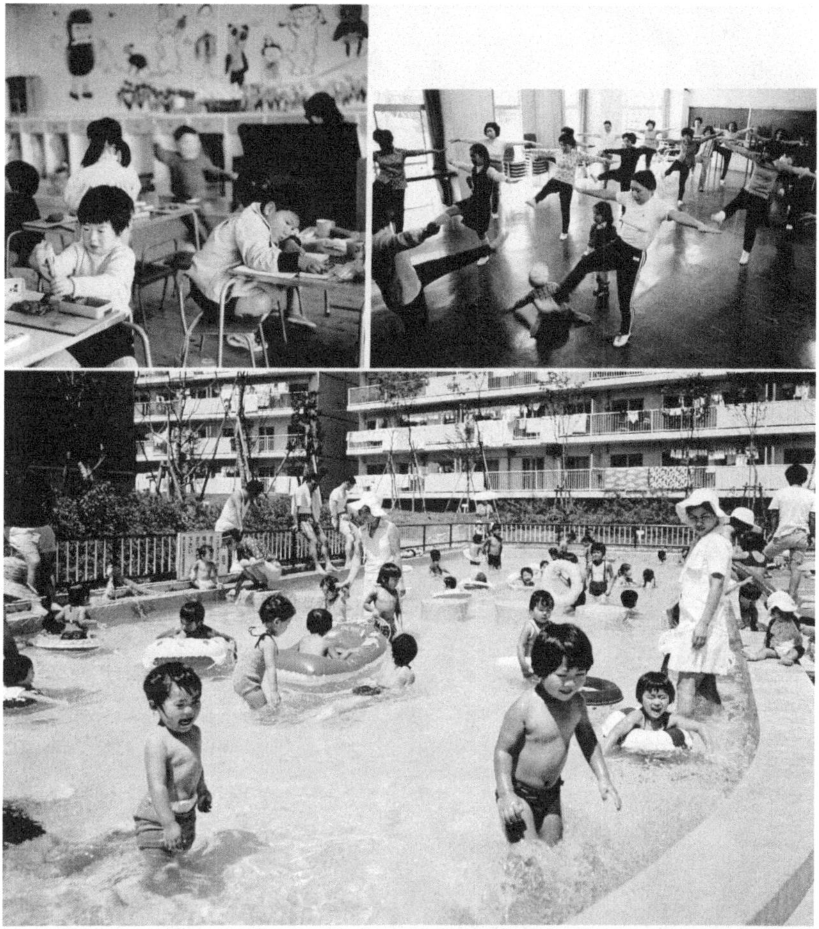

For a Pleasant Living at Danchi

Patterns of life in a standardized housing project are likely to be monotonous and stereotyped. The Japan Housing Corporation has tried to provide amenities and better environments for a satisfactory cooperative living in every sense of the word to all residents. for this purpose various facilities, such educational institutions as kindergartens, elementary and junior high schools, welfare facilities such as nursery and children's centers, medical facilities like hospitals, commercial facilities, sports and recreational facilities including meeting halls are established.

With children who enjoy playing at these nursery centers, and mothers who make good use of meeting halls for various activities, a new community that is to be their home town in the future is being formed.

Fig. 2.18 Tama New Town and its amenities. Japan Housing Corporation and Its Achievements, 1976, p. 3 (*Source* Courtesy of Urban Renaissance Agency)

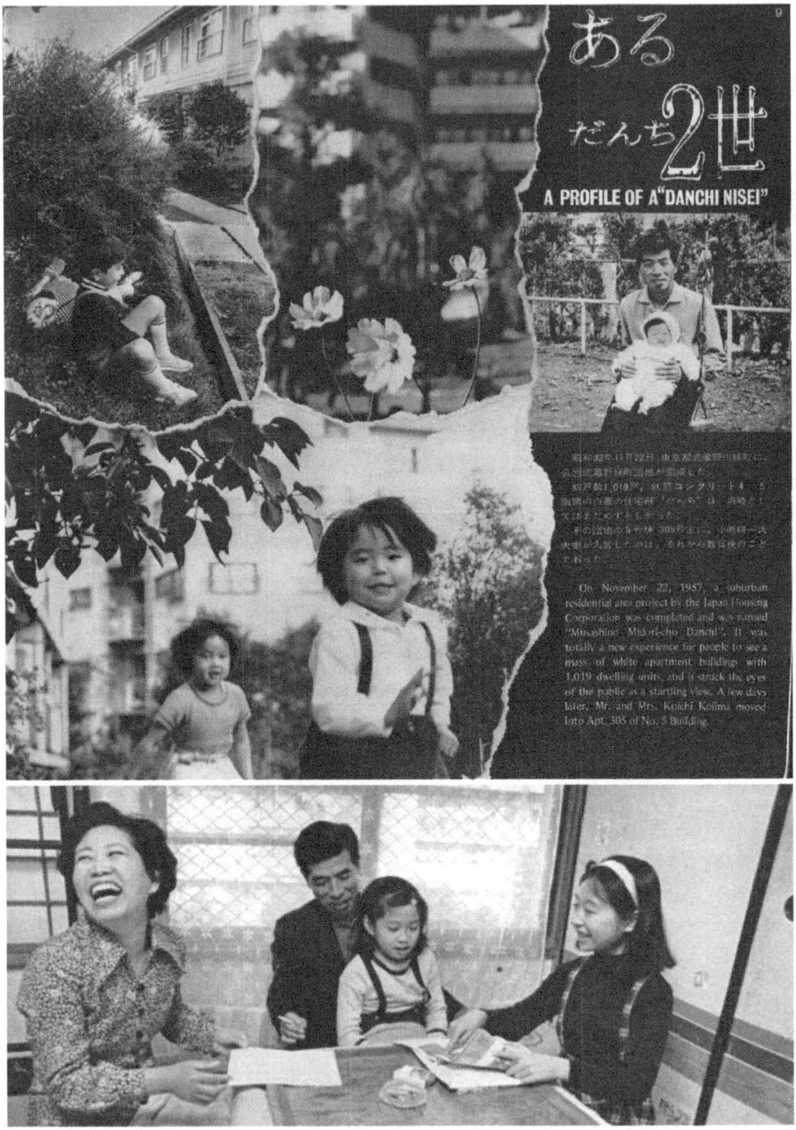

Fig. 2.19 Top: A profile of a second-generation danchi resident, telling a story of Shiori, a girl living in Musashino Midori-chō Danchi with her parents and a younger sister. 72' The Annual Report of JHC, 1972, p. 3. Bottom: 72' The Annual Report of JHC, 1972, p. 14 (*Source* Same as Fig. 2.18)

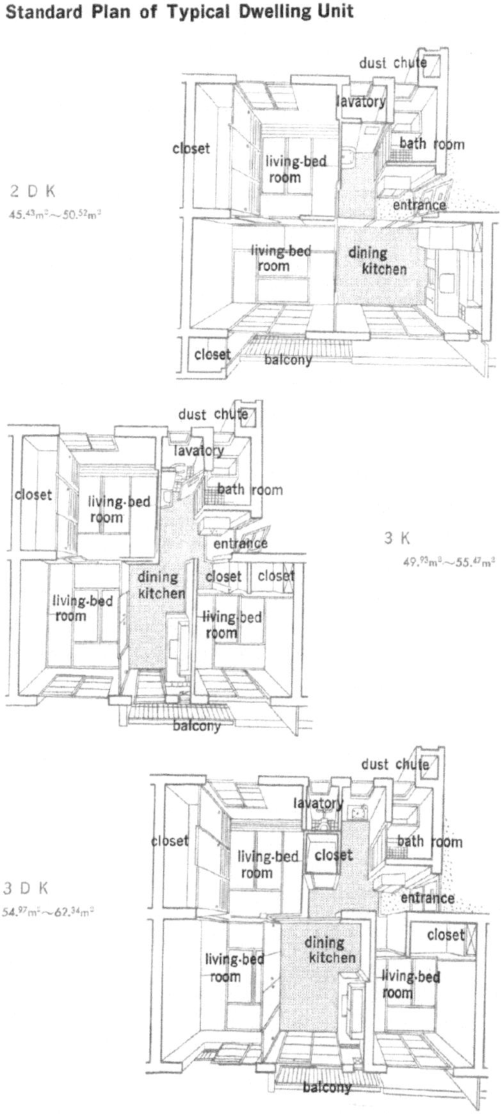

Fig. 2.20 Evolution of 2DK into 3DK. '70 Outline of the Japan Housing Corporation, 1970, p. 29 (*Source* Same as Fig. 2.18)

The Percentage of Housing Projects

Model \ Fiscal year	'55~'60	'61~'65	'66	'67	'68	'69	'70	'71
1K	6.6	2.0	–	–	–	–	–	–
1DK	15.8	15.1	3.4	4.3	6.5	9.7	15.4	17.4
2K	15.5	4.6	0.1	0.1	1.0	0.0	0.1	0.0
2DK	43.0	37.8	36.9	38.8	41.8	46.4	43.7	50.1
3K	15.8	28.2	32.7	35.5	39.4	23.1	27.2	22.7
3DK	3.2	12.2	26.9	21.3	21.3	20.8	13.6	9.8
4K (and over)	0.1	0.1	–	0.0	–	–	0.0	0.0

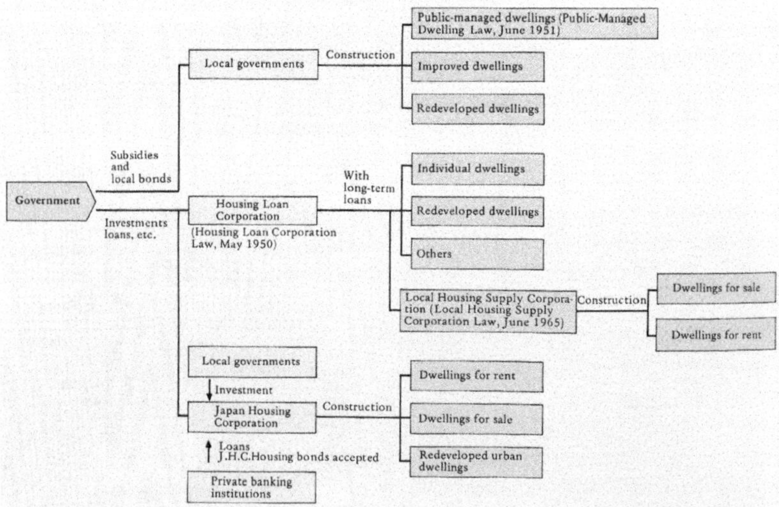

Fig. 2.21 Top: Percentage of different unit sizes built by the JHC from 1955 until 1971. Japan Housing Corporation What It Is, What It Does, 1974, p. 30. Bottom: Diagram "Types and Structures and Dwellings under National Policy", Japan Housing Corporation and Its Achievements, 1976, p. 12 (*Source* Same as Fig. 2.18)

future, and danchi were conceived as one of the steps in the "housing ladder": comfort had to be temporarily sacrificed for the sake of the future.

Still, amid the social and political turmoil of the 1960s, danchi came to symbolize security and moderate prosperity with material comfort (at least, far more than the other rental options) for young families saving to buy their own house with a garden. The popularity of both JHC-built soared; some years, the chance to win the opportunity to move in was one in several hundred (Nijū Nenshi Kankō Iinkai, 1975). With identical exteriors and slightly less sophisticated interiors, Publicly Operated danchi were similarly sought-after by less affluent young families.

The Decline of Danchi's Popularity

The Irony of the Mid-1960s: Cramped and Neurotic

The JHC's obsession with providing space for the latest technology in ideologically and financially limited floor areas became a double-edged sword (Figs. 2.22 and 2.23). Every new standard plan had to accommodate the most recent kitchen appliances on the market that promised to facilitate the housework, liberating Japanese housewives from hand labor and supposedly giving them more free time. In 1955, it was just a gas cooker and a refrigerator, but by the early 1960s, washing machines, electric kettles, rice cookers, and vacuum cleaners became common in every household. The JHC danchi plans (with Publicly Operated housing following in their footsteps) had to keep up with the emergence of the new but instantly essential technology, resulting from the governmental and industrial campaigns. After 1955, when the early postwar period ended and all industrial production levels surpassed the prewar numbers, national consumption was defined first as means to gradually improve people's lifestyles but then became an end in itself (Neitzel, 2016). Women's magazines and housewives' associations played an important part in this transformation, and the corporations took advantage of these movements to promote their goods through the media (Smith, 2018). On top of kitchen appliances, the danchi families started to purchase and equip their units with all kinds of increasingly popular Western furniture, ending up in dismayingly cramped spaces.

By the mid-1960s, various social critiques centered around danchi started to spring up in newspapers and magazines and fiction movies.

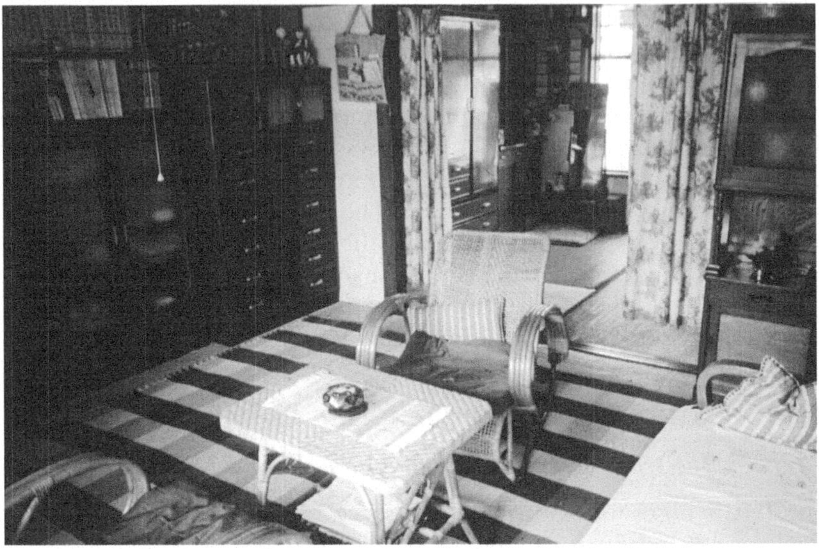

Fig. 2.22 A densely furnished tatami room in Osaka Municipal Hoenzaka Danchi, 1960. Photograph by Uzō Nishiyama (*Source* Courtesy of Uzō Nishiyama Memorial Library)

While the printed instances are best described by Nietzel in her book,[11] the movie industry shows a similar change of tone. In the 1958 film "Eternal Rainbow" (Kono ten no niji) by Keisuke Kinoshita, which focuses on the life of steel-factory workers in Kyushu, the company-built danchi are described as "beautiful apartment buildings" and given a flattering panoramic screen depiction (Fig. 2.24, top). Seiji Hisamatsu's "Urban Affair" (Kigeki: ekimae danchi) from 1961 uses danchi interiors as a pleasant background for its lighthearted main story.[12]

In 1962, however, danchi imagery in the movies lost its previous exclusively positive presence. "Being Two Isn't Easy" (Watashi wa nisai) directed by Kon Ichikawa and shot from the point of view of a toddler

[11] Neitzel, L.L. (2016). *The Life We Longed For: Danchi Housing and the Middle Class Dream in Postwar Japan*. Chicago: MerwinAsia.

[12] A wider selection of movies featuring danchi is available in Japanese-language article 'Research of utilising common space: observing the public space through the movie filmed at Danchi' by Masashi Sogabe (2006).

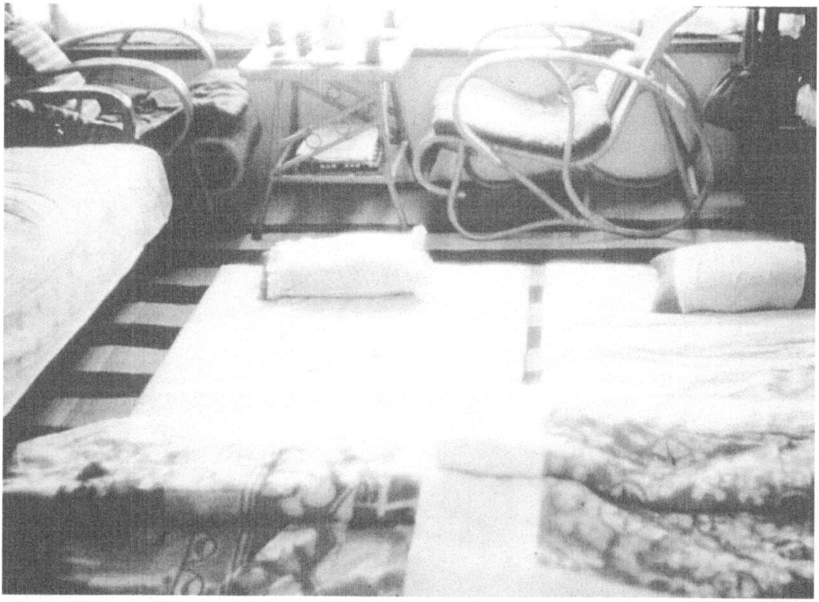

Fig. 2.23 The same room with *futon* mattresses spread for sleeping (*Author and source* Same as in Fig. 2.22)

living in a danchi district, hints at some inadequacies of the building designs and local community's "strangeness." The child often gets lost and endangered, or falls out of a window and down the stairs. Although the movie's overall tone is not critical of the danchi lifestyle, it ends with the child and his parents moving to his grandmother's house (Fig. 2.25, bottom).

"An Autumn Afternoon" (Sanma no aji) by Yasujirō Ozu, also shot in 1962, gives a similarly ambiguous perspective: a 32-year-old Kōichi, the main character's son, lives with his wife in danchi. The wife stays at home all day long and occasionally communicates with her neighbors, only to find herself envying their new electric appliances, so she pressures her husband to buy a refrigerator, forcing him to borrow the money from his father. Despite a very cozy apartment interior and a big amount of free time during the day, she doesn't seem to be enjoying herself at home alone and is not entirely satisfied with her living environment (Fig. 2.25).

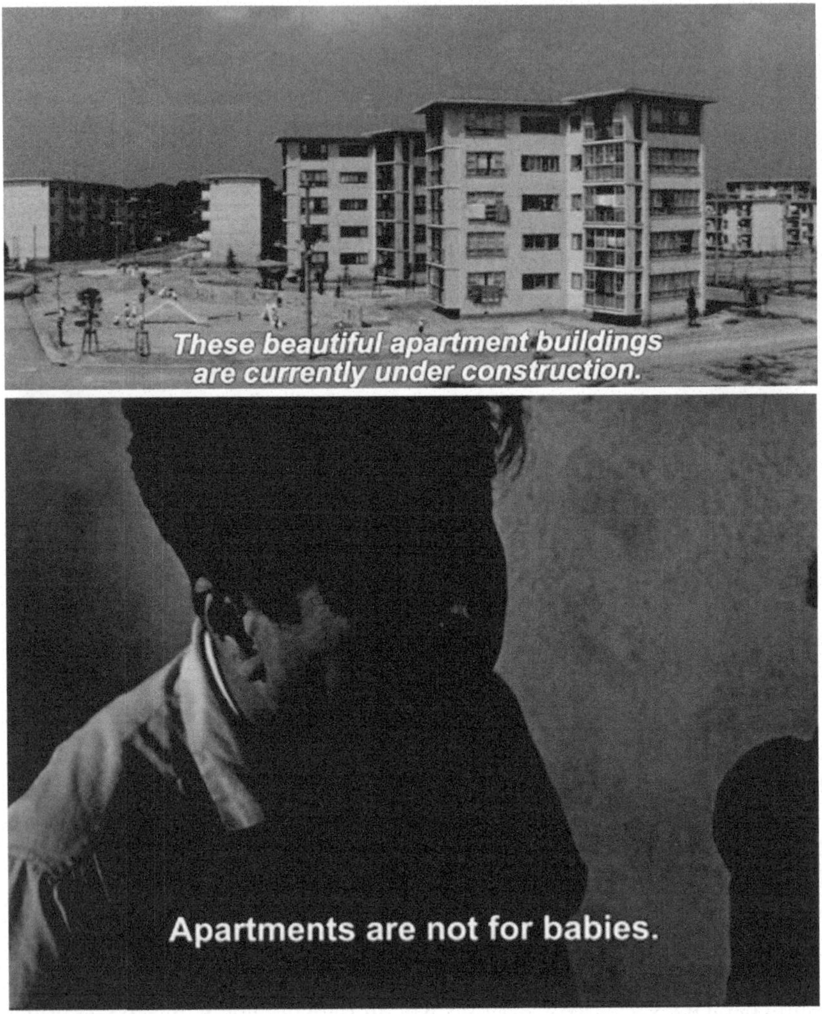

Fig. 2.24 Top: "Eternal Rainbow" directed by Keisuke Kinoshita, 1958. Bottom: "Being Two Isn't Easy" directed by Kon Ichikawa, 1962

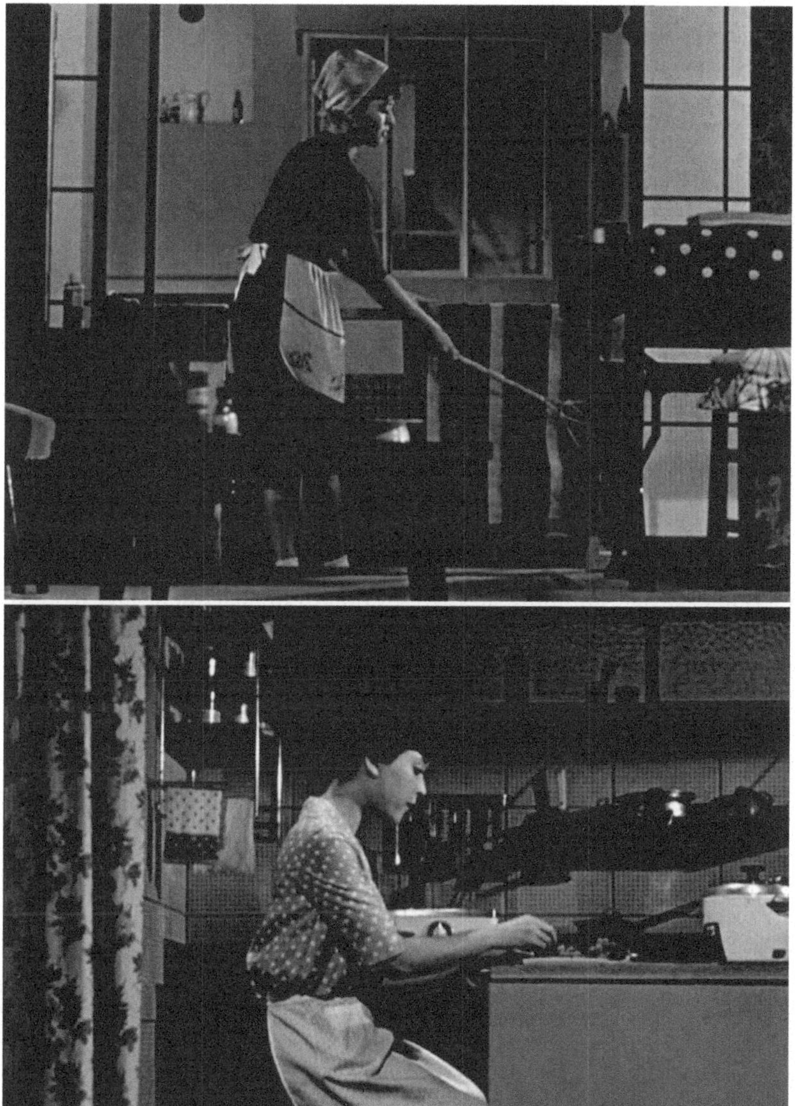

Fig. 2.25 Housewife in company housing. "An Autumn Afternoon", directed by Yasujiro Ozu, 1962

Perhaps to tackle this shifting perception of danchi life, in 1964, the Japan Housing Corporation made a 17-min promotional movie, "Invitation to Danchi" (Danchi e no shōtai). The camera follows a beautiful young woman and her husband visiting her sister's family who lives in Hibarigaoka Danchi, a model JHC project from 1959 that turned out so well that it was shown to the Emperor and his wife (Hara, 2012). As the couple strolls through the complex, they take note of all the wonders of the danchi infrastructure: there is a shopping arcade full of neatly dressed housewives chatting, a police station and smiling policemen patrolling on bicycles, a branch of municipal office, convenient garbage disposal systems and spacious playgrounds swarming with children. Particular attention was given to a community center that offers daily activities for children and housewives, such as music and *ikebana* lessons. The movie, however, doesn't address the complaints of the real residents of Hibarigaoka about the lack of kindergartens and the fact that Seibu line connecting the danchi to Tokyo had reached 240% of its capacity during rush hours (ibid.).

When the sister in a white apron finally welcomes them at her 3DK, the couple starts examining all the advantages of apartment life, from the equipped kitchen to a gas-heated bathtub and a flush toilet (Fig. 2.26, top). The DK in the movie is already so full of technology that the dining table barely fits in; everyone eats in the adjacent four-and-a-half tatami room around a low table. During their meal, the danchi inhabitants admit to their relatives that apartment life is not immediately easy: it takes time to get used to the new appliances and the potential dangers of gas and running water, and it's important to remember not to put any belongings too close to the concrete walls—the narrator explains that for the first two years after the construction, the concrete still dries off with water condensing on the walls. In fact, any type of concrete dries much faster than this, and the sad truth is that these plain concrete walls will never stop accumulating condensate in winter with gas stoves heating up the rooms: it is simply impossible without thermal wall insulation. Of course, the happy young couple doesn't know this, and after spending a leisurely day with their relatives and learning the joys of collective life (*kyōdō seikatsu*), they decide they want to move into danchi, too.

In the same year, the movie "Seven Deadly Sins in Danchi" (Danchi: Nanatsu no taizai), directed by Yasuki Chiba and Masanori Kakei, was released and showed a completely opposite side of danchi's collective life. It is a collection of seven episodes of different social "perversions"

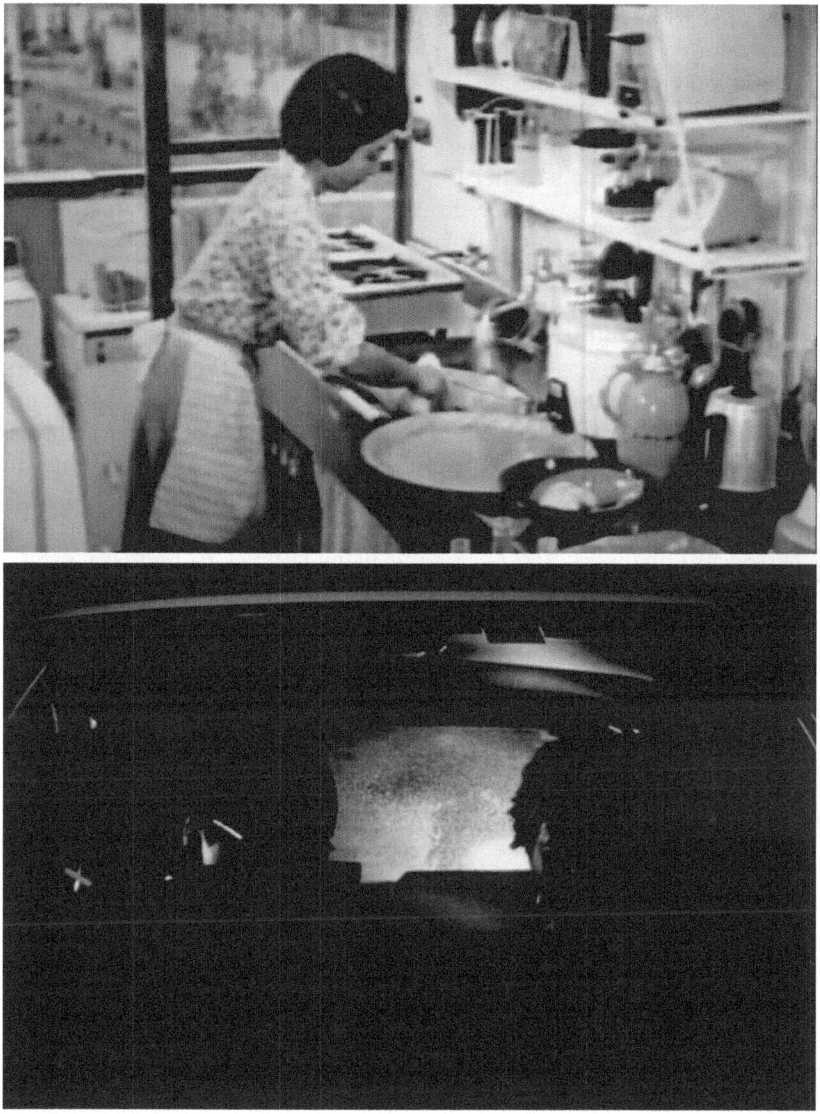

Fig. 2.26 Top: Promotional movie for JHC, "Invitation to Danchi", 1964. Bottom: "The Family Game" directed by Yoshimitsu Morita, 1983

that started to be observed in danchi districts more and more frequently. Envy, jealousy, adultery, constantly watching your neighbors, and a fear of being watched yourself, are just a few of the many "neuroses" that the danchi residents had reportedly developed. The absence of informal common spaces for outside gatherings restricted social life to the community hall with scheduled "official" activities of *jijikai*. The much-desired metal doors that allowed the housewives to leave home unattended contributed to growing social isolation. These doors destroyed the traditional Japanese "backdoor" concept where casual visitors could pop up in *genkan* during the day for a friendly chat and made all the home visits more formal and difficult. "The metal door and concrete walls might discourage spontaneous visits from neighbors, but the very anonymity of the danchi community seemed to encourage voyeurism and listening in" (Neitzel, 2016). The advertised sound-insulating walls did not absorb the noise completely, most probably due to the single glazed aluminum windows and bathroom ventilation holes opening directly into the staircase landings, so overhearing family quarrels and gossip became common occurrences (Imamura, 1987), forcing many couples to regularly escape to hourly rented rooms in "love hotels" to secure some intimacy without fear of being overheard. Led by the same fear, a married couple in the movie "Family Game" (Kazoku gēmu) by Yoshimitsu Morita from 1983 uses their car parked outside the danchi building to have any serious conversations (Fig. 2.26, bottom). This movie criticizes the already stereotyped dysfunctional danchi family, whose members are connected to each other only by means of their social roles, not by intimate interpersonal relationships.

The Disappointment of the 1970s: Perverted and Socially Isolating

Similar to "Family Game," movies with overtly negative attitudes toward danchi started appearing from 1970. For example, "The Shadow Within" (Kage no kuruma) by Yoshitarō Nomura begins as a melodrama but then transforms into a psychological crime drama with elements of suspense. The story is set in a large New Town, portrayed as culturally isolated from the rest of the urban fabric, with its high-rise beehive buildings used as a dark and ominous background.

Such a drastic change of tone was most likely the result of the government-issued White Paper in 1970, that declared that the "the housing miracle" was finally achieved: the housing shortage came to an end with every family in the country getting their own place to live. While the earlier "miracle" of the industrial success could easily be perceived and celebrated by the population in the form of consumer products and general welfare, the housing recovery was a vaguer event because it only reflected the sheer quantity of dwellings and not their size or quality of life in them. The quantity was indeed surprising, being higher than the building totals of West Germany, Britain, and France combined over the same period (Waswo, 2002), however, this victory came at the expense of individual well-being—a sacrifice that the new Japanese middle class started to perceive more consciously after 1970.

Although The Japan Housing Corporation, The Housing Loan Corporation, and the Public Housing Act became the so-called "three pillars" of postwar housing policy in Japan (Hirayama & Ronald, 2006; Waswo, 2002), they provided only 27% of all housing built between 1945 and 1973 (Fig. 2.21, bottom). The Housing Loan Corporation constructions by constituted 15%, while Publicly Operated housing accounted for 8% and danchi only for 4%. Apart from the "three pillars," there were another 8% of units built by the state as rental housing intended for public officials, civil servants, and other groups of government workers. The striking fact is that the remaining 65% of all housing was built only by the tremendous effort of the private sector with no public financing, so it was the irreplaceable "fourth pillar" of the Japanese postwar housing miracle (ibid.).[13]

Despite contributing only 12% to the housing race and having an initially temporary nature, thanks to the advertising and governmental lobbying, danchi apartments managed to get a reputation of the "universal" standard of life. With so many people looking up to danchi life in the early 1960s, all the other residential designs started copying them in one way or another and replicating the nDK pattern to the point, where it became a design bias and sometimes prevents more rational planning concepts to emerge. Shigebumi Suzuki, the creator of the DK, in his book dedicated to the history of "51C" argues that its idea was ultimately misunderstood: rather than being a model plan, it was produced as a measure to facilitate life in unavoidably small spaces, and the nDK pattern was a necessity born out of the spatial limitations and the nuclear-family life requirements (Suzuki, 2004). With the nuclear-family concept falling

[13] For more on Japanese postwar housing policies, see Waswo, A. (2002). *Housing in Postwar Japan—A Social History*. New York: Routledge.

apart after the period of high economic growth and extra square meters becoming more readily available, there seems to be no reason to stay attached to it. However, the reliance on mass production of aluminum windows, balcony parapets, electrical outlets, switches, kitchen modules, interior finishes, etc., that the JHC achieved in collaboration with other companies to optimize the construction budgets, was soon spread on private constructions of both apartments and detached housing, with some of the elements still in wide use up until now. The economic convenience of this consumption cycle continues to support the nDK pattern and its related dimensions, giving to most commercially built apartments and houses visually and technologically homogenous interiors all over the country.

Another outcome of Japanese postwar housing policies became the shift from mass renting to mass home ownership, with two negative consequences: the poor quality and small sizes of the constructed units, and rapidly rising land prices caused by constant national demand of moving into detached houses.

Due to political frictions between various parties, in the early 1970s, the state subsidies to the JHC were decreased so that to repay the private investments, the rents in danchi had to rise. Then, in the late 1970s, with the construction industry gaining capital, more spacious commercial apartments started to surpass what danchi had to offer, the market of affordable detached houses expanded, and the initial attraction of danchi life was replaced by rejection and detachment.

In 1971, the growing gossip stories about danchi housewives starting affairs while their husbands slave away at work inspired Shōgorō Nishimura from an erotic film production studio to direct a bestseller "Apartment Wife: Affair In the Afternoon" (Danchizuma hirusagari no jōji) in 1971. Depicting a bored housewife cheating on her husband with various danchi visitors behind the anonymity of a standard apartment door, it became so popular that it started a sub-genre of its own in Japanese pink films[14] ("danchi-wife" or *danchizuma*), with twenty sequels as well as many unofficial spinoff series produced ever since (the

[14] Pink film is a Japanese softcore pornography genre, usually shot on 35-mm film by independent studios, that was widely popular since the mid-1960s through the mid-1980s, when the emergence of conventional pornography started to dominate the market. Pink films are still being produced for niche audiences.

latest was shot in 2000). Receiving so much coverage in pornography, the public image of danchi was pushed even further into the "dark" zone.

The point of no return became Yoshitarō Nomura's "Writhing Tongue" (Furueru Shita) from 1980, the first horror movie to be set in danchi, this time a high-rise "mammoth" district, that the JHC invested in after the mid-1970s. A five-year-old girl is infected by an unknown disease while playing outside the cookie-cutter skyscraper-size buildings and gradually turns into a monster. The standard apartment where her family lives appears aged and uninviting; sometimes, the darkness in the rooms gets outright hostile and terrifying.

In the 1980s and 1990s, public attention almost entirely abandoned the topic of danchi. More and more commercial apartment buildings with bigger floor areas and newer designs appeared in big cities, so by 1981 the Japan Housing Corporation ceased any new construction and was renamed, first as Housing and Urban Development Corporation, then in 1999 as Urban Infrastructure Development Corporation, and in 2004 was restructured again and received its current name, "Urban Renaissance Agency." Currently, UR manages and regenerates the already built danchi units by JHC.

The Stigma of the 1990s and 2000s: Scary and Outdated

In 1991 the Japanese economic bubble burst and soon many people, who still had not bought their own house by that time, remained "trapped" in cramped and outdated rental danchi apartments for the rest of their lives. With the nationwide decrease in incomes, some residents became ineligible for any other type of rental housing. These inhabitants aged and constitute the majority of danchi residents around the country now.

Since the late 1990s, danchi also started to attract new, low-income elderly tenants who have trouble securing private rental contracts due to their age or unemployment, single parents with children, and other marginalized groups such as financially struggling immigrants that can apply for Publicly Operated units through municipal social housing programs. While historically UR-managed districts collect higher rents and have better budgets, many Publicly Operated danchi lack funds and governmental support, producing an increasing number of maintenance and social issues: dilapidation of buildings, the standard plans not suiting the new demography of inhabitants, and the growing social isolation.

The absence of elevators, which at first allowed for cross ventilation of every apartment and let young families save on air-conditioning, is now a barrier for the elderly to go out of their homes. On top of this physical barrier, as danchi residents age, some of them became unable to properly take care of their appearance, and become ashamed to regularly face the outside world. The term ***kodokushi***, which describes a situation when people die alone and remain undiscovered in their home for a long time, became an increasing occurrence in the 1980s, and from the 1990s has been closely associated with danchi. Properties where deaths occurred have a long history of being stigmatized in Japanese culture and are strongly avoided by potential renters and buyers for several years (Danely, 2019), but in densely planned danchi districts with aging residents where ***kodokushi*** tend to happen every year, the stigma is accumulated and doesn't dissolve. Horror movies "Dark Water" (Honogurai mizu no soko kara) from 2002, and "The Complex" (Kuroyuri danchi) from 2013, both shot by Hideo Nakata, are set in municipal danchi and explore dark fantasies connected to the buildings' physical dilapidation, stigma of death and social isolation, conveying the new radically negative perception of danchi in the twenty-first century (Fig. 2.27).

Still, when in the early 2000s the government started actively promoting demolition and rebuilding of "problematic" housing of the 1960s and 1970s, elderly residents of bigger UR-operated danchi districts with well-preserved infrastructure and developed *jijikai* communities started to show open opposition toward the initiative, arguing that danchi

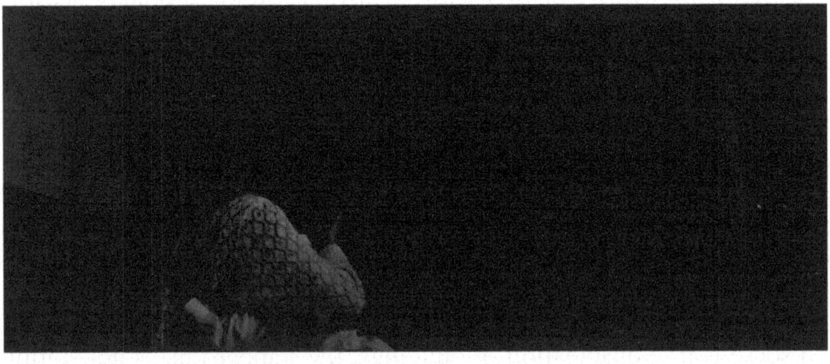

Fig. 2.27 "The Complex" by Hideo Nakata, 2013

and their abundance of greenery was a better choice than the densely built newer commercial apartments (Hara, 2012). Some UR danchi communities started tackling the problem of social isolation and *kodokushi* by bottom-up activities, such as going on apartment visit rounds, checking the number of newspapers in the postboxes of their neighbors and increasing regularity of "obligatory" community events such as clean-up days (ibid.). The situation in less-populated suburban municipal and prefectural danchi developments used as social housing for disadvantaged families is more difficult to solve. My fieldwork showed, that many elderly residents of Publicly Operated Wakamiya Danchi in Ibaraki avoid the communal activities because they feel they're too demanding, formal, or "pointless."

In addition to horror movies, from the second half of the 2010s, danchi with social housing units have been starring as a background for social critique movies. Thanks to the efforts of the JHC, *chūryū*, the concept of a mainstream middle-class Japanese family, had spread and solidified since the 1960s, and top of implying one's socio-economic status also gained the connotation of social inclusiveness (Daniels, 2010). Having successfully contributed to increasing homogeneity in Japanese mainstream identity, *chūryū* began losing its influence and stability from the 1990s when the economy and society underwent deep changes. As Publicly Operated danchi were vacated by the mainstream families, they started to accommodate the parts of the population that cannot fit into the nuclear household model for one reason or another, and became the primary location for observing the difficulties of living as an "outcast" of social mainstream, that over the recent years gets more and more difficult to define. "The Projects" (Danchi) by Junji Sakamoto from 2016 (Fig. 2.28) portrays life of an elderly couple that due to financial troubles had to suddenly move into a Publicly Operated danchi. A short feature movie "YEAH" shot by Yohei Suzuki in 2017 (Figs. 3.1 and 3.2, Chapter 3) is also set in municipal danchi and focuses on a girl with mental illness, who lives in an old unit with her most-likely unemployed brother in his thirties. A documentary "Danchi Woman" by Akiko Sugimoto of the same year tells a story of a lonely elderly woman who is forced to relocate from a Publicly Operated danchi building that is about to be demolished into a smaller unit in a newly constructed building, and cannot come to terms with the need of throwing away some of her belongings.

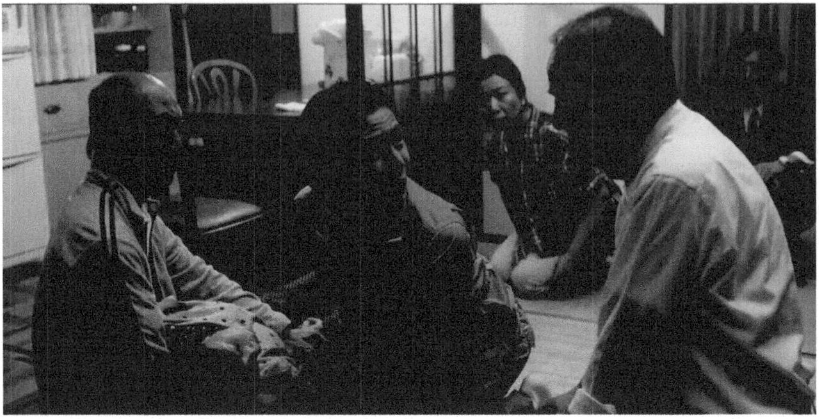

Fig. 2.28 "The Projects" by Junji Sakamoto, 2016

Thus, in the late 1990s from the symbol of bright modern life, many danchi, especially the Publicly Operated ones, gradually became a synonym for poverty, decay, and alienation. According to the Japanese building standards, all danchi built in the 1950s and the early 1960s had reached their end-of-life phase in the 1990s and were demolished. Most projects from the mid-1960s and early 1970s are facing the same fate now. However, three decades of economic stagnation in Japan that started in 1991 have significantly slowed down the construction industry, with the demand for new houses gradually slumping and many demolitions being put on hold. Moreover, the public attitude toward the built environment drastically changed after the 2011 Tohoku Earthquake, the consequences of which made the younger generation more aware of the fragility of the prevailing "scrap-and-build" ideology, unnecessary energy and material wastes, and hence the need to reuse the available resources in the future. From 2010s, both the government and architectural firms started to see danchi as an opportunity for regeneration.

The New Hope of the 2010s: Danchi Revival

The UR Renovations

Most still standing danchi in Japan belong to the Urban Renaissance Agency (UR), the successor of Japan Housing Corporation. As of March

2016, the UR owned 742,000 rental apartments in 1700 danchi districts all over Japan (Profile of UR, 2016). UR is not supposed to build new housing or freely redevelop the land it owns since the company was restructured and received its current name in 2004; instead, they are to maintain the public housing units they have for as long as possible. UR is actively regenerating big-size danchi settlements such as Tama New Town or Takashimadaira Danchi on urban scale, by improving infrastructure and promoting community activities. Moreover, they gradually undertake interior unit refurbishments, replacing outdated plumbing, air-conditioning systems, interior coatings, and infills, often getting rid of the original partitions to free up more space. Thanks to the accessibility of the UR online database of vacant units and a simplified rental system that doesn't require guarantors if one demonstrates a steady income, it attracts a large number of applicants of all ages to the most conveniently located danchi in Tokyo. Since 2011, the company has launched some radical experiments to attract more young couples to more distantly located danchi; as a cheaper and more spacious alternative to the current mass market tiny rental apartments in Tokyo, the already renovated UR danchi units were only missing a renewed public image to succeed.

In December 2011, the UR executives held a meeting with the internationally acclaimed architect Kengo Kuma and Kashiwa Satō, a famous branding specialist, to create a strategy for a regeneration project to revitalize Yōkōdai Danchi in Yokohama. Yōkōdai was built in 1970 in direct proximity to a train station and consists of 83 danchi buildings containing 3000 rental apartments managed by UR, as well as several private apartment buildings and detached houses. Currently, more than 30% of these danchi tenants are older than 65 years old.

> Naturally, the vitality of the city is being lost. The Future of Housing Complex (Danchi no Mirai) Project was initiated in 2011 to invigorate the entire area with danchi as the core. We aim to improve the attractiveness of the area and increase the number of young residents.
> —Mitsunori Ōgami, a manager from East Japan Rental Housing Office of UR for an article on the website of the Public Relations Office of Japanese Government (Sakurai, 2017)

It took several years for the first stage of the project to begin. In 2014, UR representatives launched a social initiative in a store on the ground floor of one of the danchi buildings in Yōkōdai.

> A vacant store space in the danchi in front of the station is available for a limited period as a base for the Community Challenge Lab, where groups or individuals can perform activities for regional revitalization. A wide variety of activities are offered, including exercise classes for the elderly, cafés, concerts, and art exhibitions, as well as many events with the cooperation of local groups.
> —Hiroshi Sakurai, in 'The Danchi Renaissance' article for Public Relations Office Website (Sakurai, 2017)

Three years later, in 2017, Kengo Kuma's office completed the renovation of the facades of several Yōkōdai danchi buildings facing the main square by repainting the walls and introducing decorative aluminum panels that cover the protruding air-conditioning units (Figs. 2.29 and 2.30). In 2018, a roofed promenade structure going around the perimeter of the buildings in the square was introduced to encourage commercial and social activities. In European architectural history walls usually shaped and sustained spaces for social activities between the buildings, but in Japanese traditional architecture due to a different climatic

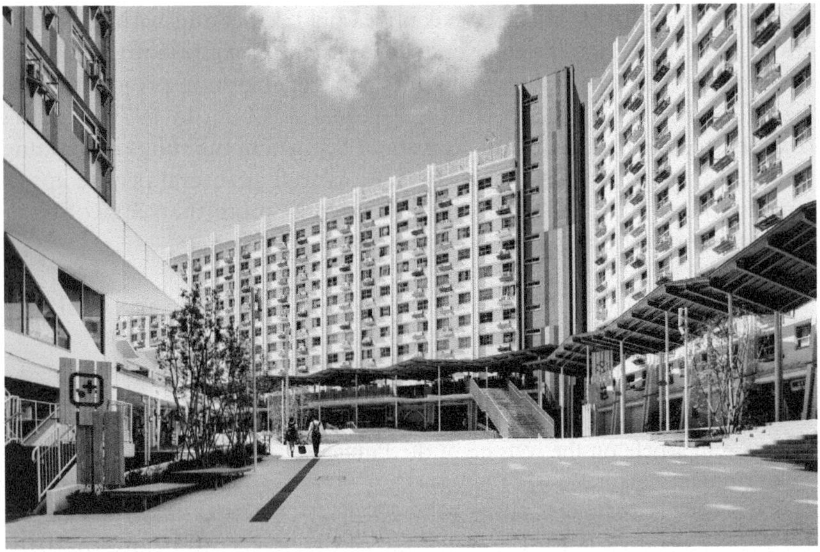

Fig. 2.29 Yōkōdai Danchi main square, Yokohama, 2017 (*Source* Courtesy of the Urban Renaissance Agency)

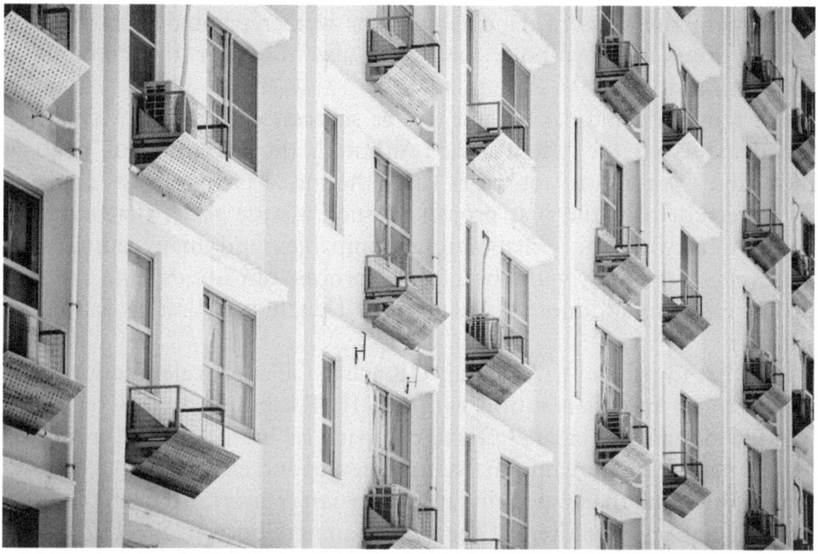

Fig. 2.30 Yōkōdai Danchi exterior renovation detail, Yokohama, 2017 (*Source* Courtesy of the Urban Renaissance Agency)

situation it's the roofs that play this role, which Kengo Kumo tried to highlight with this intervention. Trees, benches, and cascades of wide stairs were added to form a European-style urban plaza (Interview with Kengo Kuma, 2018).

> The Yōkōdai housing complex in Yokohama City will be a model project, but with the huge stock (750,000 units in 1,700 housing complexes) spread throughout the country as a future target, we will aim to revitalize the Japanese society itself.
> —Kengo Kuma & Associates Website, 2018

In 2021, the five-story Kita Yōkōdai Danchi nearby were added into the project: their balconies received more fashionable wooden parapets instead of the original aluminum poles, the outside public space was redesigned with new wooden urban furniture added, and the paving around the green areas got significantly improved. A new community building, a café and a library connected by a stepped public plaza and a large unifying roof were built in the distinct Kengo Kuma style. The numbers on the sides of danchi buildings were repainted with the new branded fonts and symbols, that were also used for the community building interiors.

The renewed Yōkōdai became a sure success, with its units always in high demand on the UR website. Although the execution of Yōkōdai renovation took almost ten years since the initial proposal was made, it was expected from the first project of such a wide scale, that required negotiations with the collaborating companies and many administrative levels. Hopefully, with the pioneer process already executed, it will become easier to add more districts to the Danchi no Mirai project in the future.

In 2012, in parallel to Yōkōdai, UR started a large-scale interior renovation project in collaboration with MUJI (Ryohin Keikaku Co., Ltd.), a worldwide-famous Japanese retail company selling household products. MUJI's main values are minimal natural design and emphasis on reuse and waste reduction, that especially appeal to *satori sedai*, literally "enlightened generation," children of the baby-boomers born in the 1970s who have witnessed and learned from the failure of the economic excesses of the 1980s. Accordingly, the slogans for the MUJI×UR project are "Don't break too much, don't add too much" and "Danchi will become your ideal home." The project description agrees that postwar LDK layouts cannot accommodate the new varied lifestyles of the younger tenants, so MUJI designers revised the standard JHC plans by getting rid of the most partitions and creating a more open "zero-infills space," while preserving the caramel color of the original timber *kamoi* framing whenever possible. The result is a photogenic yet delicate balance between the contemporary minimalist design and hints of the original danchi "retro" elements (Figs. 2.31 and 2.32).

The project highlights the pre-existing benefits of living in danchi, such as the abundance of greenery in the surrounding areas, optimal cross-ventilation, and south-oriented windows in the apartments; at the same time, the original shortcomings such as small rooms, deteriorated interior finishing, outdated kitchens and bathrooms, are fully taken care of by the designers without ruining the original "danchi charms." For example, the original tatami are good-looking but deteriorate fast: they get replaced with a visually similar linen-covered alternative.

> Imagine you could put your favorite ingredients in an empty lunch box. The same applies to MUJI×UR. For example, by placing MUJI storage

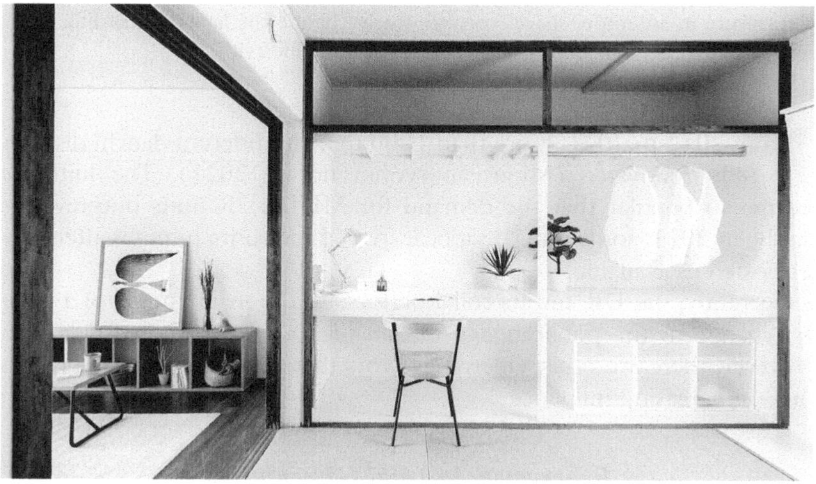

Fig. 2.31 MUJI×UR Re061 standard plan renovation from the original 2DK. Tatami bedroom (*Source* Courtesy of the Urban Renaissance Agency)

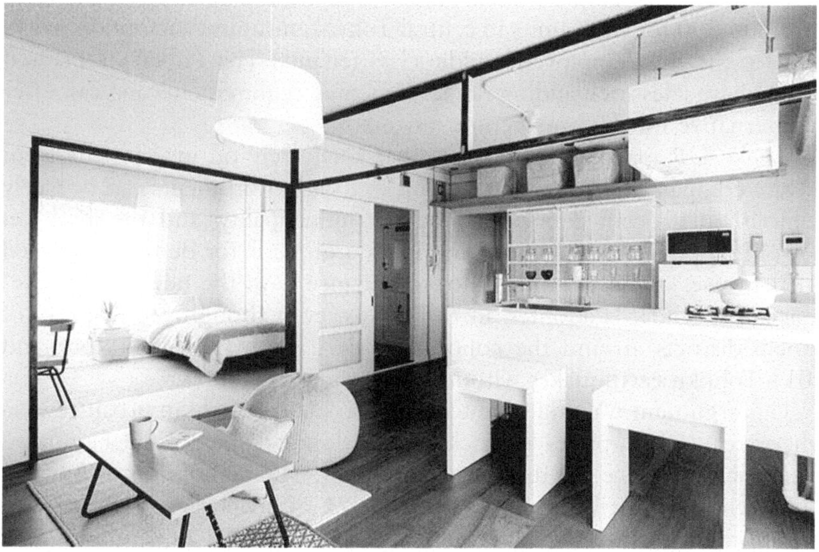

Fig. 2.32 MUJI×UR Re061 standard plan renovation from the original 2DK. Living-dining-kitchen (*Source* Courtesy of the Urban Renaissance Agency)

furniture in an empty space, you can freely change the layout according to the growth of your family and changes in your lifestyle.
—Mujirushi ryohin website, 2014

From 2012 to 2021, more than 1000 units in different danchi districts were fully renovated (Mujirushi ryohin no ie, 2021). The initiative became so popular that the demand for MUJI×UR units outgrew the supply: in 2021, some units disappear from the website minutes after they get posted as available.

Currently, the UR and its collaborators are the main engine of a positive change in the public image of danchi housing in the past decade. However, there are other emerging actors that contribute to the process with an increasing influence.

Renovations by Local Governments

All UR units have strict requirements concerning the applicants' minimum income, which should be at least four times higher than the rent, normally ranging between 55,000 and 80,000 yen per month (and over 100,000 for 2DK units in central Tokyo), meaning the option works best for the fully employed middle-class tenants. The Publicly Operated danchi have a less demanding range of income requirements and can offer an alternative for the low-income tenants.

Unlike UR-managed complexes that partly rely on investments from private companies, danchi that belong to local governments can be freely demolished if deemed necessary by the municipality, and the land can be sold to private companies. The main argument for demolitions used in such cases is the buildings' noncompliance with the new earthquake-resistance standards adopted in the 1980s, even though the majority of danchi districts around the country survived both the 1994 Kobe and 2011 Tohoku earthquakes without any structural failures.

This argument was still used to demolish many danchi in urban centers where real estate prices skyrocketed, and unoccupied land became a bigger scarcity since the time they were built. The demolition of Aoyama Kitamachi Danchi take took place in 2021 at the heart of the trendy Aoyama district in Tokyo had the same scenario. The government sold the land to a developer company on the condition that along with the two planned commercial towers, it would build an apartment block that could accommodate the same amount of public housing units that were previously located in Kitamachi Danchi. In such cases, the tenants are given a choice to move into a newly built public housing unit, which will be significantly smaller in size and will have a higher monthly rent due to the costs of the new construction.[15]

While danchi demolitions are very common in central Tokyo, where the government greatly benefits from the subsequent land redevelopment, the municipalities of smaller cities and suburban areas do not have other choices but to keep the old apartments maintained for the low-income tenants, especially because there is no new public housing built in Japan apart from the forced compromises when old units are demolished on redeveloped land. Due to the lack of funds, small municipalities only resort to the most basic interventions such as restorative exterior repairs and occasional tatami and wallpapers replacements in the interiors. Still, there are some examples when bigger cities such as Osaka and Kyoto initiate municipal danchi projects renovations with more far-reaching goals.

In the mid-2010s, Asako Yamamoto, one of the founders of Alphaville Architects studio based in Kyoto, was asked by a semi-private danchi management company connected to Kyoto City Government to join a team of architecture consultants and researchers from Kyoto University and work on a project centered around the design of new child-care spaces inside the existing danchi apartments (personal interview with Yamamoto in 2019). The danchi management company wanted to find a way of renovating rental apartments in Katagihara Danchi in Kyoto to attract more young families with children.

After several months of research, Yamamoto's team concluded that it was nearly impossible to restructure the interiors into now popular Western-style rooms because of the insufficient floor areas and low ceiling heights that restrict the use of Western furniture. They insisted on keeping the *fusuma* partitions to allow the flexibility that is needed when parents have to look after small children and do housework at the same time, advised on adding bigger washbasins, arranging special refrigerator spaces, and introducing other small improvements into the original plan. However, the research team argued that when the children grow up, a single danchi unit will be not enough for the family, so it seemed necessary to combine two units. Since calculating the risks of making an opening

[15] For more details and an ethnography of relocating danchi tenants see "Danchi Woman", a short documentary film by Akiko Sugimoto, 2017.

in the dividing structural wall between the apartments was too expensive, they proposed either sharing one public staircase landing access or connecting the balconies. The client company decided that this renovation will pose a financial problem: if one family needs to occupy two connected units (around 100 square meters), the total combined rent will become higher than the average for this size of the property in the city, while the cost of renovations cannot be efficiently returned to the managing company, so in the end, the project was never approved.

Osaka Prefectural Housing Corporation, on the contrary, has managed to implement the idea of unifying two apartments in Chayamadai Danchi, a part of Senboku New Town in the suburbs of Osaka. As a large successful prefecture-financed company, their budget and business connections surpass that of a city-run danchi in Kyoto, so an impressive initiative, "Senboku New Town Advanced Housing Renovation Model Project," was proposed in 2015 in collaboration with several commercial and non-profit organizations.

Chayamadai district consists of 26 five-story rental danchi blocks completed in the early 1970s, with most of the buildings located on hills overlooking Osaka Bay. Chayamadai is not a part of the prefectural social housing program, so the rent here is quite high—around 45,000 yen per month for a 3DK apartment. This allowed the local administration to collaborate with the Prefectural Housing officials in launching some community regeneration practices in 2015.

The first step was establishing a DIY school: all residents were invited to learn from invited professionals how to repair a danchi apartment, and with the common effort, five empty units were remodeled and rented out to the new residents. Then a permanent DIY showroom and a workshop were opened in the ground floor units of a fully vacant block under renovation at the moment, in order not to disturb the residents with the noise. An employee from a private company supplying the working tools and materials supervises the workshop and assists the residents with their DIY projects approved by the administration.

Shortly after that, the Chayamadai community hall was repurposed into a small public library, Chayamadai Toshokan, where the residents could gather informally, share books and organize their own events (Fig. 2.33). The bookshelves for the library were made by the residents as a part of the abovementioned DIY initiative. Another important result of the DIY activity was the creation of Yamawake Kitchen—a cafeteria located in a vacant apartment on the ground floor in one of the buildings, where

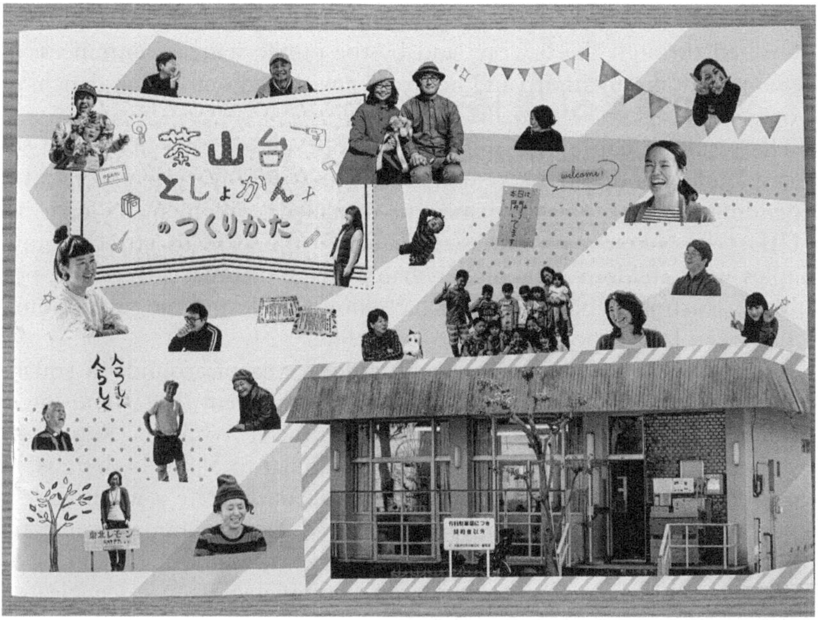

Fig. 2.33 Chayamadai Toshokan Pamphlet by Osaka Prefectural Housing Corporation, 2019

young housewives could work part-time while their children are at school. The main purpose of Yamawake Kitchen is serving lunch for the local elderly residents, creating an opportunity for them to socialize. At the entrance, the residents that do not want to walk a long way to the nearest supermarket can buy fruit, vegetables, and other food.

Not stopping at the level of the social activities, in 2015, Osaka Prefectural Housing Corporation employed several architectural firms and launched two interior renovation projects: Nikoichi and Renobe45. The vacant units in Chayamadai and later other government-managed danchi districts in Senboku New Town and Senri New Town were to be emptied from the infills, leaving only exposed concrete walls. In the case of Nikoichi, literally "two making up one," every two units within one staircase landing were to be combined into one apartment depending on the original plan and the building's structural system. Most units were connected through the balcony and by the public staircase entrances, in the same way as Yamamoto and her team envisioned renovating danchi in Kyoto.

The resulting combined units have a floor surface area of around 90 square meters and can be rented for 75,000–85,000 yen per month, depending on the finishing and the installed equipment. Similar to MUJI×UR, Nikoichi promotes open plans and seeks to attract young couples with children with higher-than-average income, advertising not only the apartments but also the rich community life and the surrounding scenic green landscape, perfect for family life.

As for Renobe45, the original unit's floor area of around 45 square meters was left as it is with 50,000-yen monthly rent, but some interesting apartment zoning solutions were introduced. While the Renobe45 apartments in Chayamadai Danchi are very similar to Nikoichi designs, in Senriyamadanishi Danchi, in an attempt to accommodate a wider variety of tenants' lifestyles, nmstudio architects and Nozoe Shimpei came up with a much more radical concept. They designed multifunctional raised-floor plywood islands to be inserted into a completely open space, cleared of all the infills (Figs. 2.34 and 2.35).

The islands' walls are made of pegboards and can be equipped with shelves, while the raised wooden platform can contain storage drawers. Some islands can be closed with a curtain, and if a mattress is put on top of the raised floor, they act as bedrooms. The flexibility of the islands' functionality and therefore of the whole apartment increases so much that it's hard to tell that the interior is located in a danchi building.

Private Renovations

While the majority of danchi units belong either to the Urban Renaissance Agency or the local governments, there were some cases when the apartments got sold to private individuals. Several buildings in Tama New Town contain privately owned units that in the 2010s started to be actively purchased and renovated. It takes more than one hour on a train to commute to central Tokyo from Tama, so the popularity of the district among commuting workers has decreased over the years, however, there is a growing number of young professionals working fully or partially from home away from the city in a general tendency of avoiding office careers with long hours or living in cramped conditions in central Tokyo or both.

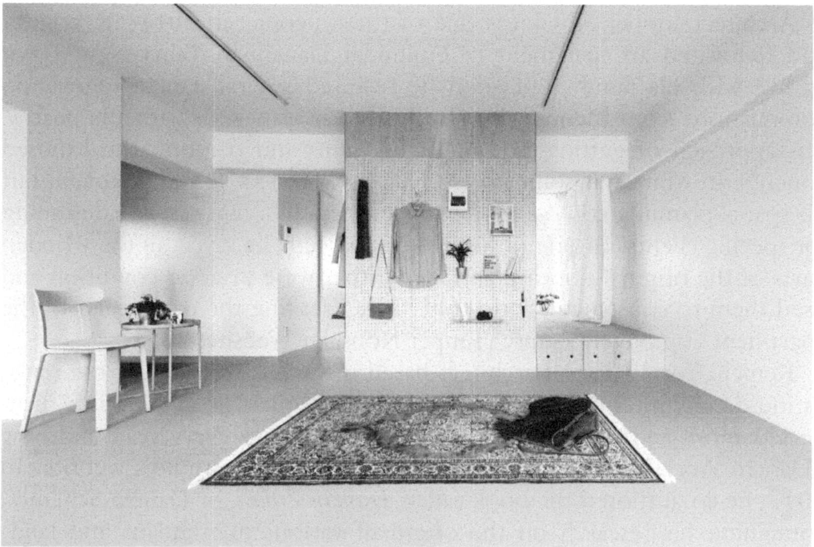

Fig. 2.34 Renobe45 in Senriyamadanishi Danchi. Architect: nmstudio architects and Nozoe Shimpei Architects. Photographs: Forward Stroke/Koji Okumura (*Source* Courtesy of nmstudio)

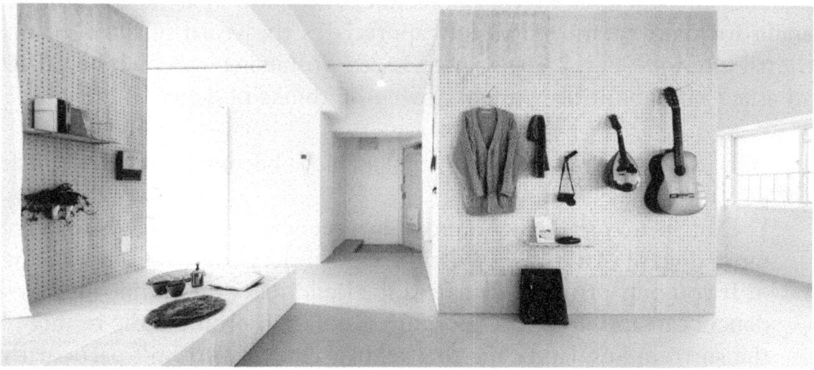

Fig. 2.35 Renobe45 in Senriyamadanishi Danchi. Architect: nmstudio architects and Nozoe Shimpei Architects. Photographs: Forward Stroke/Koji Okumura (*Source* Courtesy of nmstudio)

Architect Junpei Nōsaku is one of these people: in 2011, he bought and renovated an apartment in Fujimidai Danchi in Tama New Town to live with his family, but soon he received several danchi renovation commissions from friends who also moved in danchi apartments nearby. His approach of getting rid of all the infills and painting the exposed concrete in white was somewhat similar to MUJI×UR and Nikoichi, but his spatial planning could get more experimental because he was designing for specific clients. In one of his danchi projects, he saved all the wooden parts of the original flooring and *kamoi* that were in good condition and used them to construct a bathroom "box," leaving the other parts of the apartment completely empty (Junpei Nousaku Website, 2011).

Kenichi Yoshinaga, an architect based in Osaka, has also started renovating danchi interiors because of a friend's request in 2006. Since then, he got more and more private danchi commissions every year, and now "Danchi Works" became a separate directory on his studio's website. In 2017, he co-authored the book called *Danchi Zukai*, or Danchi Schemes, containing his research on the origin of various masterplans and landscapes of danchi districts, as well as some insights on the history of the standard plans (Shinozawa & Yoshinaga, 2017). He sometimes consults the UR in Osaka as an independent researcher.

Yoshinaga's renovation works focus on preserving the original aesthetics of danchi as much as possible, and show that he has studied danchi for many years and deeply appreciates the visual qualities of the original interiors (Fig. 2.36). I interviewed Yoshinaga in September 2019 and asked him about his work and what he thinks of danchi in general.

- Why do you think moving to danchi is becoming more popular nowadays?
  Y: Danchi are usually surrounded by greenery, and the landscapes are more diverse than those inside the city fabric, people started noticing it. If you only promote danchi as the buildings with flexible interiors, danchi can appear as too "boring". But if you promote the beauty of the surrounding landscape to a regular citizen who isn't particularly fond of danchi, the overall opinion can become more positive.
- So what plays a decisive role for people choosing to move into danchi?
  Y: The difference between reality and people's low expectations of what danchi are supposed to be. In my opinion, there are two types of danchi: the well-designed ones and not so well-designed ones,

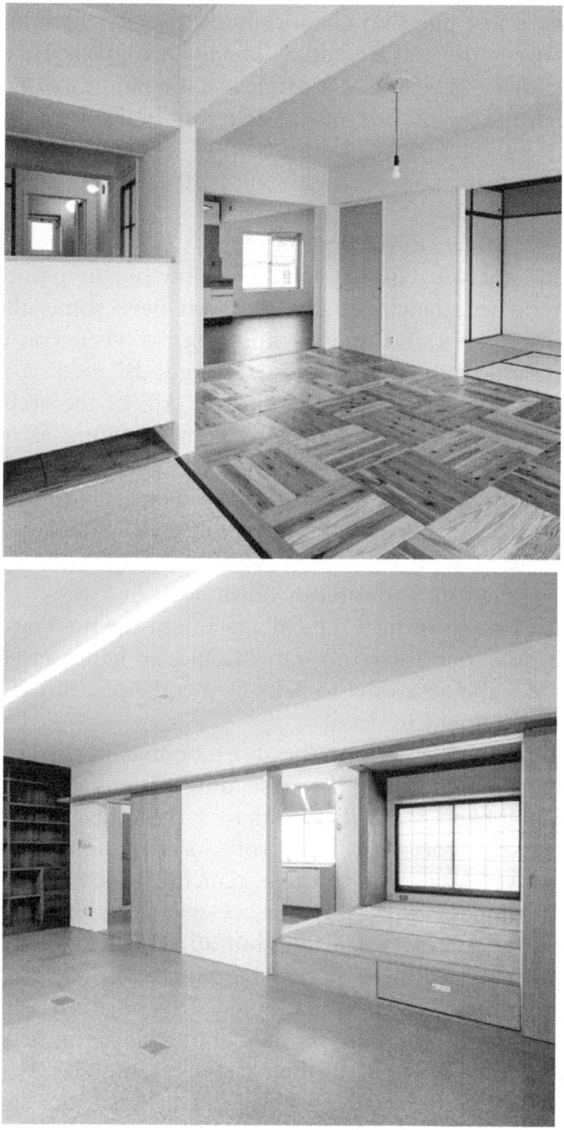

Fig. 2.36 (Top) (Bottom) Examples of danchi interior renovation by Kenichi Yoshinaga (*Source* courtesy of Kenichi Yoshinaga)

which were just piled up chaotically on the plot without the necessary infrastructure and amenities. The former type is usually designed with the idea, "If we made it carelessly, it wouldn't work, so let's do it properly." The interior design planning is also thoughtful in such cases.

- Could you share your thoughts about the interiors, their pros and their cons?
  Y: First, the quality of the equipment may vary. For example, Publicly Operated danchi are usually filled with low-quality plumbing, unlike privately-owned danchi estates that can have some above-average quality equipment and interior finishing, so when you come there, you sometimes wonder: "Why is it this good?".
  And interior design depends on the skill of the architect. Some plans try to fill the apartment with as many rooms as possible, and there are cases where privacy of spaces was wisely planned. Of course, the high number of individual rooms was usually the primary goal, but nevertheless, there are some excellent examples where the space could be used well according to the residents' needs, with good design, ventilation, and interior finishing.
- When did you renovate a danchi apartment for the first time?
  Y: 2006. My friend lived in danchi, and he had wanted to reform some spaces and asked me to help. It was the first time I could study a danchi apartment in detail.
- Was it difficult to overcome the shortcomings of the original plan?
  Y: When I entered for the first time, I was genuinely amazed because it looked much better than I thought. I remember from my university years that our professors' opinion on danchi was very negative. According to them, danchi districts were "inhuman", concrete jungles. After the war, people chose to live in danchi because it was pretty reasonable, but after the 1970s, danchi started to be associated with low-social standing, and people became more attracted to *mansions*, more fashionable commercial apartments.
- What was the turning point for danchi to receive this negative image? Why did people start to call them "concrete jungles"?
  Y: When danchi projects were being constructed, the buildings were raised in parallel with the landscape design, including plants and trees, so when the first people moved in, the scenery had a very desert-like appearance because the trees grew very slowly. So after

the first wave of residents moved out, nobody really wanted to live there anymore.

- But now it's full of greenery, isn't it?
  Y: Yes, but the image is already ruined.
- Do you think danchi were not the best place to live when they were just built?
  Y: Yes, I think so. Just imagine, the surrounding area was full of well-grown trees, and in the middle, you have a concrete island. Another significant point was that your apartment entrance door was made of steel, and the walls were made of concrete, which provided you with 100% privacy. Everybody ended up living in their own world, without socializing with the neighbors.
- If you have to renovate a danchi interior for a young client, what aspects would you change?
  Y: Let me think. There aren't too many things to complain about, and most of the clients I have had were usually happy with the original design in general. The only problem is the old plumbing and kitchen equipment, but it's easy to fix.
- So you didn't know anyone who wanted to reform the unit completely?
  Y: In my first renovation project, I initially proposed making quite a lot of changes. I designed several options for the new floor plan, but the client actually preferred the original floor plan when we discussed it. The client was running a design office, and he had to work from home, so we first thought that the floor plans didn't work very well. He wanted to make the office room bigger, and since he was single then, he didn't need a large sleeping room. At first, we decided to make the big rooms bigger and the small rooms smaller. However, the result did not seem much different, so we returned to the original plan. In fact, most young people are satisfied with the original plans because they are very comfortable, there are many available floor plans. It is essential to consider how the old designs can fit the present lifestyles, but we should avoid changing the attractive points. It is better not to destroy the balance.

- Looking at the recent renovations of the state-owned danchi, I feel that the younger generation is given preference over the elderly. Do you think there is any way they could actually live in danchi together?
  Y: I always thought attracting young people to live in danchi is a good idea, but following only the latest innovations and design trends leads to nowhere. About ten years ago, such approaches were widespread, and I was disappointed by them. First, for elderly people's comfort, barrier-free systems are the most essential thing to think about. If you only follow the young generation's preferences and focus on decorations, elderly people will feel that they are left out. During the "danchi mania" (danchi *otaku*) time (the early 2010s), the UR employees came, and we had a discussion on how we should renovate danchi. We interviewed some young people in their 20s and 30s who thought that there is no need to change the original style, it's good as it is. Afterwards, we encountered more and more people with similar opinions, so I think we don't really need to readjust danchi interiors for different generations. Speaking of MUJI, the strength of their concept is that being visually flashy does not make a design unique. Being unique depends on its internal qualities, so they advocate for simple, well-designed, but not so expensive features. Originally danchi were created with this concept in mind as well. I told UR that they should work with MUJI when I consulted them.
- Are there many elderly people now that move to UR-managed danchi?
  Y: When elderly people try to find rental housing, they often come to UR because they can't move into private rental apartments. They are required to have guarantors and a certain minimum income. Many of them have enough savings, but their applications still get rejected, so it looks like UR and municipal units are the only alternative. Even if there are no elevators... I suppose that if you can still walk normally, you are likely to choose danchi as the only option when you look for a rental place from where you can reach both shops and a hospital. If you don't have to work at the office, you don't have to care whether you live near the city center or not. So, most people can confirm that

it is convenient to live there. Although some say they don't really have any choice... but still most people say positive things.

- What about social activity in danchi districts? Is it possible to attract people from other areas to visit them?
  Y: Well, usually, "outsiders" don't have any reason to go there. So often, rather than doing something about the building or apartments themselves, we try to change a shopping street or some vacant unit into a new communal or commercial facility, just like the project in Chayamadai, Senboku New Town. City governments always tended to provide mass housing of bigger sizes, well-equipped and surrounded by greenery, which most private apartments lack. However, danchi meant for low-income social housing aren't given that much attention.
- To summarize, to change the current negative image that some people have about danchi, how should we renovate these complexes in the future?
  Y: First of all, if we consider the buildings, this is my central belief: I don't think you need to change much. Reforming can be harmful to danchi. For example, some *machiya* in Kyoto were renewed entirely. It was fashionable at some point. People sold them with these fully renovated interiors, but the designs turned out to be uncomfortable, and I think this business didn't work as well as expected. Rather than reforming, I believe the old features should be left as they are because they are essential to *machiya*. The same goes for danchi. They should be discussed on the same level with *machiya* because they were built more than 50 years ago. Whatever you do, physically, danchi are danchi, so it makes more sense to change the image of what danchi stand for. Of course, I think danchi don't fit every lifestyle, but generally they work just fine. When I take clients to look around some good danchi estates, some instantly say they want to live there, and almost everyone who said that went on to move in.

Unlike similar modernist districts in France or the United States, danchi neighborhoods are relatively safe, quiet, and clean, but as we could see in this chapter, until recently, their media image had negative connotations and there was a prevailing public determination to demolish and completely rebuild them. However, it is becoming more and more evident that a sharp decline is awaiting the construction industry after the

2020 Tokyo Olympics with colossal investments not returned as originally planned. As the coronavirus pandemic hit the world's economies in 2020, and the new housing demand declining, state-subsidized danchi districts will continue supplying Japan with rental units several decades longer.

With greater media attention and the success of large-scale renovations by the UR, the public perception of Publicly Operated danchi will hopefully change for the better, too. However, if we really want to save these residential complexes of epochal urban memory, how exactly should we renovate the apartments to respect the needs of the current tenants when the funds are limited? The fieldwork in next chapter will attempt to find the answers.

References

Atkins, T. (2017). *A history of popular culture in Japan*. Bloomsbury.

Danely, J. (2019). The limits of dwelling and the unwitnessed death. *Cultural Anthropology, 34*(2), 213–239.

Daniels, I. (2010). *The Japanese house: Material culture in the modern home*. Berg.

Daniels, I. (2015). Feeling at home in contemporary Japan: Space, atmosphere and intimacy. *Emotion, Space and Society, 15*, 47–55.

Guthrie-Shimizu, S. (2012). *Transpacific field of dreams: How baseball linked the United States and Japan in peace and war*. University of North Carolina Press.

Hara, T. (2012). *Danchi no kūkan seiji-gaku*. NHK Publishing.

Hirayama, Y., & Ronald, R. (Eds.). (2006). *Housing and social transition in Japan* (1st ed.). Routledge.

Imamura, A. (1987). *Urban Japanese housewives: At home and in the community*. University of Hawaii Press.

Itoh, G. (1950). *Postwar housing situation and policy of Japan*. Ministry of Construction Housing Bureau.

Izuhara, M. (2000). *Change and housing in post-war Japanese society: The experiences of older women*. Routledge.

Kaneko, Y. (1958). Multi-story housing in a city growing upward. *Shinkenchiku: New Architecture of Japan, 33*(12), 18–21.

Koizumi, K. (1979). *Kagu to shitsunai ishō no bunkashi*. Hōsei Daigaku Shuppankyoku.

Matsumoto, S. (2017). *Shōwa no Nihon no Sumai: Nishiyama Uzō Shashin Akaibuzu Kara*. Sogensha.

Neitzel, L. L. (2016). *The life we longed for: Danchi housing and the middle class dream in postwar Japan*. MerwinAsia.

Nishiyama, U. (1989). *Sumai Kōkongaku: Gendai Nihon Jūtakushi* (2nd ed.). Shōkokusha.

Otake, E. (1958). Two Multi-story Apartment Houses. *Shinkenchiku: New Architecture of Japan, 33*(12), 24–30.

Sakurai, H., (2017). The Danchi Renaissance. *Public Relations Office* (website). https://www.gov-online.go.jp/eng/publicity/book/hlj/html/201711/201711_06_en.html. Accessed 30 Sept 2021.

Shinozawa, K., & Yoshinaga, K. (2017). *Danchi zukai chikei zōsei randosukēpu jū-tō madori kara yomitoku sekkei shikō.* Gakugei shuppansha.

Shō, A. (1958). High-rise apartment houses today. *Shinkenchiku: New Architecture of Japan,* 33(12), 1958, 22–23.

Smith, M. D. (2018). *Mass media, consumerism and national identity in postwar Japan.* Bloomsbury Academic.

Sogabe, M. (2006). Danchi eiga o tōshite miru kōkyō kūkan no katsuyō ni tsuite no kenkyū. *Science Reports of Research Institute for Engineering Kanagawa University, 29*, 27–34.

Suzuki, S. (2004). *"51C" kazoku o ireru hako no sengo to genzai.* Heibonsha.

Uchida, S. (2002). *Kieta modan tōkyō.* Kawade shobō shinsha.

Waswo, A. (2002). *Housing in postwar Japan—A social history.* Routledge.

Reports and Articles with No Author

(1959). News and Comment. *The Japan Architect: The International Edition of Shinkenchiku, 34*(2), 3.

(1959). News and Comment. *The Japan Architect: The International Edition of Shinkenchiku, 34*(4), 3–5.

(1965). A Complete Look at Senri New Town. *The Japan Architect: The International Edition of Shinkenchiku, 40*(5), 68–79.

(1965). *Housing in Japan.* Ministry of Construction Housing Bureau.

(1965). *Jū Nenshi Kankō Iinkai.* Japan Housing Corporation.

(1975). *Nijū Nenshi Kankō Iinkai.* Japan Housing Corporation.

(2014). Danchi rinobēshon purojekuto, Mujirushi ryohin (website). https://www.muji.net/ie/mujiur/. Accessed 30 Sept 2021.

(2016). Profile of Urban Rennaissance Agency. *Urban Rennaissance Agency* (website). https://www.ur-net.go.jp/profile/english/pdf/profile_en_all.pdf. Accessed 30 Sept 2021.

(2016). The Future of Danchi. *Kengo Kuma and Associates* (website). https://kkaa.co.jp/works/architecture/the-future-of-housing-complex/. Accessed 12 May 2020.

(2017). Interview with Kengo Kuma. *Danchi no Mirai* (website). http://www.danchinomirai.com/news/news180630.html. Accessed 30 Sept 2021.

(2021). Danchi marugoto rinobēshon chōin-shiki o okonaimashita. Mujirushi ryohin no ie (website). https://house.muji.com/life/clmn/danchi_renov/marugoto_210316/. Accessed 30 Sept 2021.

CHAPTER 3

Dissecting the Danchi of Today

"Yeah": Finding a Case Study

Wearing a cooking apron on top of her oversized sweatshirt and old pair of jeans, Ako, a girl in her early 20s, is wandering around a deserted danchi neighborhood, limping and stumbling in rubber boots clearly too big for her feet. The camera follows her as she walks in a daze from one building to another, goes up one of the dilapidated concrete staircases leading to a tiny apartment door squeezed under a low ceiling, and pushes her ear on its scratched blue metal surface. She carefully rotates the unlocked doorknob and enters the apartment, giving up on trying to hear what's going on behind. Inside, a startled middle-aged woman leans over a kitchen cupboard that she uses as a dressing table and looks at the *genkan*. "How many times do you have to do this? You're trespassing," she says with a frustrated but strangely unalarmed tone. "She's not my mother," concludes Ako to herself, takes the boots off with a habitual motion, and slowly proceeds into the living room while calling for her sister. Instead of her family, inside she finds a young man listening to music on the balcony, who recognizes her and greets the flustered uninvited guest with a lighthearted smile. Before Ako can respond, the woman catches up and pulls her back toward the entrance with a tired resignation on her face, as if she somehow understands the logic behind the girl's disturbing behavior. It looks like Ako, who lives in the same

T. Knoroz, *Dissecting the Danchi*,
https://doi.org/10.1007/978-981-16-8460-9_3

danchi with her older brother, keeps mistaking neighbors' apartments for her own from day-to-day, but no one judges her: the interiors, the doors, the entrance stairs, and all the buildings do look eerily identical (Fig. 3.1).

As Ako loses herself in the sterile whiteness of buildings' freshly repainted exteriors, barren lawns, and rows of empty parking lots, she shouts something between an English "yeah," "*iie*," that means "no" in Japanese, and "*ie*," the word for "house" and "household," into the distance—a perfect combination of meanings to describe the absurdity of the current state of danchi neighborhoods that function as social housing. Watching her stroll through faded remains of a 1970s children's playground in-between the buildings, the other residents don't appear to be living a better life than poor confused Ako (Fig. 3.2). Most of her neighbors are in some way excluded from mainstream Japanese society and bear similar feelings of drowning in homogeneity and isolation of this danchi district. Some even react to Ako's apparent insanity with a hint of envy—at least she doesn't seem to be completely aware of the hopelessness of their living situation.

When I first came to Japan to collect data for my research on postwar mass housing regeneration, I wasn't yet aware of how synonymous danchi's media image had become with social isolation. My initial plan

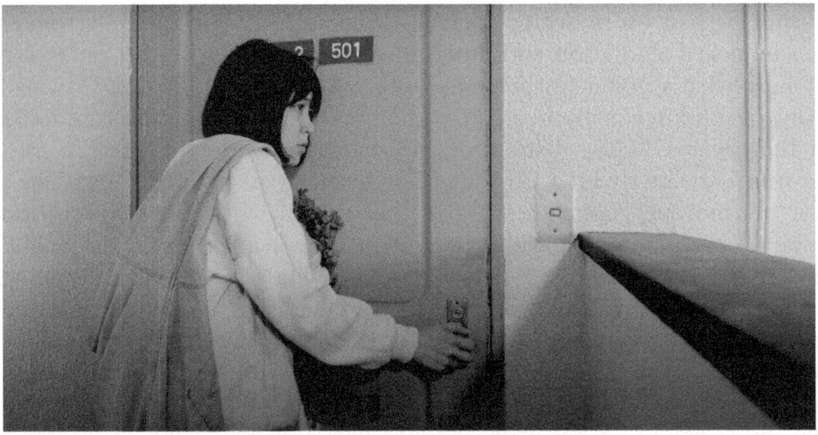

Fig. 3.1 Ako listens in before opening the door to a neighbor's apartment. YEAH, directed by Yohei Suzuki, 2017

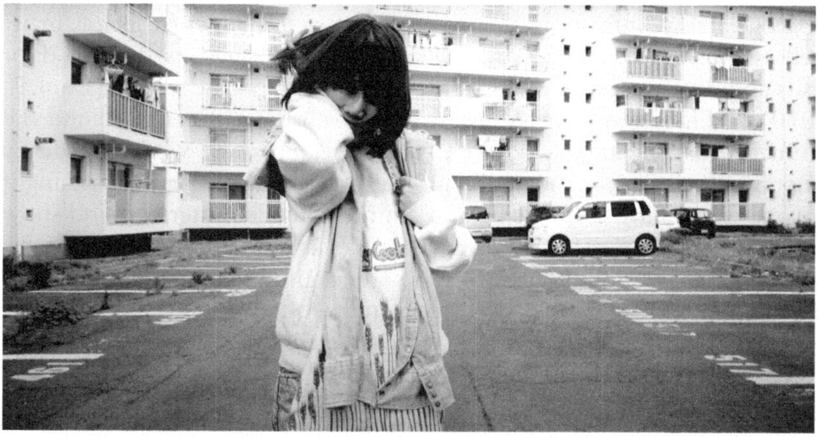

Fig. 3.2 Lost Ako in despair. YEAH, directed by Yohei Suzuki, 2017

was to find several danchi inhabitants for conducting interviews and apartment visits within the first two or three months of my stay through university colleagues. To my surprise, in an entire department of architecture of Tokyo University of the Arts, no one knew anyone living in danchi; even reaching out to friends of friends didn't help. Most students reacted to my research plan with disbelief and kept asking why I would be trying to study something so "ugly," "outdated," and "soon to be demolished anyway." Some of the professors and teaching assistants strongly advised changing my topic completely. According to them, danchi had no further research potential as Japanese scholars had already documented the phenomena in the 1970s from every possible perspective.

Later I realized that this kind of denial was specific to TUoA that focuses on esthetics rather than social issues and practicality and that architects from technical universities can be more encouraging toward discussing postwar mass housing and renovation. Still, ordinary Japanese people I met outside of universities made similar comments about danchi, distancing themselves from the topic. It was hard to believe—during my daily commute to Tokyo from Chiba, the train passed dozens of gigantic danchi neighborhoods, and I've seen New Towns with 1000s of units with my own eyes. Apparently, the social circle that I tried to extend so much was still too far from intersecting with danchi people, so I decided to change tactics and go into the field directly.

As Daniels points out in the introduction to *The Japanese House*, many well-established fieldwork strategies in the West such as door-to-door visits and distribution of posters or letters fail in Japanese setting (Daniels, 2010). My idea was to make day trips to both the UR managed and the municipal danchi in Tokyo and Chiba prefectures and work outside by stopping the locals for short talks in a safer public atmosphere, checking if anyone was willing to participate in a more extended interview and show their unit. Since the UR housing is less of a gray area in the contemporary Japanese media due to active renovations and higher financial requirements for tenants, I tried to go more often in the Publicly Operated social housing with lower budgets, which become target setting of horror movies and urban legends nowadays and are less studied by both anthropologists and architects.

On top of language concerns, in suburban areas where foreigners are a rare sight, my face was already a big problem, so I always took a Japanese friend with me for a smoother approach and communication. Another obstacle was the high percentage of elderly tenants, making danchi quieter and more deserted than surrounding low-rise neighborhoods, with barely any social activity visible outside the buildings. Some people were alarmed enough already when they saw us approaching, cutting us off as soon as they could, while others reluctantly continued the conversation until they heard the part about apartment visits, where the interviews would always finish with an awkward decline.

After several months of demotivating failures in my pursuit of fieldwork, I was almost ready to give up when a chance encounter changed everything. While looking for a part-time job, I got acquainted with Yohei Suzuki, a young film director from Ibaraki prefecture, and mentioned I was studying danchi. Much like all the other Japanese people I talked to before, he was taken aback by my desire to meet current danchi inhabitants, but this time it was because he was deeply involved in a danchi-related project himself.

After describing my unsuccessful attempts at infiltrating public housing in Tokyo, Suzuki sent me a link for his 45-minute fiction movie "YEAH" that he presented at the Japan Cuts Festival in 2018. Similar to Suzuki's previous highly controversial feature movie "Ow," "Yeah" is a surreal critique on contemporary Japanese society, which pushes for the exclusion of anyone who doesn't fit in, despite the fact that the boundaries of normality have been getting increasingly blurrier since the 1990s. The main character, Ako, tries to make sense of her life in a government-subsidized danchi neighborhood. According to Suzuki's description, danchi's orderly structures and homogenous environment represent the power of "history" and "authority" that overwhelm and confuse the girl, pushing her to look for a mental escape.

Fascinated by the unusual ghostliness of the danchi estate in the movie, I decided to inquire Suzuki about the setting. He didn't hesitate to send me the precise location—a Google Map pin in a place called "Wakamiya Danchi," somewhere in the suburbs of Mito, Ibaraki prefecture, two hours by train north from Tokyo. Mito's population is slightly over 250,000 people; born and raised there, Suzuki has a tight-knit local friend network. His close friend had a kindergarten classmate living in Wakamiya, a social housing danchi managed by Ibaraki Prefectural Government, so despite the neighborhood's secluded location and stigmatized status, they could get familiar with some residents through their contact. Suzuki's team had to get permission from the local administration and Wakamiya's residents' council to set the movie there.

Suzuki was very empathetic about my project and invited me to visit Wakamiya Danchi with him to see if we could find anyone willing to show their apartments. Mito was a long train ride from where I lived at the time, and I could only come for the weekend, so I asked if we could secure the possibility of some interviews beforehand to avoid the risks of my previous attempts at engaging danchi residents on the spot. After helping me obtain the filming permission for outside areas from the local administration in the same way he did for his own movie the previous year, Suzuki called his contacts connected to Wakamiya, and the municipal office that manages the estate, and told them about my research. To my surprise, apart from one tenant, Akane, and an ex-tenant, Yoshimura, agreeing to be interviewed, the municipal official who helped with the permissions invited us to attend and observe the monthly residents' council meeting in the community building with the possibility to ask some questions in the end. It seemed like a solid starting point for connecting with someone, who may be able to invite us inside their unit, so we confirmed the dates and contacted a local interpreter to assist us with the interviews in case Suzuki won't be able to make it.

One Saturday morning in December 2018, I packed my camera, a tripod, a microphone, a laser distance meter for the architectural survey and boarded the first train to Mito.

Wakamiya Danchi

Before every danchi visit, I usually did some preliminary information gathering on the Internet to check its media reputation, see if it's managed by UR, a private company, or the government, and approximate what kind of people will live there. Most UR and municipal danchi in and around Tokyo are easily traceable online both in English and Japanese, thanks to the recent interest in social housing of international journals such as Japan Times, and most importantly, to online subculture known as "danchi *otaku*": people who appreciate either the Shōwa period esthetics of danchi interiors or romanticize the decadence of dilapidating buildings—preferences best described with a popular Twitter hashtag, "danchi *moe*," translated as "danchi charm." With the continuing economic stagnation, there is no surprise that nostalgia for the thriving 1960s and 1970s is getting stronger, especially among the generations that never actually witnessed this period, and danchi, a trademark and a symbol of that lost success became a fictional past to return to for many Japanese in their 20s and 30s (personal interview with Yoshinaga 2019). There are some blogs that collect photographs of danchi all over Japan (http://codan.boy.jp/ or http://danchi100k.com/), well-known artists portraying danchi in their works (see Cody Ellingham's "Danchi Dreams" photographic project https://danchi-dreams.com or Japanese rapper Anarchy's songs about his childhood in danchi), and small communities of architects interested in danchi in one way or another. However, despite knowing the precise location of Wakamiya, I couldn't get any information from asking around, and in my online search, so I had to find out everything on site.

Suzuki and his friend Ōtsu, who agreed to be our backup interpreter, met me in front of Mito Station on top of a lifeless entanglement of pedestrian overpasses surrounded by shabby office buildings from the 1980s. Ōtsu ironically introduced himself as "an ordinary Mito salaryman, who lives a meaningless life and is bored out of his mind on the weekends." Half-jokingly he admitted that hanging around extravagant and artistic Suzuki usually gets him to participate in exciting "unusual" activities, just like our fieldwork endeavor that day. The duo's instant friendliness and desire to help a stranger contrasted with Mito's depressing townscape and struck me as something I had never experienced while living in Tokyo. We got into Suzuki's car, and after a 15-minute drive through dusty low-rise suburbs and drive-in chain shops, we approached the first row of Wakamiya Danchi blocks looming over a carpet of tiny detached houses on both sides of the road. The interviews were scheduled in the afternoon, and we still had plenty of time, so camera in hand, I took my first walk around the neighbourhood (Figs. 3.3, 3.4, 3.5, 3.6, 3.7, 3.8, 3.9, 3.10, 3.11, 3.12).

Wakamiya, like many danchi designed in the 1950s and 1960s, is a cluster of four- and five-story slab buildings, without elevators, located on rice fields along the Naka River at the edge of an agricultural settlement in the outskirts of Mito. While most danchi in Kansai (Osaka and Kyoto) area tend to be built in hilly areas with buildings' sides following natural topography, danchi in Kanto plains, Wakamiya included, are usually arranged in rigid grid masterplans based on an East–West axis, with most buildings providing South and North exposure for every apartment (Figs. 3.13 and 3.14). Still, looking at the aerial map, the masterplan differs from the standard Japan Housing Corporation layouts, with the East–West axis being more tilted toward SW-NE, following the existing streets directions, which are influenced by the river. Some buildings are

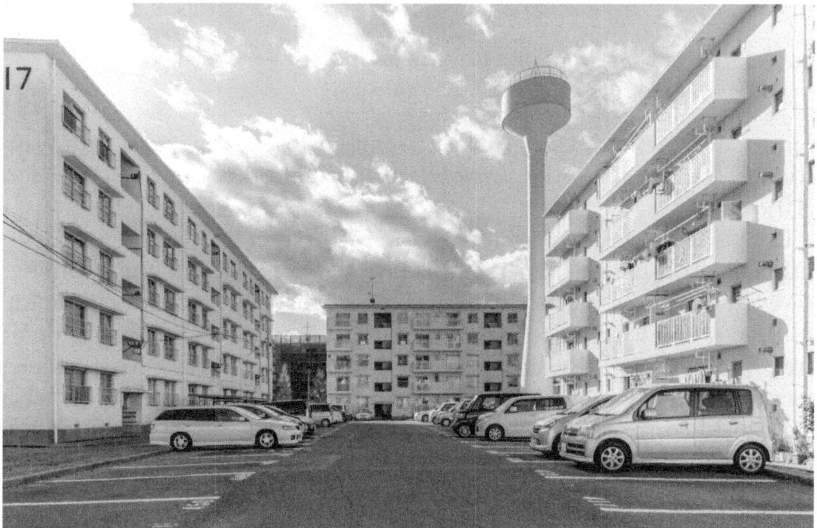

Fig. 3.3 Wakamiya Danchi Watertower, December 2018. All images below are by the author

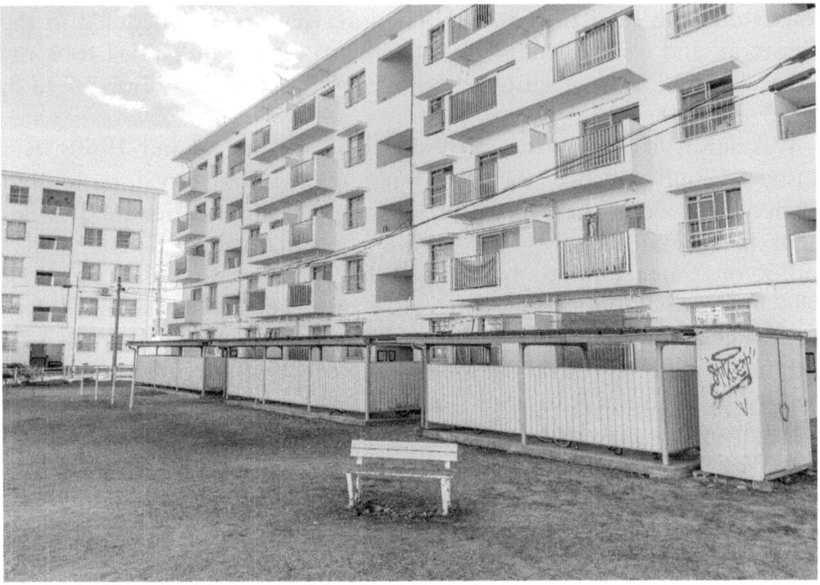

Fig. 3.4 A bench in front of a playground in a semi-enclosed courtyard

even rotated by 90 degrees to create semi-enclosed courtyards with playgrounds, similar to Soviet *khrushchevka* neighborhoods (Figs. 3.4 and 3.10).

The plot is in direct proximity to the Jōban train line, leading to Ueno station in Tokyo from where I made my way earlier in the morning; however, the closest station, Mito, is only reachable by car or a 20-minute bus ride. A one-way trip to Tokyo on public transportation can take up to three hours, so the district was mainly developed to house local people, especially those who worked in nearby factories such as Hitachi. After a round of the area, it became clear why Wakamiya didn't appear in the web search. Unlike most danchi in Tokyo metropolitan area, this housing estate is neither managed by the Urban Renaissance Agency nor by the local municipality—Wakamiya was built, is owned and maintained by the prefectural government, a situation much rarer than city-built complexes, is used exclusively as social housing and does not accept tenants easily, and therefore is not listed on Japanese housing websites.

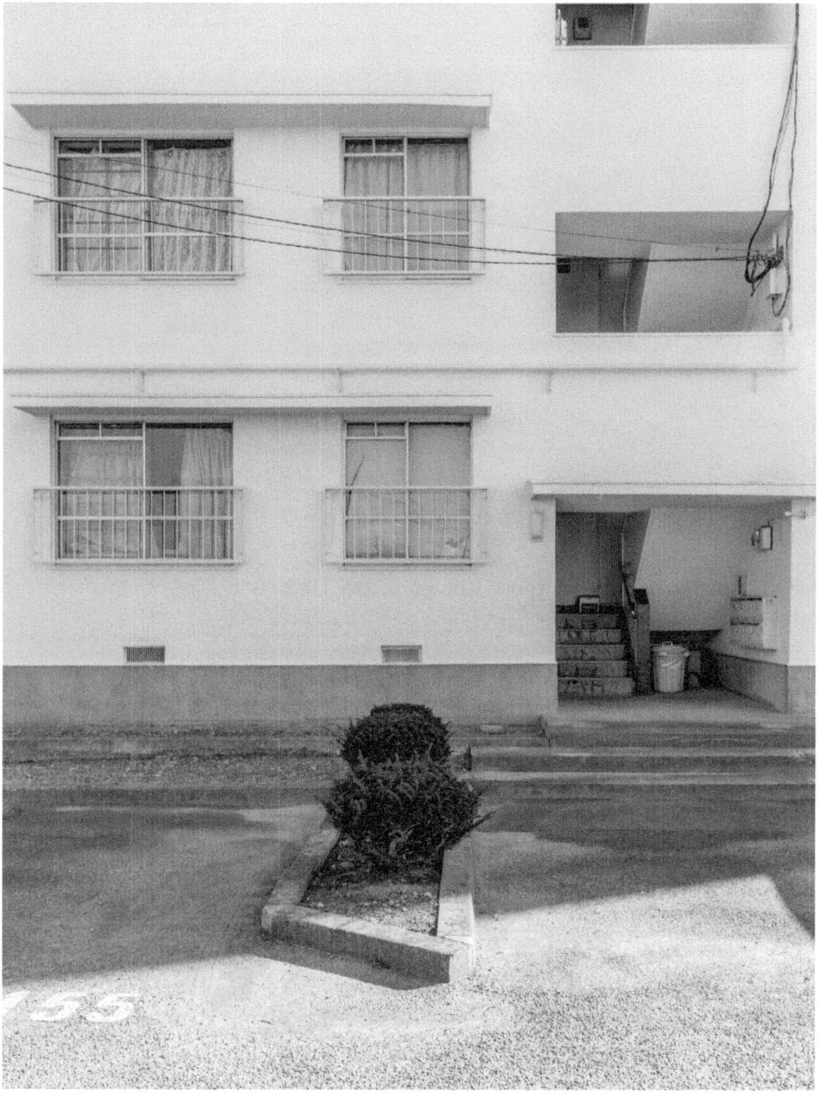

Fig. 3.5 Entrance of one of the buildings. The frames of old *shōji* screens are visible in the windows

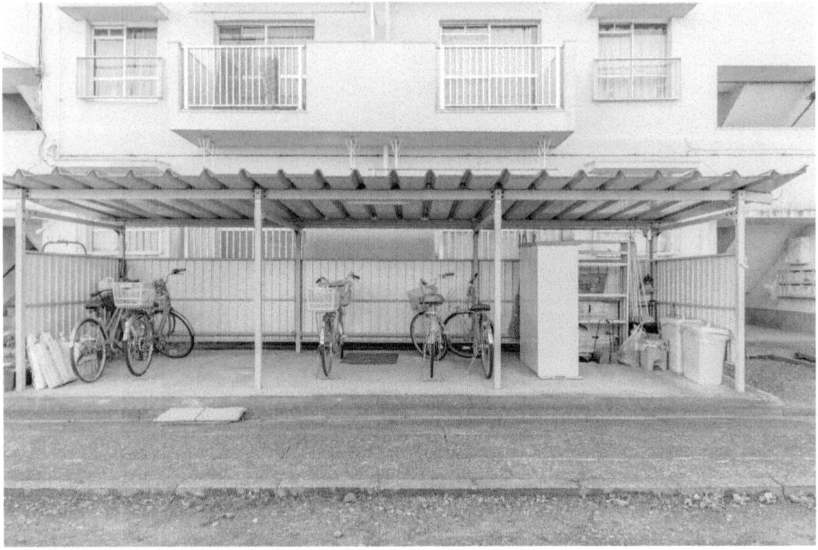

Fig. 3.6 External multipurpose storage sheds. There is at least one per staircase in front of every building

In our later trips to Ibaraki Prefectural Library and Ibaraki Government Office, we discovered that Wakamiya was planned and built by Ibaraki Prefectural Housing Bureau, with the government subsidies allocated in the framework of Public Housing Act from 1951, and just like the other Publicly Operated estates was originally designated as rental public housing for young lower middle-class families. Now it provides social housing apartments for the most financially struggling applicants, with the monthly rents ranging from 3000 (30 USD) to 10,000 (120 USD) yen depending on the tenant's income, family size, and the year of application. When I interviewed employees of the Ibaraki Prefectural Housing Bureau, who are in charge of social housing maintenance in the prefecture, Wakamiya included, no one had any materials or information on the details of its history, apart from three original project drawings kept in their archive; some employees could not even immediately recall the existence of this danchi district.

Old city maps depicting the development of Mito and its suburbs that I found in the Ibaraki Prefectural Library provided the most important

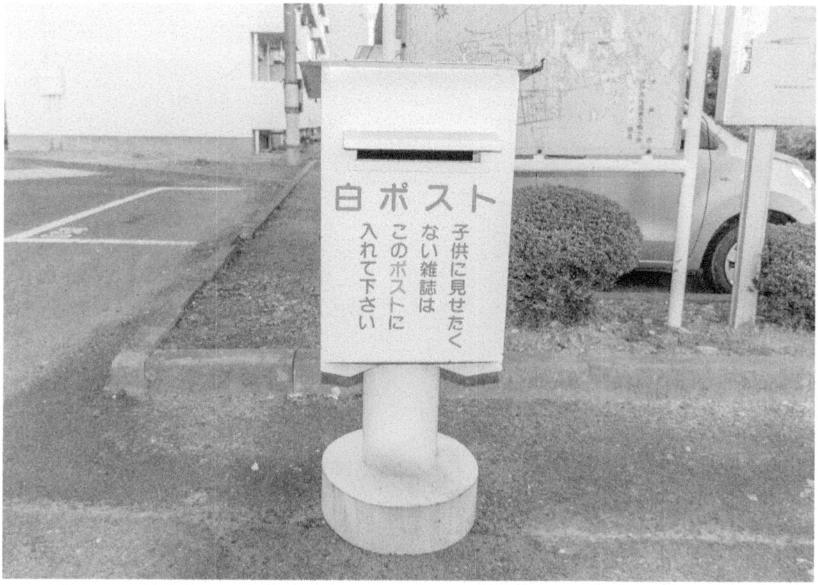

Fig. 3.7 Shiroposuto, "White Mail," a box for adult magazines disposal is a trademark of danchi districts. The inscription states: "Please insert periodicals that are not to be viewed by children"

insights into the history of Wakamiya Danchi. A map from 1965 showed that the housing complex's land was previously empty and belonged to the government, and the district around it was a sparse rural settlement. In the area closer to the main road leading to central Mito, four predecessor apartment buildings had already been built by that time, all under three-story height and the largest consisting of only 33 apartments. These buildings are treated by the mapmaker as some sort of exception: the outlines of the plots are in bold, and the information about the names of every apartment resident is placed into special tables on the sides of the page. This might seem strange compared to the usual anonymity of Western urban maps, but most Japanese urban maps include names of the house or business owner on top of every patch of land. In 1971, when the first seven buildings of Wakamiya Danchi were completed, seven more tables were added at the corner of the page, showing the resident name for every apartment organized by floor number, with some

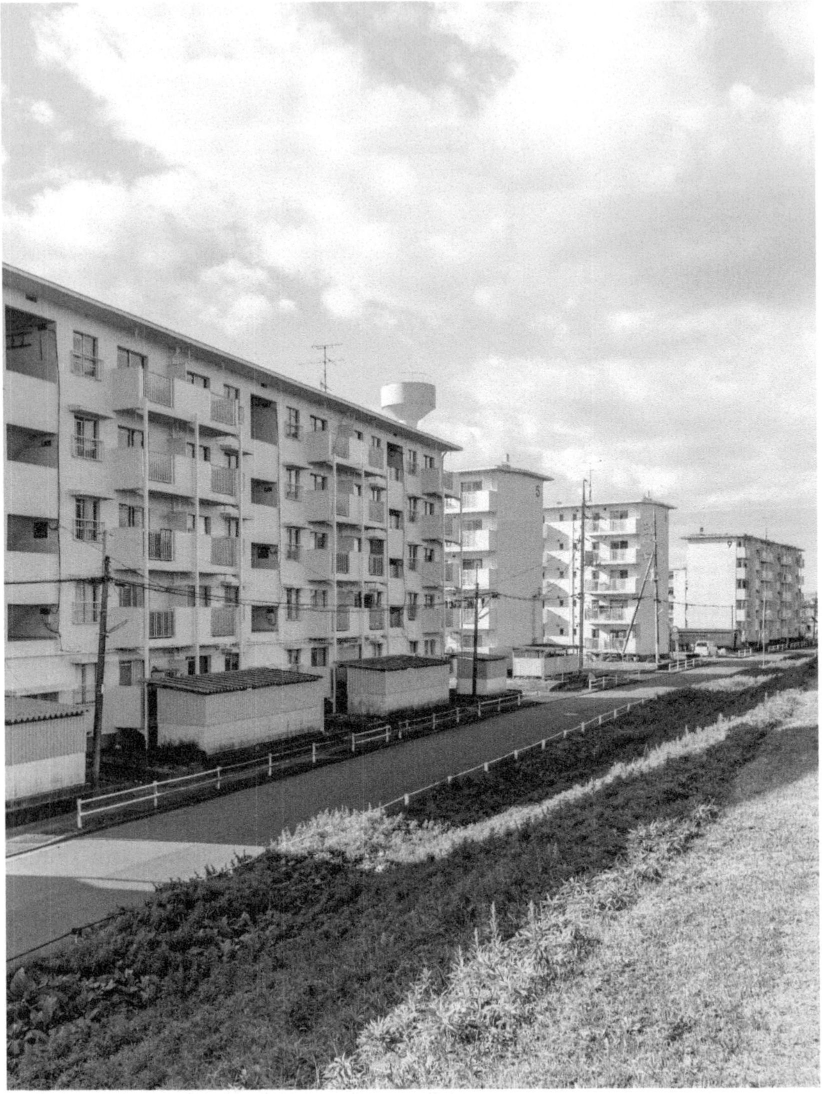

Fig. 3.8 The view from the riverside road. Storage sheds on this side are more enclosed

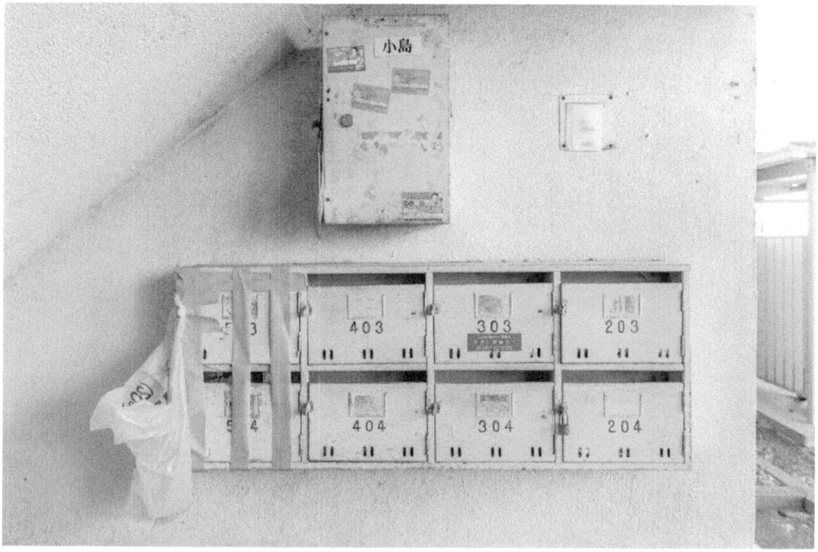

Fig. 3.9 Mailboxes in one of the buildings. Mailboxes of vacant apartments get taped to avoid accumulation of printed advertisements

units left blank as they were still vacant (Fig. 3.13). As we know already, Wakamiya Danchi was designed as rental housing, so it seems pointless to include names of temporary tenants on an urban map that will be in use for years to come, but this was a natural attempt to "regularize" the unprecedented typology of residential buildings and make them into the existing order of the city, representing it in a comparable way to the usual detached houses. By 1975, when the construction of Wakamiya Danchi was finished, mapmakers gave up on the idea to list every resident in a special table, most probably due to the lack of space on the page and the changing perception of apartment housing as a completely different mode of land use compared to detached residences.

As we explored the neighborhood with Suzuki and Ōtsu, I counted 33 buildings forming semi-enclosed courtyards with minimally equipped playgrounds, all flanked by parking lots, now half-empty most of the time (Fig. 3.14). The buildings' lengths differ depending on the number of standard units and stairs, the only variety in the otherwise completely homogenous exteriors. The buildings had a simple slab shape with flat

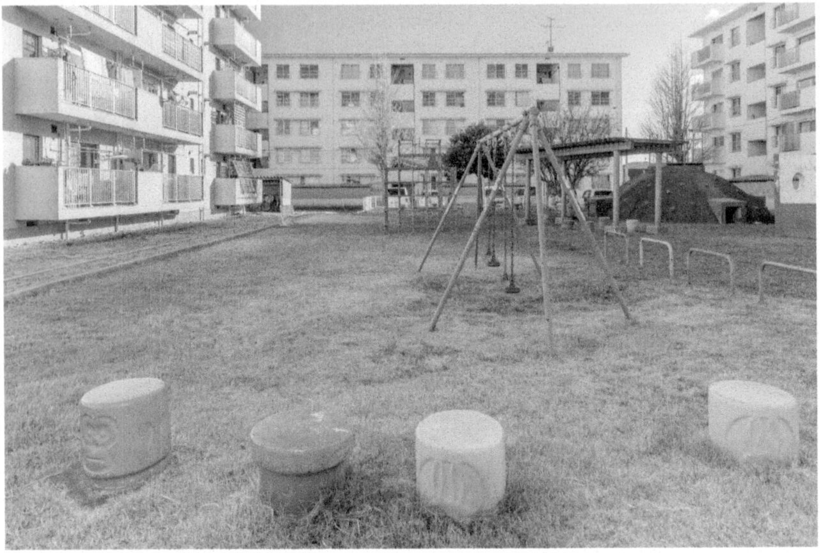

Fig. 3.10 Playground in one of the semi-enclosed courtyards

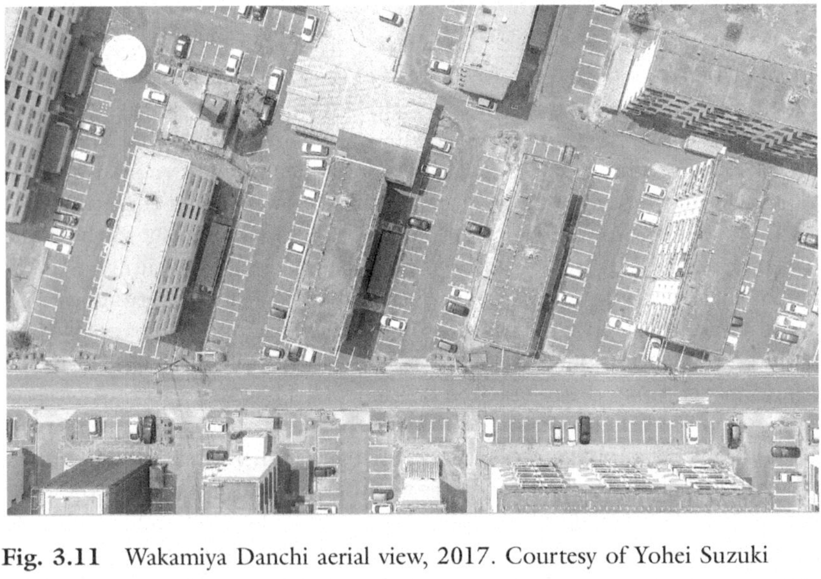

Fig. 3.11 Wakamiya Danchi aerial view, 2017. Courtesy of Yohei Suzuki

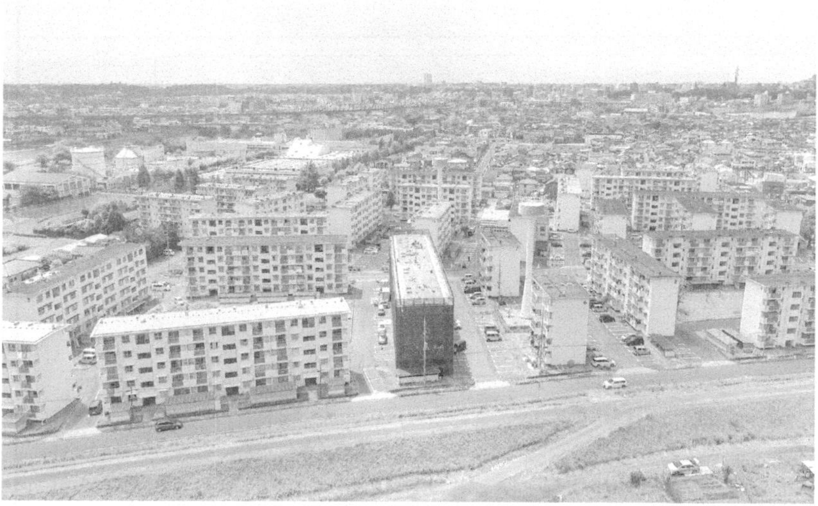

Fig. 3.12 Wakamiya Danchi aerial view, 2017. Courtesy of Yohei Suzuki

roofs and narrow rows of balconies on one or both longitudinal sides, all made from cast-on-site monolith reinforced concrete. In some windows, original worn-out *shōji* screens were still installed, separating the curtains from the glass (Fig. 3.5). Just like tatami, they were a remainder of traditional Japanese architecture to be inserted into concrete shells, providing complete visual privacy and reducing sun glare yet letting enough light inside for daily needs. Ubiquitous in the Japanese housing industry, single glazing aluminum horizontally sliding windows with their low thermal performance now seem like an obsolete choice for mass construction, but in the early 1960s, when aluminum just started being produced in large quantities in Japan, they were the only alternative to timber frames and became one of the danchi's exterior hallmarks. Another is parapet railings made out of vertical aluminum rods for balconies and non-balcony facing windows, a feature first implemented in Dōjunkai apartments for *futon* drying and child safety and present in Wakamiya in its classic form.

Apart from several dilapidated buildings with the highest number of vacant apartments on the district's periphery, the exteriors looked neat and structurally safe: later, we discovered that the plaster was recently repainted during the prefectural renovation. However, after entering

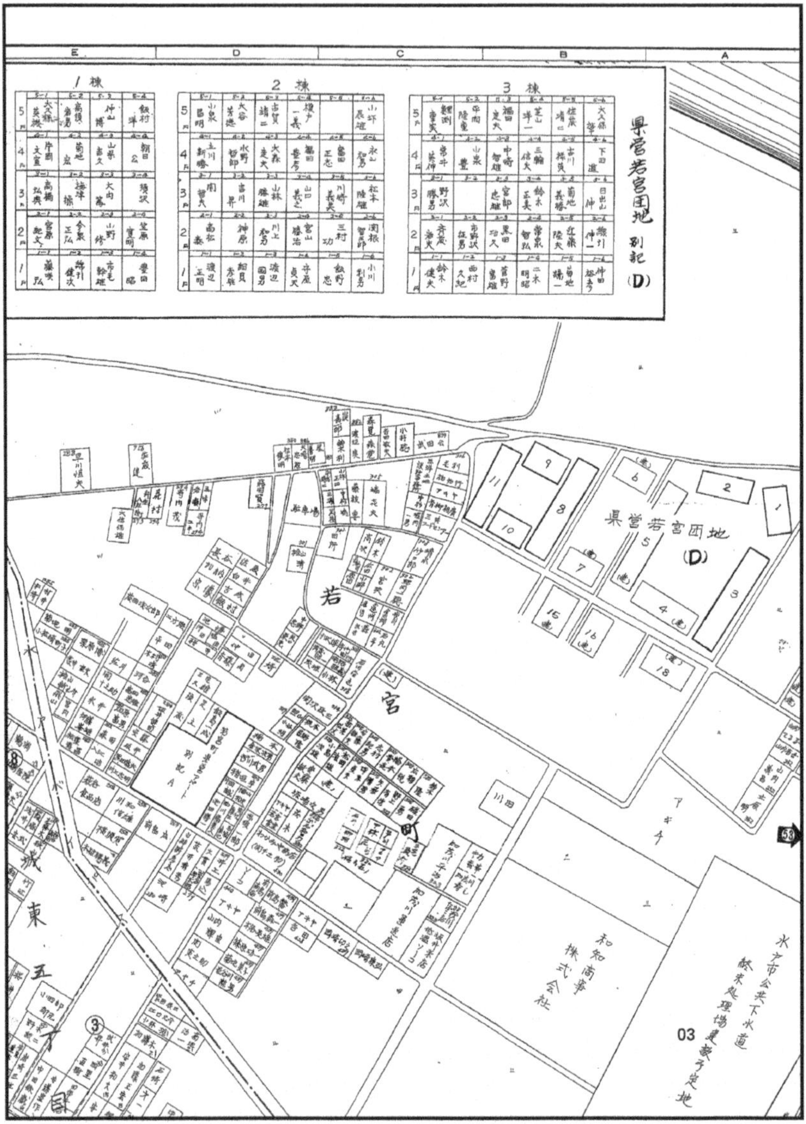

Fig. 3.13 Map of Wakamiya district, 1971. First half of Wakamiya Danchi completed (*Source* Mito Urban Maps, Ibaraki Prefectural Library)

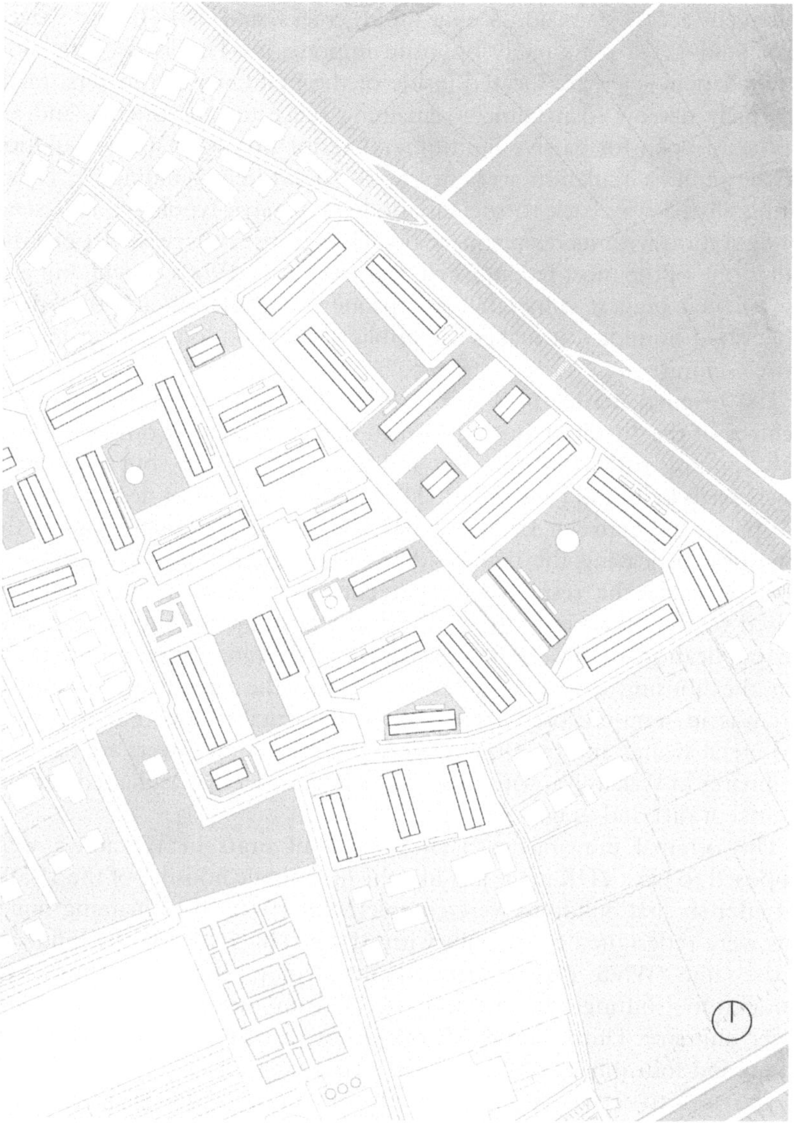

Fig. 3.14 Wakamiya Danchi masterplan, 2018

apartment access stairs and seeing mold, cracks, and dark, humid spaces, one could get a completely opposite impression. This is because most 1960s danchi stairs are located inside of the buildings' perimeters, made extremely narrow to maximize remaining space for apartments, and are kept semi-open for passive lighting and ventilation—a standard solution for the public circulation areas in low-rise apartment buildings in Japan, dating all the way back to the variations of *nagaya* typology. This stairs configuration with its deep square openings in the otherwise flat exterior wall is one of the most recognizable features of the 1960s danchi, but also one of their biggest vulnerabilities—prone to weathering and the effects of elevated humidity, it makes the public circulation look dangerous and unwelcoming.

The original master plan from 1969 that we later requested in the archives of the Ibaraki Housing Bureau depicted exciting outdoor spaces with winding paths through rich and varied vegetation, but these were nowhere to be found (Fig. 3.16). They became victims of design changes that happened between 1970 and 1972, apparent in the city maps of the same period, leaving the new residents with simple lawns and asphalt—most probably the result of budget cuts in the construction industry caused by the oil crisis and the shift in the housing subsidy policies after the publication of the 1970 government's "White Paper" announcing that the housing crisis was officially over. In the end, five simple playgrounds in semi-enclosed courtyards with brutalist concrete structures and metal swings and two monumental water-serving towers are the only landmarks in Wakamiya, with other outside spaces left as asphalted parking or unkept dirt and grass.

The original drawings also show that all units in Wakamiya were supposed to have 2DK plans just like the first public housing of the 1950s, but after six first buildings were completed in 1970, the remaining buildings were redesigned to be built with 3DKs. This is clearly the influence of the same "White Paper" that brought ideological changes to housing production, shifting the industry's goal from quantity to quality and larger unit size. During my fieldwork, I got to visit only the 3DKs—one vacant and four inhabited units (Fig. 3.15).

The door to each unit opens directly into a tiny version of a traditional *genkan* entrance hall integrated with the dining-kitchen area, and *fusuma* sliding doors open onto a small bathroom, all with south-eastern or south-western exposure. The DK has direct access to a small balcony and to the other rooms: the four-and-a-half-tatami (7.4-square-meter) living

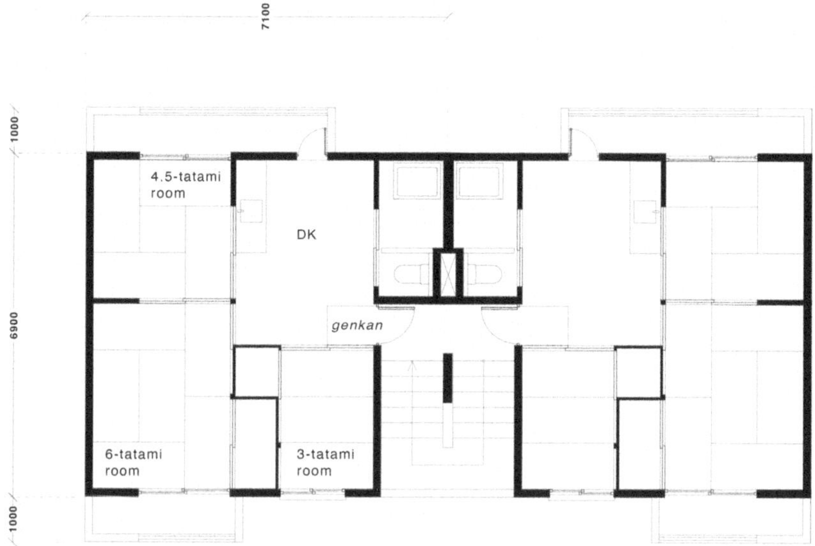

Fig. 3.15 Wakamiya Danchi: two 3DK units in a typical one-staircase building plan

room with the same sunny exposure, the six-tatami (9.7-square-meter) parents' bedroom with an *oshiire* closet, and the three-tatami (4.9-square-meter) children's bedroom with another smaller built-in storage with a pivoting door. Despite the small sizes of the tatami rooms, all the *fusuma* doors could be opened to create a single large space (Fig. 3.16).

3DKs in Wakamiya, although similar in size, do not fully correspond to any of the standard 3DK plans published by JHC in their annual reports from 1965 until 1973 that were aiming at greater efficiency for kitchen spaces that needed to contain more electric appliances and higher privacy for family members. Publicly Operated housing plans, Wakamiya included, were more simple and slightly smaller during that period, but they allowed unobstructed views from one side of the apartment to the opposite, providing more natural light and ventilation than some newer JHC options in high-rise danchi with corridor access layouts. There is considerably less planned storage space as a result, but at the same time, it is possible to take out the sliding *fusuma* partitions and transform the original design into a semi-open space, but during the community

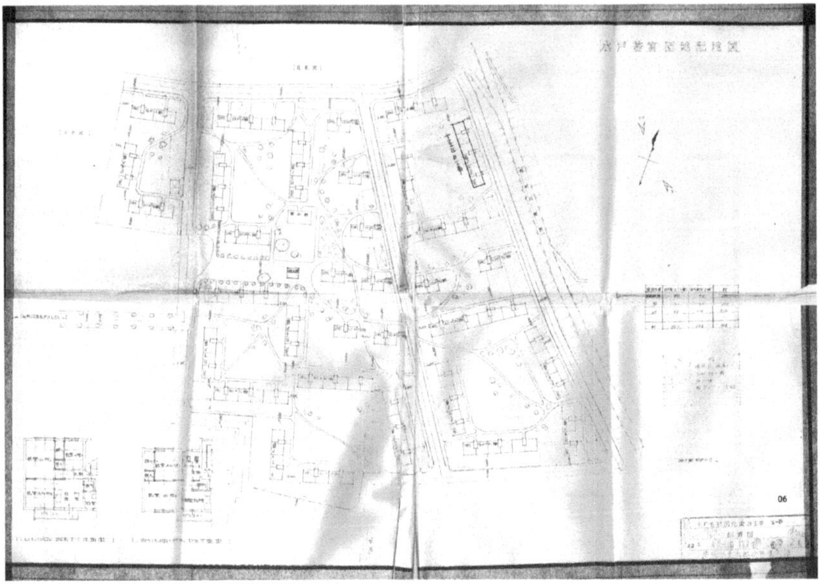

Fig. 3.16 Original masterplan of Wakamiya Danchi, 1969 (*Source* Ibaraki Housing Bureau)

meeting, I was told most tenants avoid doing so because of inefficient building insulation: to save on air-conditioning and heating costs they usually maintain the appropriate temperature in the smallest room with all the *fusuma* closed.

When we almost finished our external inspection and walked past an old fish shop next to one of the blocks, the owner recognized Suzuki from his prior movie-making visits, invited us in, and gave us a small interview. "We get less and less customers every year, especially those from the danchi … I am not close to anyone from the buildings, so I can't help you get inside the apartments, but be careful with your project. You must know, they allow criminals to move in there, people like credit debtors and others …." It was easy to believe what he said: apart from a couple of elderly women waiting at the bus stop, that December morning Wakamiya was eerily deserted, unlike the neighboring residential areas we passed on our way there. However, I already knew danchi for low-income families are covered in rumors and stigma in Japan and waited for the interviews with the residents to get a better perspective.

We met our first interviewee, a 75-year-old Yoshimura, a first-wave tenant in Wakamiya, in the local soba noodle shop for lunch. He lived there in a 3DK with his wife and two kids from 1970 until they purchased their own house in 1985. He shared his memories of the Wakamiya's playgrounds swarming with children, air filled with happy voices, the joys of living in a tight community of young working families with similar interests, and anecdotes about his parents always refusing to visit their apartment, that was way too small for a family of four.

According to Yoshimura, most of the first-wave residents from the 1970s left the place after buying a house, and now Wakamiya's demographic situation is far from the originally intended. As a consequence of Japanese ownership-oriented housing market development, most Japanese rental housing now is only available for either students with guarantor parents, working singles, or couples with a maximum of two children both in terms of square meters provided and financial eligibility requirements, therefore subsidized danchi are the only affordable rental opportunity for the more neglected financially struggling social classes (Hirayama & Ronald, 2006; Izuhara, 2000). As a result, young nuclear families in Wakamiya were completely replaced by elderly singles or couples who didn't have a chance to move out before they retired, elderly singles who moved in after being unable to secure a house or find a reasonable renting opportunity after the economic crash, and single parents with kids who moved in recently with the help of the regional social housing programs.

After the interview with Yoshimura, I was sure I wouldn't encounter the ideal middle-class, nuclear-family housewife polishing the kitchen sink in the Wakamiya danchi, but I couldn't have imagined how different an actual apartment would be from my expectations based on the original plan.

Community Meeting

The next morning, we returned to participate in the Wakamiya Danchi residents' community meeting, an opportunity arranged by Suzuki through his acquittance in the Ibaraki Housing Bureau administration. We thought that the meeting would be held as usual, while I was to film it, take notes and ask the resident council members some questions at the end. However, when we entered Wakamiya community hall at 9 a.m., we realized that this meeting was not a regularly scheduled occasion: after a planned neighborhood cleanup, they met up in the hall with the only purpose to give us a group interview, so the atmosphere was stiff and almost too formal. While the government official responsible for social housing in the city showed us in and introduced himself, 11 elderly Wakamiya residents watched us silently, sitting on cushions around a long low table. No one started speaking before I set up my camera and asked the first question; it seemed that it was an extraordinary event for all the residents involved, and they were not sure what to do and how to behave.

Suzuki helped me introduce my project and my intentions. We explained that I was doing a preparatory study to come up with a design regeneration strategy for danchi in Japan and that I wanted to hear their ideas about any possible improvements both of the interiors and the outside areas. There was a long pause, so Suzuki rephrased the question, but people were still fidgeting and looking around in hesitation. I changed tactics and asked what everyone liked about living in danchi first to postpone more negative topics that might frighten the participants. Later we realized that the reason for the initial confusion was the council president's absence. From my experience of living in Japan, I knew it is impolite to be the first one to offer an opinion before the highest-ranked person in a group does, so when Katsuko, a lady sitting beside the government employee, spoke up and everyone started nodding in relief, it became clear that she was the unofficial leader of the council today. She seemed to have been delegated a certain authority by the group and chose her words carefully at first, retaining neutrality and occasionally glancing at the Mito city official.

The government employee, Mr. Nishino, was another reason for the general reluctance to answer my questions; he worked for Mito City administration and was responsible for monitoring social issues in Wakamiya Danchi, among other state-subsidized housing in the city, so he wasn't a regular at the local meetings and was perceived as an exterior supervisor by the residents. In the beginning, he sometimes moderated the conversation by cutting into what everyone was saying and putting a more positive spin to their descriptions of danchi life, but it wasn't necessary most of the time: no one seemed eager to complain anyway. Below I relay the most relevant parts of the interview.

— What do you like about this neighborhood?
Katsuko: There are plenty of good things here. The green areas are beautiful. We all get along really well and help each other. Life is simple here.
— What is your apartment like? Do you have your own room?
Katsuko: My own room is four-and-a-half tatami big.
Nishino: It sure is simple to live there.
Katsuko: Four-and-a-half tatami is enough, right?
— What about the kitchen?
Katsuko: It is small as well. Anyway, we all ... Although it is small ...
Nishino (cuts in): It is compact and convenient.
Katsuko: I mean, you can sit anywhere and have everything there at hand. I am quite old already, actually. When we just got married, our parents would come to visit us. They used to live in a big country house, so ... They complained about how cramped it was. And never stayed long. But the place gets convenient as long as you get used to it. It is nice.

Her answers reassured the other participants, and they started nodding and murmuring agreeably. Then, after a short pause, a 66-year-old man sitting at the center of the table, Shigeru, said:

Shigeru: One more good point. The air.
Katsuko: It's fresh indeed.
Shigeru: And transportation. Buses go frequently. Transportation is important, you know. One bus in 20 minutes.

Daichi, a man sitting between Katsuko and Shigeru, added:

Daichi: In the morning and in the evening, there are more buses, though. It takes 20 minutes to get to the station. So 20 minutes to Mito station, it is not that much, right? We are also blessed with a hospital nearby.
Nishino (cuts in): We are in the center of a lively district, so buses come often.
Shigeru: I can't think of any problems here. (Everyone nodding actively.)
Katsuko: The closeness of Mito station is sure great.

Nishino's comment sounded strange. He had never lived in Wakamiya but wanted us to get a positive impression about the area, which was objectively very far from being lively and central—no wonder everyone was so happy about the direct bus.

— What facilities do you wish were built in Wakamiya?
Daichi: Probably a park for children to play in.
Katsuko: But there are fewer children nowadays! We rarely hear children's voices. Even if they play, they rarely do it outdoors.
Kimiko: There used to be a lot of shops around here, but many of them closed. Restaurants, a shop selling seafood, butcher's, stuff like that. I wish these places could be brought back. The supermarket is around 20 minutes' walk from here, but it would be nice to have more places nearby where you could buy lunch.
— There are some vegetable gardens by the river, can you use them?
Katsuko: They are not for danchi people. Maybe some people from danchi rent them, though. Municipality lends these patches of land. There is even an office, you can go and find out how much it costs a year.
Kimiko: 3000 (30 USD) yen per year. But the price changes depending on the size of the patch, can be 5000 a year. People used to keep gardening tools in the exterior storage units here in danchi. And everyone here had a personal flower bed for every apartment, around one-and-a-half square meters. You could grow vegetables there. Yes, usually not flowers but veggies. It would be nice to have them again.
Katsuko: Some people grow flowers in the areas surrounding ground floor balconies. Actually, it is not prohibited. About half of the residents do that.
— What is the main responsibility of the Wakamiya resident council?
Katsuko: Every month, we choose a cleaning day and pick up trash in the outside public spaces together. Actually, today was such a day. Going to the previous question, people here are allowed to plant small trees themselves. Before there used to be quite a lot of young families, but now there are mainly elderly people so planting trees has become more difficult.

From the recent news articles about danchi (Murakami, 2018; Ōnishi, 2017), I knew there was a problem with single elderly people living in isolation and not going out of the apartment for days, so I was curious if the council or the municipality were aware of that.

— Is there anyone who lives here on their own?
(Daichi and Kiichiro raise their hands)
— How often do others confirm that you're feeling okay? Or is it done by the prefectural government employees?
Nishino: No, the prefecture is not involved. They rely on their friends.
Daichi: Right.
Nishino: In our danchi, mainly residents check on each other. If there is something wrong, like many newspapers piled up in someone's mailbox, others call social workers, so it is impossible not to notice for months if someone dies.
— Do social workers come here regularly?
Katsuko: It depends on the person. Helpers or social workers visit some apartments from time to time. Our president is a nice person. We hold these regular meetings once a month. During the meetings, he tells us to take care of the elderly and help them with throwing out the trash, so it is okay. We support each other like that.
— Are there any tenants who avoid going outside?
Shigeru: There must be people like that.
Katsuko: When we have regular clean up days, some people never come out because of physical problems. Still, we go see them in their apartments just to confirm their safety.

Here Katsuko is talking about the prevention of ***kodokushi***—people dying alone and remaining undiscovered for a long time. Everyone became tense because of the topic, so I decided to finally shift the focus to the main point of the interview—interiors of the apartments; a 61-year-old woman, Kimiko, was the first to share her thoughts.

— Have you ever altered or renovated anything in your units?

Kimiko: No, actually. My apartment has two spacious tatami rooms for living.[1] As for the toilet and bathroom ... They appear to be two separate rooms but are still somehow together, so it is better to call it a single space. So, yes, I have only two tatami rooms, but ... I feel like they are spacious because they are semi-open. Also, when the toilet and bathroom are separated, it makes them easier to use.
Daichi: Yes, separating them goes without saying in the modern world.
Kimiko: That's true! But did you know that the designers had some problems with plumbing in the first Japanese hotels after they tried to separate them? In the end, they merged them into one small room, and they still went on to become first-class hotels. Therefore, I think there is nothing wrong with merging. Surely, it may be more comfortable to have more space in the bathroom ... But in Japan, it is more common to separate these two. But if you go abroad, bathrooms and toilets are often united and more spacious. Maybe we could borrow some of their ideas.
— So now your bathroom and toilet are separated, right?
Kimiko: Yeah.
— And you would be happier to have just one but more spacious space, right?
Kimiko: The local government will probably think about it in the future.
— Do you have the right to change wallpapers or tatami?
Kimiko: It is not impossible.
Nishino: There are some regular renovations provided by the prefecture. Replacing old wallpapers and tatami is their job. Some people do it themselves, too. I don't know if anyone among us at the table did this, though. Is there anyone?
Others: No, no.
Kimiko: I used to do it when I was younger. Now it's just bothersome.
Shigeru: This is subsidized housing, so I'd rather ask for help from the government. But there are plenty of people who do it themselves.

[1] Here Kimiko means that out of three tatami rooms she uses two for living. The smallest room is most probably used for storage.

Nishino: Well, I agree that it might take decades if you depend on the prefectural government (some people laugh).
Daichi: Doing small cosmetic renovations is possible. It's like a hobby.
— Do you need to report such repairs to the municipality?
Nishino: I don't think you need to.
— What about exterior repairs? We can see some works are being carried out.
Nishino: To maintain these buildings, you need repainting and also waterproofing. It lasts for a long time. We are also replacing aluminum handrails for the balconies.
Shigeru: Also, toilets and bathrooms.
Nishino: Yes, we are gradually replacing the equipment and installing walls separating the toilet and the bath, but only 12 out of 33 buildings have been finished so far.
Shigeru: Bathrooms used to be separated from the toilet only by a low wall and a curtain instead of a full-height plastic wall.
Katsuko: Yes, bathrooms and toilets used to be in the same room. The prefecture decided to separate them.

The topic of toilet and bathroom separation seemed to be a particularly important notion for the residents. Toilets, similar to traditional dirt-floor kitchen, and *genkan*, discussed in Chapter 1, are strongly associated with impurity and can only be included in the psychological concept of home with the condition of its firm spatial separation from the rest of the house (Ozaki & Rees Lewis, 2006). In the traditional Japanese homes bathrooms, on the other hand, are "clean," and cannot coexist in the same space with the toilet, but since the introduction of Western housing models and limitations of concrete mass housing, this concept has been destabilized. While in Wakamiya the government decided to re-introduce the generally desirable separation, Kimiko questioned it's necessity in the light of limited space available.

— Is the government working on external repairs and separating all toilets and bathrooms in Wakamiya right now?
Nishino: Yes. There are 33 buildings and 767 units. About half is already done. We started more than three years ago.
Katsuko (confidently): Because it costs so much, it takes a long time.

Nishino: Maybe it will take 10 more years … (everyone laughs).

A 63-year-old man Kichiro, who seemed uninterested in the conversation before, suddenly joined the discussion.

Kichiro: They are also working on fixing the entrance stairs and replacing entrance lights with LED ones.
Nishino: The goal of the repairs is just to prevent general aging. These are the first repairs since the time of Wakamiya's construction. The big earthquakes in the recent past didn't damage the buildings. They only affected the furniture inside.
— I saw there are some vacant apartments when walking around. How many are there?
Katsuko: About 110 out of 767 units are empty.
Nishino: There are more vacant apartments on the upper floors. Mostly fourth and fifth floors.
— Is it a problem for the management?
Nishino: Yes, it is. It is better to have more tenants, of course. But the budget is limited, so thinking of fairness, we cannot dedicate too much effort to solve the issue of the empty rooms.
Daichi: I have heard that there should be some empty rooms to help people in need in case of natural disasters.
Nishino: It is not necessary; we won't keep those apartments vacant on purpose. (in a low voice to Daichi) However, two or three rooms are kept specifically for DV (domestic violence) victims.
— Is there anyone who wants to renovate their apartment by changing the existing layout, getting rid of the gypsum walls or constructing new walls for example?
Daichi: No, it is basically prohibited.
Nishino: I guess no one wanted to do so (laughing).
— Anyone tried detaching *fusuma* partitions?
Daichi: Not me, but my son did. He took out all of his *fusuma* doors and then brought them to my apartment for storage.
— Does he live in Wakamiya, too?
Daichi: That's right. He lives here with two children. I don't know why he got rid of the partitions … To have more space for the children I guess. (Later, Daichi showed us his son's apartment briefly).

— Everyone else here continues to use *fusuma* as they were designed originally?
Kimiko: Yes, especially because in winter it is very cold. So *fusuma* serves as a barrier to keep the heat in the room where you have the heater.

A cheerful 70-year-old woman Hiroko contributed more on *fusuma*:

Hiroko: When your children are small, you need to separate the rooms, so now the DK and four-and-half mat room are separated by the wall, but if it was not separated, we could easily put a table there and talk to each other. You would be able to watch the TV from the kitchen ... LDK-style.
Kimiko: Talking about improvements, we also need more outlets to plug in air-conditioners.
— Wasn't there any air-conditioning when you moved in?
Kimiko and others: No, there was nothing at all. No bathrooms, no air-conditioners. We used the small window to let out the tube of self-bought air-conditioners. If you do so, you cannot open the window. Normally, the air-conditioner is attached to the wall, but we didn't have one when we moved in.
Kimiko: The fact that we don't have enough outlets is pretty inconvenient. There are just two in every room, right?
Katsuko: Yes, and only in the renovated rooms. But you know, fifty years ago, when this place was built, they installed the latest Western flush toilets here. Back then, it was very convenient to live in these apartments. It was very nice.
— How well do you think these buildings have been preserved?
Katsuko: Of course, they are aging, but I think it is still fine for living.
Shigeru: Most new apartments now are built for sale, but our case is different, so we cannot change whatever we want here like they do in other countries. When considering old buildings like ours, we should always follow what the administration decides, so we cannot really change any interior fittings or walls in our rooms right now. There are many historical buildings in Italy, for example. Those are preserved well. However, in Japan, danchi apartments are harder to preserve.

Apart from Hiroko's notable dream about the LDK-style room and common technical points like electric plugs and air-conditioning problems, I still did not have much information about Wakamiya danchi's adaptability to the new demography of tenants. Normally, attempts of self-renovations would be an important hint about what the current inhabitants lack or need changing, but in this case, they weren't possible. I expected the participants to go into more detail when they talked about their personal use of the apartments, but they were more focused on the common points as a group. I asked Suzuki to translate the question, "What would you personally change in your apartment if you had unlimited possibilities and resources?" When he asked this without rephrasing, everyone answered that they couldn't change anything because of the municipal rules and did not need to anyway. When there were so many constraints in their reality, it might be psychologically traumatizing to seriously think about a better life they may never have. However, in my previous fieldwork experiences in Italian modernist mass housing and Russian *khruschevkas*, it was much easier for me to get residents to list their wishes and complaints in similar kinds of interviews because being negative about what you have was more culturally acceptable there. It was difficult for Japanese people to fantasize and imagine a better living environment because I, Suzuki, Nishino, and even the other tenants could judge their possibly naïve wishes as negativity toward their present and discredit their gratitude for being accepted into the subsidized housing.

We had to come up with a different way of asking the same thing that could lift the weight of responsibility for daydreaming from everyone in the group. Then, I remembered that the day before, we briefly talked to a bunch of kids riding bicycles nearby Wakamiya bus stop, and they answered the question about what they wanted to have in the neighborhood without any hesitation.

> — Before we came to this meeting, we were walking around the area and happened to talk to some children. They said they wanted to have a game arcade[2] in Wakamiya danchi. What about you?

[2] A popular type of entertainment venues in Japan, usually in large buildings with neon lit facades, loud music at the entrance, and a wide variety of gaming machines inside, especially popular with teenagers.

An absurd image of a lit-up entertainment center standing in the middle of deserted Wakamiya worked well: some people smiled in amusement; sudden lively discussion started among the participants.

Kimiko: For me, it is a shopping center.
Daichi (surprised): Right inside the danchi district?!
Kimiko: Yes, a park and a shopping center. Because there aren't many residents who own cars like there used to be.
Kimiko and other women: And a hospital, hospital![3]
Daichi and Shigeru (in disbelief): A hospital?!
Hiroko: Elevators.
Kimiko: Right, right, barrier-free!
Shigeru: Barrier-free danchi? (laughs with a hint of irony)
Kimiko: We don't need to put them in too many buildings, just 20 elevators in total, maybe?
Hiroko: I know it is a big luxury to ask for. We are just saying careless things…
Kimiko: Big dreams, huh … Yes, a shopping mall …
Kichiro: A restaurant or a cafeteria. I would go every day.
Others: Yes, it would be very convenient.
Daichi: A public bath and a gym, preferably in one building. For old people, it will be great for stretching, and young people could come, too. (everyone loudly agrees)[4]
Katsuko: And there could be a clinic, too. That would be the best.
Nishino: From my point of view, sound insulation is necessary.
Kichiro: Yes, even if you close the door, you can hear all the noises from your window. Footsteps, doors shutting, even sneezing.
Daichi: If you talk loudly when your window is open, people next to your room cannot hear you, but those who live across the courtyard or stand in the parking lot can hear you clearly.
Kimiko (quietly to other women): I wish we had a pool …
Hiroko: This is such a silly dream …

[3] It's peculiar that the vicinity of a big hospital was mentioned at the beginning of the interview, but in fact, it take a 15-min bus ride to reach it.

[4] As briefly mentioned in Chapters 1 and 2, *sentō* represent an important socializing opportunity, especially for the elderly. Wakamiya Danchi is located far from the neighborhood *sentō*.

The way we phrased the last question using an example of a kids' game center was an effective tool to go around the cultural blocks, but it also backfired: the residents only talked about missing public facilities, which they never mentioned when answering my direct question at the beginning of the interview. Now, with the same "childish" attitude that masks the adult responsibilities, we needed to get back to the interiors.

— So, if you could completely rebuild your apartment, what kind of interior spaces would you make?
Hiroko: I need a dressing room outside of the bathroom (*senmenjo*). Maybe a I could keep the washing machine there ...
Kimiko: Speaking of the washing machine, if it could be inside, next to the bathroom, it would be very convenient. Now it is on the balcony, we have to use an extension cable. Nowadays, in most apartments, there is a *senmenjo* and a washing machine set next to the bathroom. Also, a washbasin, we don't have that either.
— Do you wash your face in the kitchen sink?
Shigeru: We used to have a sink in the bathroom, but they had to get rid of the sink to build a new separating wall. Actually, the bathroom became bigger. It is easier to use the bathtub like that.
Katsuko: I need more storage space.
Shigeru: Now we have a normal Japanese *oshiire* closet and a smaller half-tatami-sized built-in storage.
Kimiko: I also need a free-standing closet to hang my Western-style clothes.[5]
Daichi: What a luxurious thing...
Kimiko: Not really, because those new apartments don't use *tansu* (Japanese-style chest) for clothes storage. It is convenient. You don't have to fold up your clothes. But if there is a closet, the room will get much smaller...
Shigeru: We sure talked a lot.
Katsuko: Maybe we don't really need the three-tatami room. It is just too small for a room. Also, it is a bit difficult to use, so we need a bigger one.

[5] Mentioned in Chapter 1, Japanese *oshiire* storages are designed for keeping *futon* mattresses, bedding, and folded *kimonos*. They normally have a waist-high shelf throughout their length and no wardrobe rail, so it's impossible to hang western-style clothes inside.

Hiroko: If the three-tatami-sized room was not separated from everything else completely, it could be more useful.
Kiichiro started drawing a typical Wakamiya 3DK room layout on the blackboard to make it easier for us to understand (Fig. 3.17).

— If you could choose between tatami or Western floors, what would you choose?
Multiple people at once, confidently: Flooring would be better.
— Why not tatami?
Daichi: Flooring is just more comfortable, I guess.
Kichiro: But I like tatami. If you drop something, it won't be damaged.
Daichi: For the living room, flooring is better. For the sleeping room, maybe tatami is fine.
Kichiro: It is more comfortable to sleep on the bed, so western-style flooring is better.

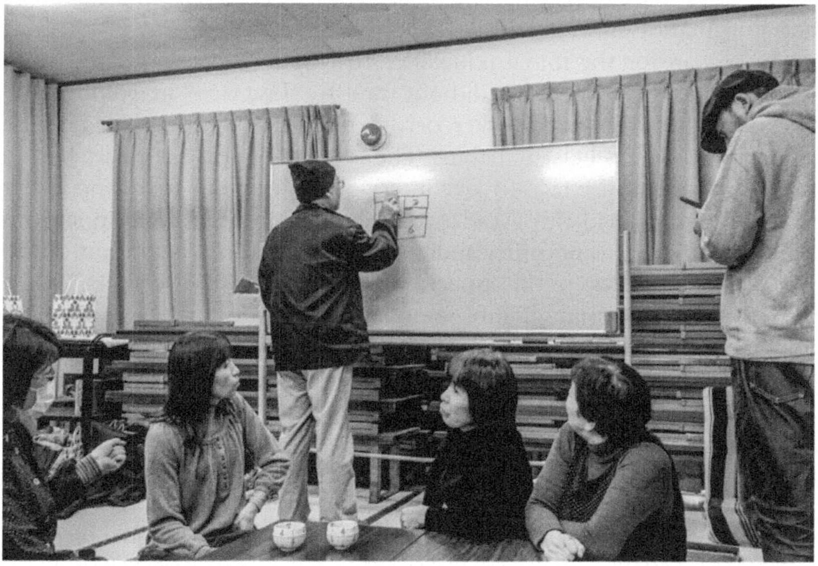

Fig. 3.17 Community meeting, December 2018

— Let's vote, who would like to have Western floors at their ideal house?

Everyone raised their hands. They looked around and laughed.

The interview took around two hours. In the beginning, I was constructing my questions from the point of view of an architect who needed to understand the situation in the neighborhood and see if there were any problems in the buildings and interiors to see if a design renovation was necessary. However, straightforward questions of this character couldn't get danchi residents to open up about their personal problems right away. It took one hour to get to the point where we could discuss the first inconveniences: insufficient number of electric plugs and air-conditioning setups. Even such obvious issues as the absence of elevators and bathroom sinks could only be raised at the end of the interview when I had to transform the conversation from the factual statement dimension to a "daydreaming" game by switching the focus from the real danchi to "what if." When everyone could feel enough distance from their own everyday life reality, they started to open up to the possibilities and use their imagination more freely.

The reason for the initial reluctance to talk about their desires could be that the participants either did not want to "lose face" in front of each other and the municipal worker or did not want to complain because of their personal beliefs or habits. The second option seems to have a stronger basis because face-to-face interviews during our following apartment visits confirmed this avoidance of complaints after direct questions even when there was no other audience. There is also a significant difference between genders in this aspect: in the phase of "daydreaming" when women were proposing highly impossible scenarios such as pools and shopping malls in Wakamiya, men would strongly react with skepticism and disbelief. Men also preferred to engage in more affirmative conversations about the outside areas and the efficient management and were not active during less positive moments, for example, when women were pointing out the plug or the air-conditioning problems. Only women voiced the issues with space management such as washing machines on the balcony, the uselessness of the three-tatami room, and inadequate storage spaces, even if they were only mentioned when talking about their "ideal apartment" at the end.

Another interesting point is that some tenants not belonging to the council that I later interviewed individually told me they were not fond of the Wakamiya council president, who was praised by everyone during the meeting. Two people had heard rumors of him illegally staying in his position for many years by avoiding re-elections and misusing the community budget. The president was the only member of the council who did not come to our meeting, so it was indeed intriguing.

From the constant remarks about the endlessly long prefectural repairs, it was easy to see a problem with renovation funding. When we interviewed employees of the Ibaraki Housing Bureau a few months later, they confirmed there weren't any strategies for danchi regeneration in the region because there is neither budget nor public interest for improving social housing, so the Bureau merely provides non-systematic exterior repairs when specific dilapidation complaints arise from the resident councils. However, with the continuing economic stagnation and current housing policies, danchi will most likely remain the main social housing provider in Japan for years to come. If soon the state-managed danchi districts will need to shift from cosmetic repairs to interior renovations for the new types of residents, what will be the basis for their research? How can social housing experts see behind all the cultural facades and distinguish "careless" remarks from what the residents really need? To find answers, we set off to inspect the inhabited apartments with our own eyes.

Apartment Visits

Endo

"I live alone here. A decade ago, I severed all relationships with my children. I told my daughter and four sons that we shouldn't see each other anymore, they agreed. It's fine for me," said Endo, a widow in her 70s, smiling brightly as she placed a tray with two cups of instant coffee on a wobbly low table for Suzuki and me. I understood barely 20 percent of the woman's old-style Japanese, and Suzuki didn't have time to translate complete sentences before Endo moved on to another topic, which turned out to be a good thing. When I later received the translated transcriptions of the recording, I realized that if I had understood everything she was saying, I would have been unable to focus on the main topic of our interview: her lifestyle in the apartment and the housekeeping habits.

After our council meeting was over, Suzuki helped me start conversations with more than a dozen residents from the council and on the streets around the buildings, and although some of them shared short stories about their life in Wakamiya, they were very cautious and refused to show us their apartments. We almost secured a case study when one elderly man approached us himself, curious about my foreign appearance and the filming equipment. The man willingly shared a lot of personal housing history, and after 20 minutes of a very friendly talk, we even exchanged business cards. He agreed to a longer interview inside his apartment and gave us his address; we made an appointment to visit him the next day. However, when we came knocking on his door, the man seemed to have completely forgotten about us and, through the narrow crack in the door, asked us to leave, threatening to call the police.

Wandering around the blocks and failing at getting people to trust us for hours, I began to lose hope of entering an apartment when Suzuki pointed toward Endo, walking her dog in front of the Wakamiya community center: "We should try talking. She can be our lucky catch!" With my foreign face and professional film equipment, I knew to hang back while he approached her. I couldn't imagine why this woman might be any different from those who had already rejected us, but after a brief chat, Suzuki waved at me to come closer. The woman was unfazed when we asked if we could film the interior of her apartment, and she invited us in right away.

Following close behind Endo and her dog, we ascended the narrow concrete stairs to the fourth floor and squeezed through her low, rusty door. Crossing the threshold, I felt the space compress due to the low ceiling, dim lighting, and an incalculable number of objects visible in every direction. It was hard to find a place to stand. We took turns taking off our shoes in the narrow *genkan* entrance hall that barely fit one person in (Fig. 3.18), then followed Endo into the living room while trying not to knock anything over. She told us to sit around the low table, shrouded by an old blanket held down by a piece of plywood,[6] as she disappeared behind a curtain to make some coffee. Though the room contained a massive, dangerous-smelling gas heater on a wheeled wooden platform, the air seemed even colder than outside. Unwilling to remove

[6] An attempt at imitating a *kotatsu*, a low table with an electric heating device attached to the bottom, covered with a thick blanket to preserve the heat. In this case there was no electric heater below.

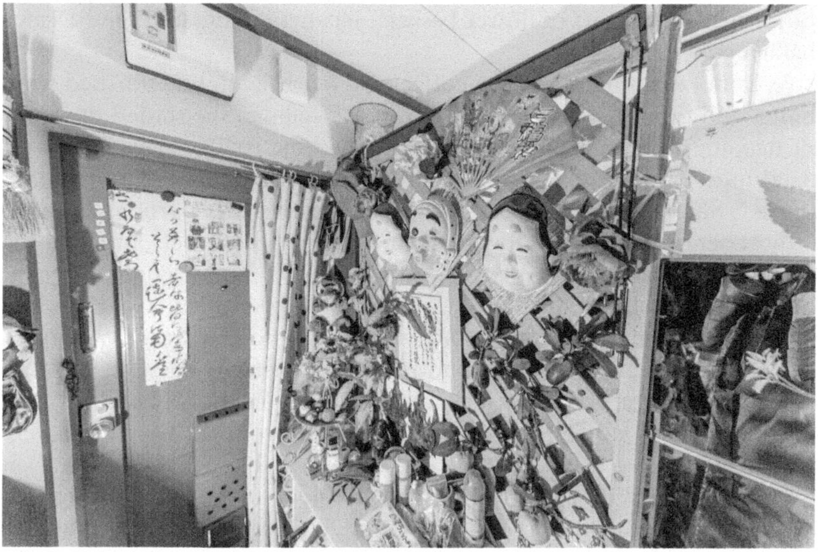

Fig. 3.18 Endo's apartment. *Genkan* and the entrance door. The improvized screen separates them from the DK. The curtain is probably left from the old times when Endo used to leave the door open and casual visitors could drop by. The interior photographs have the shadows and colors enhanced to reflect more details

our winter coats, we struggled to find enough space to sit down on the floor. I squeezed between a cupboard and the table, set up my camera, and studied the interior (Fig. 3.23).

The four-and-a-half-tatami space where we sat, which Endo used as a combination living/dining room, was crammed with objects of all scales and purposes. The floors were barely visible underneath heavily worn rugs and carpets, which Endo said were to protect the tatami mats and to provide additional insulation. A small rug beside the gas heater was occupied by a cat, who observed us curiously while the dog stayed under the table. Next to the table stood a low puffy sofa, unevenly wrapped in three different fabrics, and a bench-like structure with a blanket and a couple of cushions on top, which Endo called a "napping bed"—another DIY object (on the left in Fig. 3.23). Fluorescent lighting illuminated the accumulation of fabrics, shelves of plastic figurines, as well as walls decorated with magazine cutouts of flower baskets, Japanese calligraphy, and Disney characters.

As Endo was bringing in the coffee tray, her head lightly touched wind chimes and other trinkets hanging from the ceiling. She settled down on her napping bed while an eerie clinking filled the room. "This is where I spend most of my time every day. I read, listen to the radio, and nap, of course." She suddenly looked under the improvized *kotatsu* and smiled softly at her dog. Publicly Operated danchi do not allow pets, but after the death of her third husband around ten years ago, Endo acquired her cat and dog to keep her company. She keeps quiet about them, avoiding close relationships with her neighbors and walking the dog far away from home. Pets are not the only reason Endo keeps to herself: her late husband worked for a local yakuza gang, and it was probably his conflicts with city officials that led to their move into Wakamiya when they both were in their 50s.

Endo grew up in a low-rise apartment block in Tokyo. Throughout her life, she held many part-time jobs, ranging from waitressing in nightclubs to assembling telephones in factories, but after her final marriage, she wasn't able to find work. "This is the reason I have to rely on my pension"—rolling up one of her sleeves, Endo showed us a small "protection" snake tattoo on her forearm. "Even if I live alone here, I still don't feel sad or lonely. My dog can instantly make friends outside, and we exchange a few words sometimes. Danchi residents don't gather to socialize anymore, but I can still meet people when I go to the hospital. Such moments make me and my neighbors happy."

Endo named her dog after a famous Edo period Japanese swordsman Musashi, but she most often referred to him as "this person" and talked about him as if he was human, sometimes even comparing his character traits to her late husband's. "You know, this person never lets me stretch my legs under the table or sit on the sofa. Even when I sleep on the big bed in the other room, I have to lie diagonally with my head next to his legs because he takes up too much space."

The six-tatami room, where Endo sleeps, was visible from where we were seated. A double bed piled with blankets took up almost half of the area, set on DIY legs that lift it high enough to prevent her knees from hurting, but not as high as a Western bed due to the 2.2-meter ceiling height. The *fusuma* doors that originally separated the living room and the bedroom were moved to the three-tatami room, which Endo uses for storage, just like some council members suggested in our group interview.

A short porous curtain attached to the *kamoi* track now divided the space, allowing natural light to enter from either side. Below the curtain sat a TV stand—a stack made of a horizontally placed triple-cube shelving unit, a chipboard panel, and another storage unit on top (Fig. 3.13). Rotated 30 degrees and filled with a figurine collection, the top unit served as a base for a wide-screen TV that faced Endo's napping bed.

The fiberboard triple-cube shelves, colloquially called *karabokkusu*, sold for a few 100 yens in home-improvement stores, were a recurring feature in this apartment and three other apartments we visited later. One sat on top of a traditional, one-piece low cupboard overloaded with statuettes, figurines, fake or real flowers in small vases, and Buddhist ritual objects (Fig. 3.13). Another was wedged into a gap between the cupboard and a tall glass cabinet in the corner; yet another was used for extra shoe storage amid chests, baskets, and plastic trays at the entrance. Two more were part of a multilevel display for a stuffed toy collection in the bedroom, hazardously stacked on rough DIY benches, with additional shelves provided by plastic, wooden, and metal boxes of varying sizes, and even some cardboard panels (Figs. 3.14, 3.19, 3.20, 3.21, 3.22, 3.23, 3.24, 3.25, and 3.26).

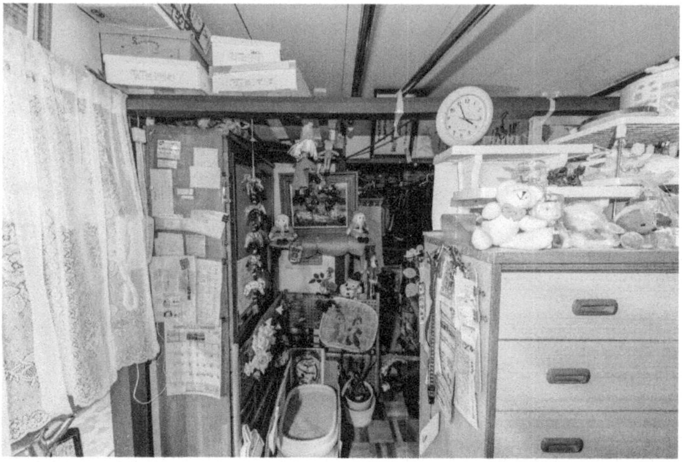

Fig. 3.19 Endo's apartment. The view from the DK to the *genkan* area and entrance of the three-tatami room used as storage. Endo placed wooden planks above *kamoi* to create overhead storage

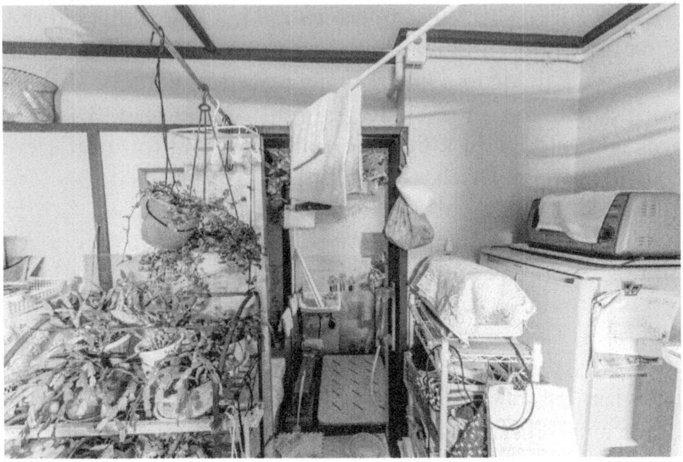

Fig. 3.20 Endo's apartment. Bathroom and toilet entrance. The sliding door is not used to have more space for the plants that Endo brought inside to protect while the balconies are being renovated

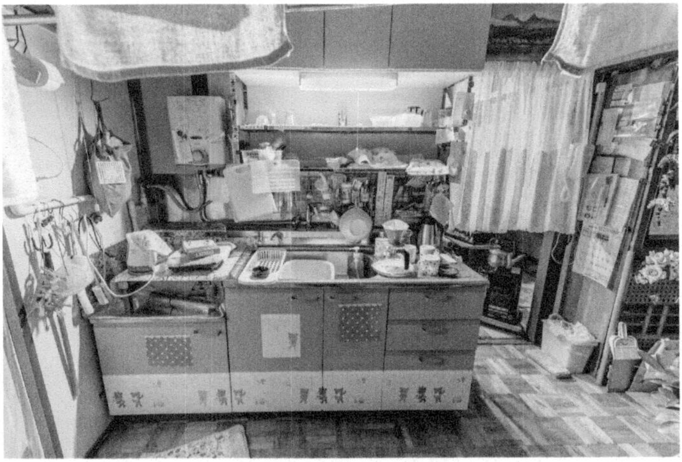

Fig. 3.21 Endo's apartment. DK, kitchen unit. Endo uses an electric hotplate instead of the original gas cooker that broke. She had to construct a DIY wooden platform to elevate the hotplate to the kitchen counter level

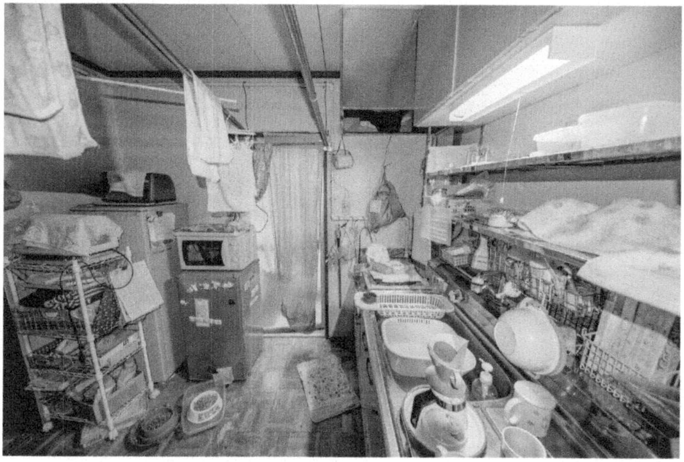

Fig. 3.22 Endo's apartment. DK. The freezer on the left can only be opened if the metal storage rack in front is rolled to the side. According to Endo, two toaster ovens on tops of them have different functions: one is for fish and the other is for bread

I only noticed these fascinating structures later while studying my photographs because, at the time, I was overwhelmed by how all these objects looked together under cold fluorescent light—disorganized and, I thought, indicative of poor quality of life. Before visiting Wakamiya, I was expecting, based on Japanese horror movies about danchi, such as "Dark Water" (Honogurai mizu no soko kara) and "The Complex" (Kuroyuri danchi), to find numerous technical issues with the buildings: poor insulation and plumbing, absence of heating and elevators, and general dilapidation. The reality wasn't too far from the movies, but having seen an actual apartment and remembering some points from the council meeting, I became more aware of the challenges of compact layouts intended for young families, characterized by mid-term tenancy planning: a lack of space for furniture, storage, and therefore movement.

— Have you ever tried improving anything in your apartment?

She didn't understand the question just like the council member at first, so Suzuki rephrased.

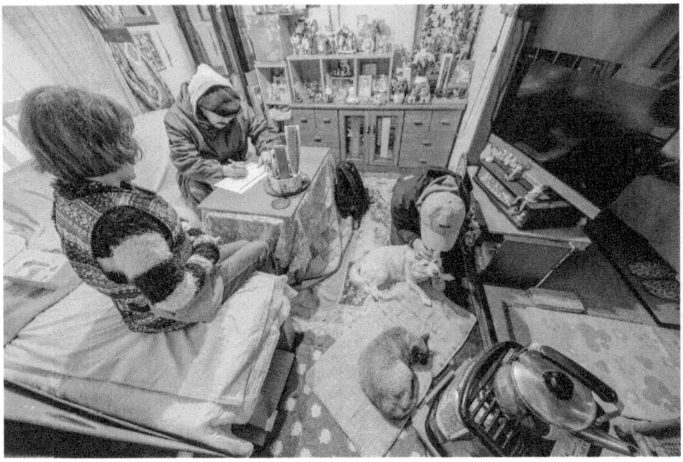

Fig. 3.23 Endo's apartment. Four-and-a-half-tatami room used as living and dining. Suzuki is taking notes on the improvized *kotatsu*, Ōtsu is next to the *karabokkusu* TV stand, two more *karabokkusu* create a complex shelving structure at the back. On the right, tatami in the bedroom is covered with a straw mat and a carpet on top

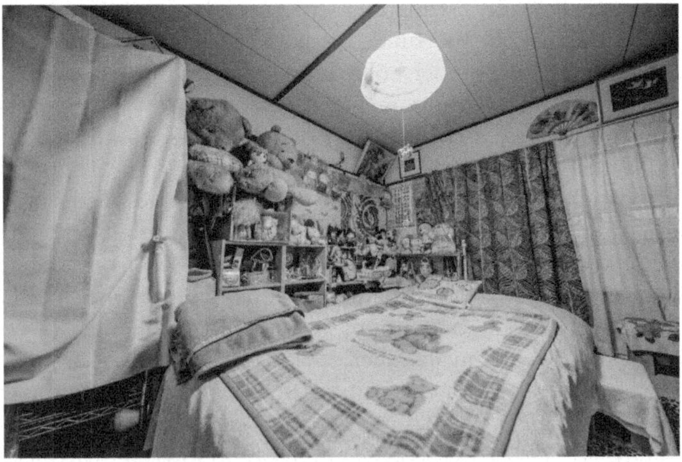

Fig. 3.24 Endo's apartment. Six-tatami room used as bedroom. An improvised closet made of a metal storage rack and a blanket held together by cloth pins

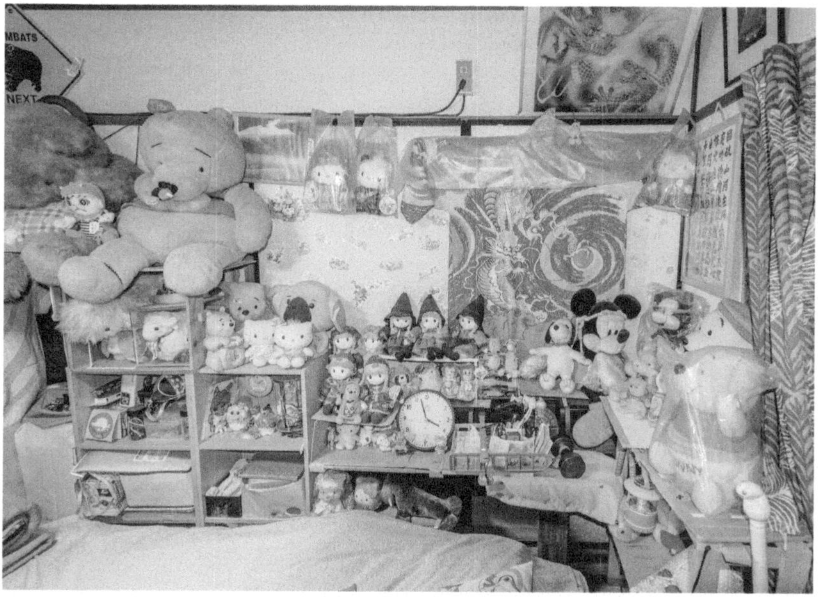

Fig. 3.25 Endo's apartment. Two different *karabokkusu*, DIY wooden benches and cardboard shelves around the bed

> *E*: Ah, no, it's impossible here. It's better to just get used to how things are. I got used to it very quickly. You know, I am 70 years old now, so it's impossible to increase the amount of stuff I have. Most of the furniture you see here is from my third husband. Once when I had to spend a few weeks in the hospital, my second husband just cleared out our apartment to the last 10-yen coin and disappeared, so I lost everything I had.

It was an incredible story, and it explained why Endo was so keen on collecting and keeping many things around her, but I didn't want to drop the question—I saw a cramped old apartment, and I was sure the tenant must have some problems.

> — If you could get the municipality to approve changes and you could receive enough funds, would you change anything?

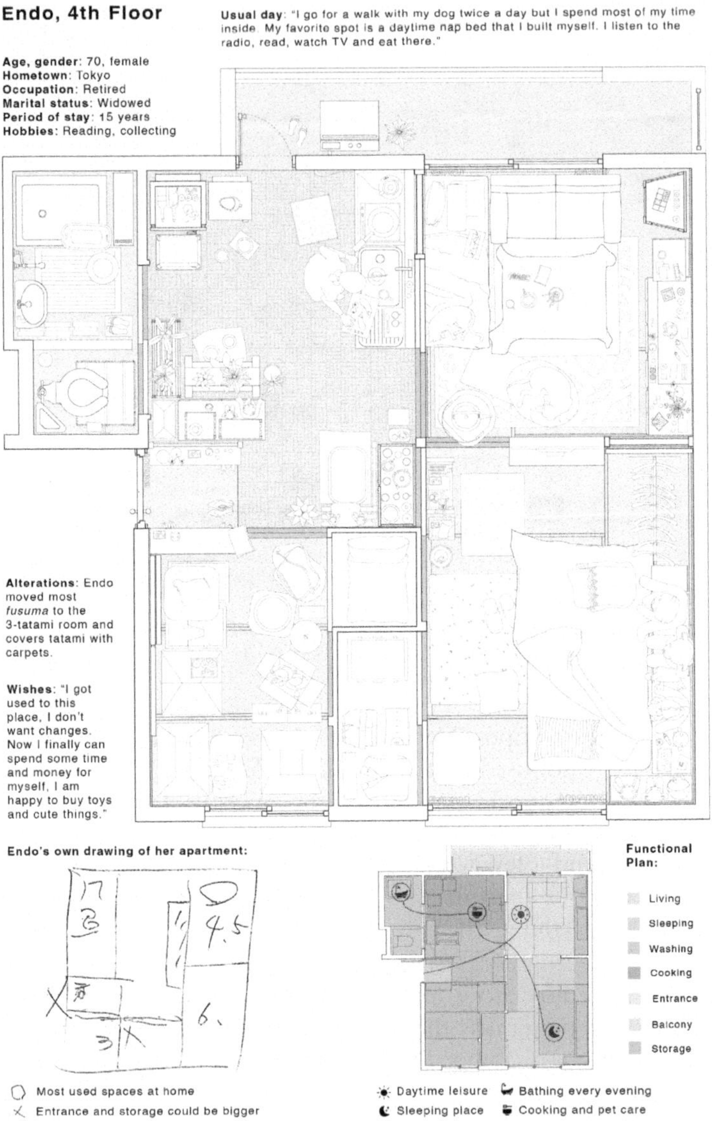

Fig. 3.26 Fieldwork data for Endo's apartment

Endo seemed troubled imagining an alternative reality in which she might have a more comfortable life. She pulled on a massive woolen cloak and moved closer to the portable gas heater.

> *E*: I have been already extremely lucky so far. Some neighbors from my block are not as healthy as I am, so they have trouble going out and taking walks. Unlimited money? I don't know. To be honest, there is too much space here just for myself. I can use the small three-tatami room as a walk-in closet like they do in Western countries. I'm grateful that the prefectural government lets me rent this place for such a good price. Around fifteen years ago many things changed. There are more and more people who live alone and danchi people don't gather as used to before. Talking about the policy of the municipal government, it's more about just placing all of us here (in old housing) but not providing anyone with new accommodation, I think.
>
> — Is it obvious for you that they don't want to resolve it?
>
> *E*: Hm ... Because the funding is needed, isn't it? That's why they are continuously doing these small exterior repairs here. Well, this thing is better not to be taken out of here. Because it's *kanhasshu* (points to the picture of her late husband).
>
> — What is *kanhasshu?*
>
> *E*: A position in yakuza hierarchy. In fact, it's a bit different. He was working for the prefecture and ... we got in trouble. When this happened ... Our life became different compared to other people's. Anyway, he did many things. That's why we moved here. The photo is older than 10 years here, so it's my talisman.
>
> — Are those ritual cups on the shelf connected to this?
>
> *E*: This is ... It's rice and salt (to commemorate the deceased). And because he was born in the year of the snake, I put a snake figurine there, too. Unlike other people, I don't have a Buddhist altar. I keep my memories in my heart. Always. Everything depends on the way of thinking. My first husband gave me my children, so I'm grateful. The second husband passed away soon after we married, but he taught me singing.
>
> — Where do your children live now?
>
> *E*: Very close by, in Mito, but we almost never contact each other. I told them we shouldn't and they agreed, it's better this way. Although I once met my granddaughter, she secretly came to see

me in kimono after her coming-of-age ceremony to the entrance of my block, I took a picture… I like when people visit. Danchi children used to come over a lot in the past. I often don't close the door, so everybody is welcome.

Hitoshi

After visiting Endo, we received a call from Daichi, who mentioned his son's apartment with all *fusuma* taken out during the council meeting and said he could let us have a look and take photographs after checking with his son. Hitoshi and his two children, 11-year-old son Yuta and nine-year-old daughter Hina, weren't home at the time, but Daichi had the key; he guided us around the unit and explained what he knew. Hitoshi's father did not want to disclose too much of his son's life story, it seemed as if he was slightly ashamed of his situation, so we could not get as much information as we did with Endo.

Hitoshi was born and raised in Wakamiya Danchi in the 1980s, when it was still a desirable place to live. After spending his childhood years in the danchi, Hitoshi moved out into a rented apartment in Mito when he finished high school and went to study in culinary college. He got married in his first year of studies and had two children soon after, but his wife left him around the time when Yuta was four years old. Hitoshi had to pause and then give up his higher education and move back to Wakamiya as a low-income single parent to save money on rent. To earn a living, he took up short-term professional courses and now has a blue-collar job at an Internet provider company installing Wi-Fi routers. Hitoshi works every day and clearly doesn't have enough time to do housework: clean and dirty laundry could be found in piles on the floor in every room, trash bags full, and kitchen utensils in disarray.

However, it was obvious that he cared about children's comfort and wanted to make their life better as much as he could. I could spot an improvised girl-care table in the living room loaded with hair products and devices to keep Hina's hair up to middle school beauty standards. Moreover, both children had their own floor study desks and little closets for personal belongings set up in the three-tatami room (Fig. 3.27). They were aligned in rows to allow some visual privacy between the kids, however, because of this Yuta's desk lacks access to the natural light from the window. Hitoshi and his children all sleep together in one room side to side: three unfolded *futon* took up the entire four-and-a-half tatami

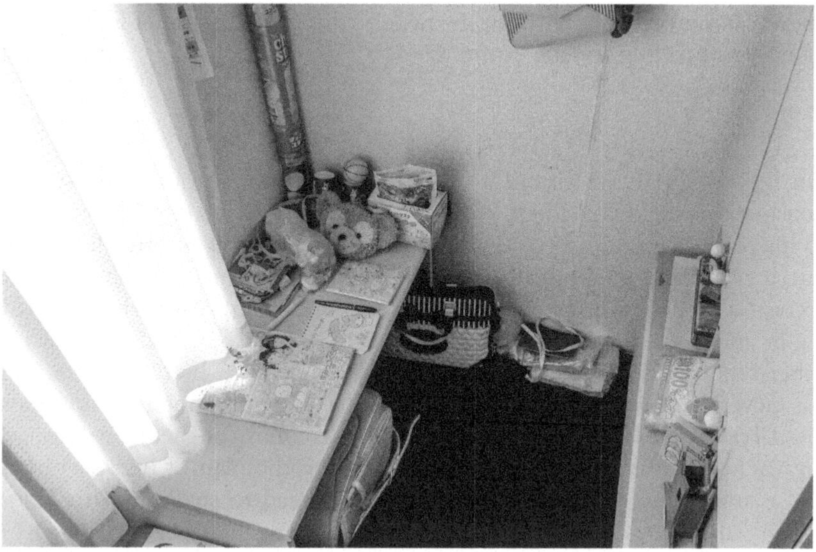

Fig. 3.27 Hitoshi's apartment. Hina's floor study desk in the three-tatami room

except for the space occupied by a tall chest of drawers. Hitoshi's mattress is in the middle between Hina's and Yuta's, judging by the choice of bedding and toys lined up by the walls.

Some details hinted that there was not enough space for storage in the apartment: toaster oven inside the *oshiire* closet in the living room, vacuum cleaner spread right beside the head of the *futon* on the bedroom floor, two soccer balls squeezed under the metal mailbox in the entrance door so that they "hang" on the door even when it gets opened. To get more open space Hitoshi detached all the *fusuma* partitions in the apartment, even the ones used as the doors of the built-in storages, and asked his father to store them in his apartment in another building. Hitoshi's unit was one of the first to be renovated, so all tatami got replaced with wall-to-wall carpeting, an intervention not repeated in the newer renovated units in Wakamiya. The bathroom and the toilet were separated after the renovation, however, the old wallpapers remained unchanged and fungus covered the bathroom walls. We could only look around for about 10 minutes, but without its owners, this cold apartment left us with a heavy sad feeling for the entire day.

Kimura

On the same day, we visited a 75-year-old Kimura, an old friend of our first interviewee, ex-resident Yoshimura, who introduced and brought us to his place. Kimura was a very reserved person, so it was difficult to dive into a conversation about his past. All we knew for sure was that he used to rent a detached house for 45,000 yen a month in Mito while he had a job, and then moved to Wakamiya in 2003 because he realized that no other rental option would be easily available for him when he retires. He has never had a spouse or children and he did not want to talk about his parents or extended family. We couldn't confirm if he even finished high school or college. When he was drawing the plan of his apartment and marking the names of the rooms, he seemed to struggle with *kanji* writing and the resulting characters looked unusual to Suzuki and Ōtsu (Fig. 3.32). Kimura's sketch of his unit plan was interesting as well: the rooms were floating in space, as if the author didn't fully understand the concept of how the walls divide the space.

It was hard for Kimura to find any personal photographs: all he could show us was a framed picture of himself in his 40s. Before he retired he used to work as a security guard at the prefectural hospital in Mito. At some point in life he became a devoted member of a popular Buddhist sect with an ambiguous reputation called "Sokka Gakkai." He dedicated most of his six-tatami room to shelves with religious objects and books as well as a *butsudan* (altar), which he bought from the sect's shop for an impressive price of 70,000 yen. The altar and a few other shelves are tied with belts to *kamoi* to prevent it from tipping over during the earthquakes. Apart from praying everyday, his usual activities included watching DVDs, listening to the radio and taking film photographs of flowers growing around Wakamiya Danchi. His favorite monthly "adventure" was taking the bus to Mito to develop the films at the specialized shop.

Compared to Endo's and Hitoshi's units, Kimura's apartment was exceptionally well-organized: we came with no advance notice for the first interview and later in March of 2019, and every time the place looked tidy, although the amount of furniture made actual livable space quite small. I could spot a variety of large brand new kitchen appliances (Fig. 3.30) and audio systems from different epochs everywhere but Kimura confessed that he was especially fond of his wide flat TV at the deepest end of the six-tatami room, which he usually watches from the four-and-a-half-tatami living room from a special low armchair which helped with his knee pain (Fig. 3.31). Kimura therefore detached *fusuma* between the main rooms, just like Endo and Hitoshi. He was the only interviewee who slept in the three-tatami room, where he also kept the detached *fusuma*. Even though the single bed took up most of the room, there is still space for more of the latest technology: a contemporary air purifier on the floor and another audio system at the bed table. It was hard to see the actual tatami in his apartment: all floors were covered with thick carpets, two of them electric. Kimura strictly controlled his budget: he reported that he always cooked his own meals, hunted for the cheapest vegetables in supermarkets and often marinated them at home to preserve for a longer time. Just like Endo, he relied on a portable gas heater in winter, but he had also installed air-conditioning for summer on his own money.

Kimura didn't like the merged toilet and bathroom so he was patiently waiting for the prefecture to separate them. However, when asked about any other wishes for renovation, much like the council members, he said that he didn't want to change anything.

— Have you ever wanted to improve your apartment in some way?
K: My apartment?
— Yes, for example, removing some walls or having more space or furniture in a certain room?
K: This is a rental unit, so I can't do that.
— But if it wasn't, what would you do?
K: I don't know, probably nothing much.
— Have you ever tried to carry out small changes with furniture and *fusuma* re- locations?
K: Yes, a little, but I cannot break that wall (points to a wall between four-and-a-half and six-tatami rooms). If I break it, I will be blamed by the government, so I don't want to try.
— What do you like about living in Wakamiya?
K: I like socializing with my friends the most. Encouraging each is happiness.
— Do you have friends that come over to visit?

K: Yoshimura-san, the one who introduced you to me, comes sometimes. He is a tea friend. But others do not come as often.
— So you mostly meet outside?
K: Yes, on the benches.
— Would you like to have some improvements in the outside public space or the buildings?
K: There are some chairs and benches, but I wish we had some space where old people could meet up more easily.
— What about the community hall?
— *K*: We can't use it freely. The community space is only for the residents' council, for example they use it for cleaning days. I never join, but the responsible people meet there and collect the membership fee from us.
— Is there anything you don't like about this danchi?
— *K*: I don't like gossip. I don't like when I hear people talking badly about me. Women are doing this a lot here.
— What do you think about the absence of the elevators?
K: Of course, I want one. I am getting old. I think many people want to have them.

Akane

In the afternoon, we finally got to our pre-scheduled interview with Ōtsu's childhood acquittance, a single mother Akane staying in Wakamiya with her 9-year-old son Yusuke. After meeting us briefly for lunch and hearing about my project, she invited us over for tea.

Akane was born and raised in Mito. She and Yusuke moved to Wakamiya in 2013 with the help of the prefectural social housing program targeting low-income families, earning less than 33,000 yen per month. She worked part-time as a nurse and although she had an opportunity to transfer to a better full-time job at the same hospital, she chose not to do that because a slight salary increase would mean that they will not be eligible for the social housing program anymore. Renting a subsidized 3DK in Wakamiya costs 3000 yen per month plus electricity and gas, which can amount up to 10,000 yen in winter and summer months. Similar size rental properties in Mito area start from 45,000 yen per month, so Akane cannot afford moving out.

She didn't want to get into details about her marital status, all she said is that Yusuke's father left them when the boy was very young. When it happened, she moved to her parents' detached house in a suburban area a 30-minute car ride from Wakamiya but soon their family house got damaged by an earthquake and she decided to move out. Akane maintained a regular schedule and went into great detail when we asked her about their daily routine. On weekdays they wake up at 7:00, eat breakfast together, and get in the car by 8:20. She drops Yusuke at school and got to work around 9:00. Yusuke would return from school by public transport and Akane by car later by 18:00. She always cooks dinner, and then they eat together in the four-and-a-half tatami room equipped with a low table and a TV. An important daily event in winter was filling the bath at around 20:00, with both taking turns bathing, because "it makes it easier to keep your body warm in the evening." Before sleep Akane watches TV and sometimes helps Yusuke with his homework in the four-and-a-half tatami living room, switching on the electric carpet under the low table in winter. At 22:00 she rolls out one big *futon* for both of them in the six-tatami room and they go to bed. On weekends she either takes Yusuke to see his grandparents at their new smaller detached house, or her sister or friends come for dinner at her place.

Yusuke wasn't at home when we visited. Akane shared that she was slightly worried that he didn't have his own private room: his toys and school books were stored in the six-tatami room along the wall in *karabokkusu* shelves and plastic containers (Fig. 3.33). He would always use the low dining table in the four-and-a-half tatami room as a desk for drawing or doing his homework. The three-tatami room, originally meant as an individual space for children, wasn't equipped with air-conditioning by the prefecture, so Akane thought it was impossible to use it as a bedroom for Yusuke. Like all the previous apartments we saw, Akane's unit was missing *fusuma* doors separating the four-and-a-half-tatami living room and six-tatami bedroom because she put them away to facilitate frequent access to the storage in the bedroom. Since they slept on one *futon* together,[7] one air-conditioning unit was enough to heat these two rooms on winter nights. During the day they both spent most of their free time on the heated electric carpet.

In general Akane was satisfied with her apartment. She didn't have any particular image of the "ideal home" because she "got used to living in danchi." When I asked her to draw her own plan of the unit and mark

[7] Sharing *futon* by parents and children until they turn 11 or 12 years old is common in Japan.

all the places she likes and dislikes, she suddenly remembered she always wanted to have a *senmenjo* space for changing clothes before and after bath, because now she has to do it in the kitchen in front of the bathroom door, which is visible from all the tatami rooms (Fig. 3.35). She also marked the lack of hot water in the kitchen sink as a problem, unlike Endo and Kimura, who didn't mention it as something bothersome. Her biggest wish, however, was installing air-conditioning in the three-tatami room so that grown-up Yusuke could have his own place to sleep and study.

Inventing Devicology

"It's Better to Just Get Used to It": The Gaman Mentality

The main goal of the interviews was to answer a specific question: what issues should be solved in the inhabited built environment of Japanese social housing so that the residents could become more satisfied with it? It seems easy when you think about it as an architect: "I should just go and ask these residents themselves." The unexpected problem that I encountered during the interviews is that most people I met in danchi, except for Akane who said she wished for a *senmenjo* room, were not able to answer this question concisely within an architectural context. Even if someone would finally admit they wanted some change after an hour of questioning, it would be mostly technical: more electric plugs or an air-conditioning unit in a certain room. These issues should be normally solved by civil engineers rather than architects and interior planners.

However, inside the rooms, one sees cramped, dark spaces (Endo), the inadequacies of the original planning in relation to the lifestyles of elderly people (Endo and Kimura), an obvious lack of planned storage due to original short-term rental policies (all case studies) and the lack of privacy between the family members (Akane and Hitoshi). With the elderly tenants it was not possible to demonstrate the need for renovation using the statements of the residents when phrases such as "It is better to just get used to it" and "We can't make any changes because it's not allowed" were their main way of answering all my questions concerning the interiors.

By the time of my first apartment visit, I knew that the strive to maintain a good public image and conform to the community's expectations shouldn't be underestimated in the Japanese context, so I made sure to talk to the inhabitants casually and explained that the recordings would only be used for academic purposes in English language media. However, face-to-face interviews didn't prove to be more outspoken than the talk at the community meeting. Even the "daydreaming" question strategy did not work that well in individual conversations: Endo, Kimura, and Akane kept repeating that they got used to everything even when asked to "imagine their ideal home." At first, I couldn't get my head around it: these people lack hot water in their kitchens, live with excruciatingly cold temperatures in winter, store their belongings in piles on the floor, yet they do not complain? (Figs. 3.28, 3.29, 3.30, 3.31, 3.32, 3.33, 3.34, and 3.35).

I turned to Suzuki and my Japanese colleagues for an explanation, and we concluded that the inability of danchi residents, especially the elderly, to admit their unsatisfactory living conditions most likely arises from the

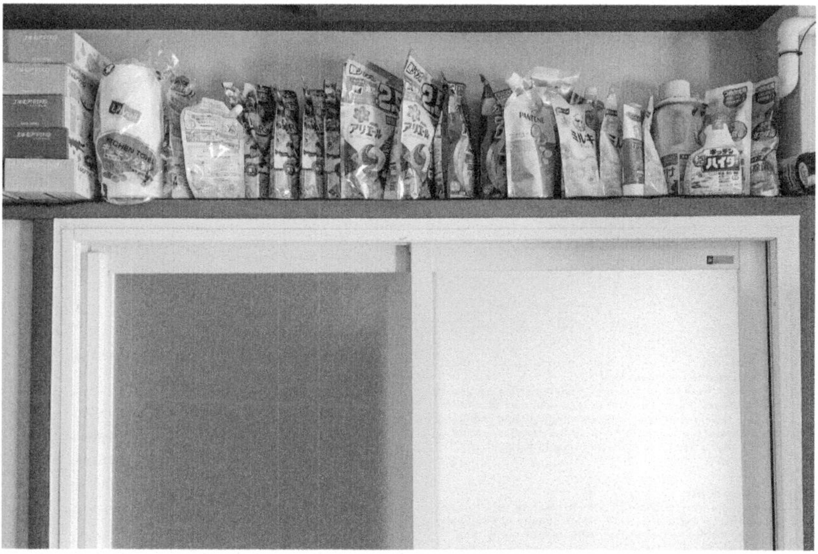

Fig. 3.28 Hitoshi's apartment. Improvised household item storage on the frame of the renovated bathroom entrance

Hitoshi + Hina (9) & Yuta (11), 4th Floor

Age, gender: 32, male
Hometown: Mito
Occupation: Electrician
Marital status: Divorced
Period of stay: 6 years
Hobbies: Soccer, guitar

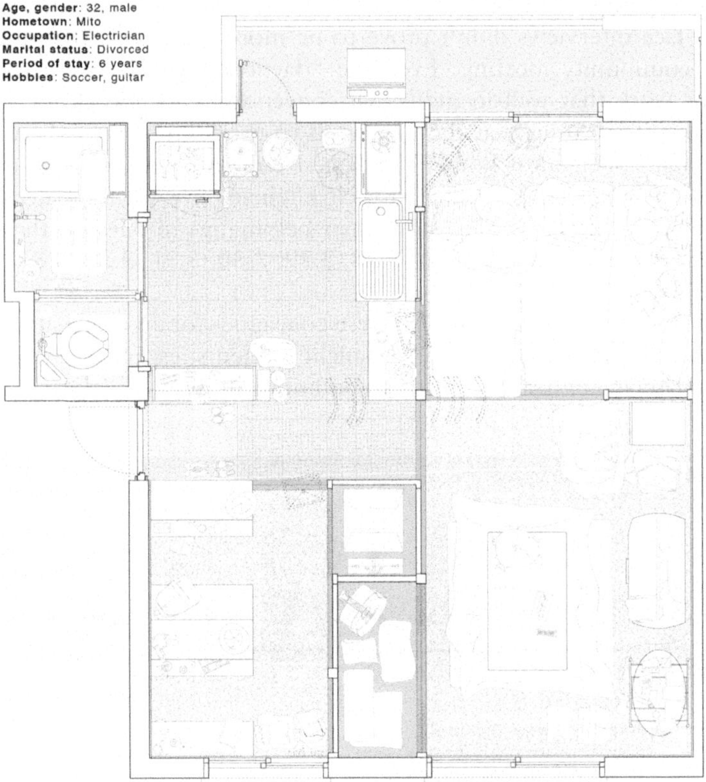

Usual day:
[Hitoshi's father about him]
"Hitoshi works a lot now and often doesn't have time to do housework, but he still tries to spend as much time as possible with kids in the evenings. I don't really understand why he got rid of all the partitions in the unit, but it seems to work for him so I am glad to support it."

Alterations:
The unit was renovated by the prefecture before they moved in: there are carpet floors instead of tatami and toilet-bathroom separation. Hitoshi took out all the fusuma partition panels and asked his father to keep them in his apartment in order to have more space for the kids.

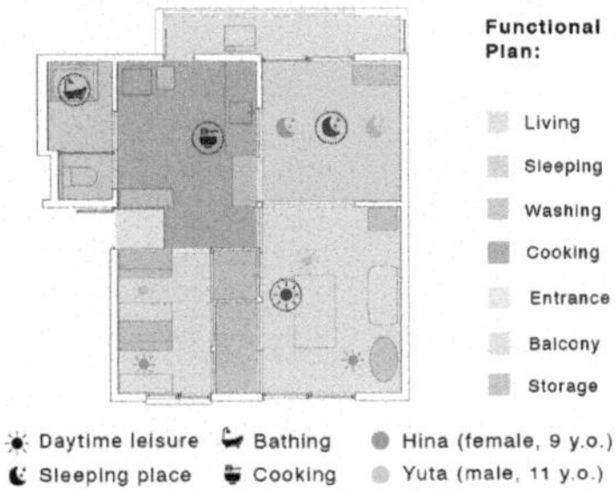

Fig. 3.29 Fieldwork data for Hitoshi's apartment

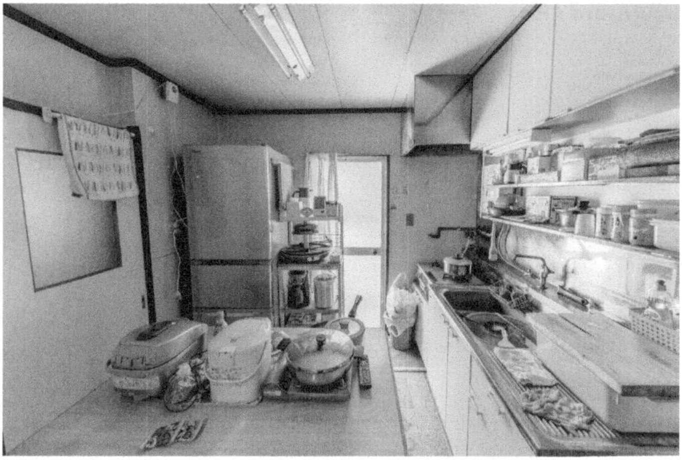

Fig. 3.30 Kimura's apartment. DK. Kimura uses the table as a counter for cooking and keeping his kitchen appliances. December 2018

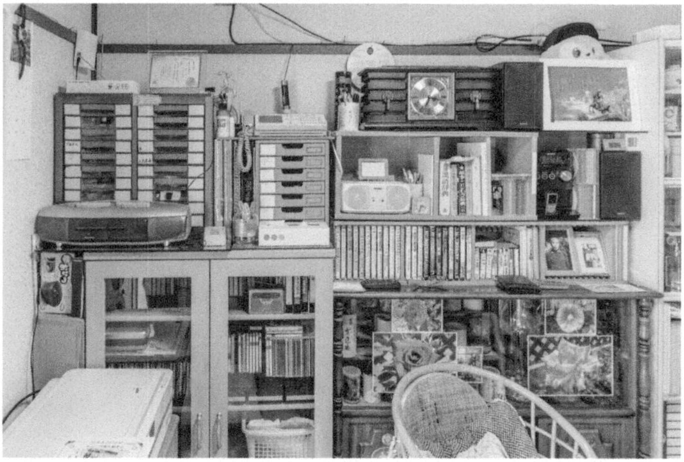

Fig. 3.31 Kimura's apartment. Four-and-a-half tatami living room, low armchair below

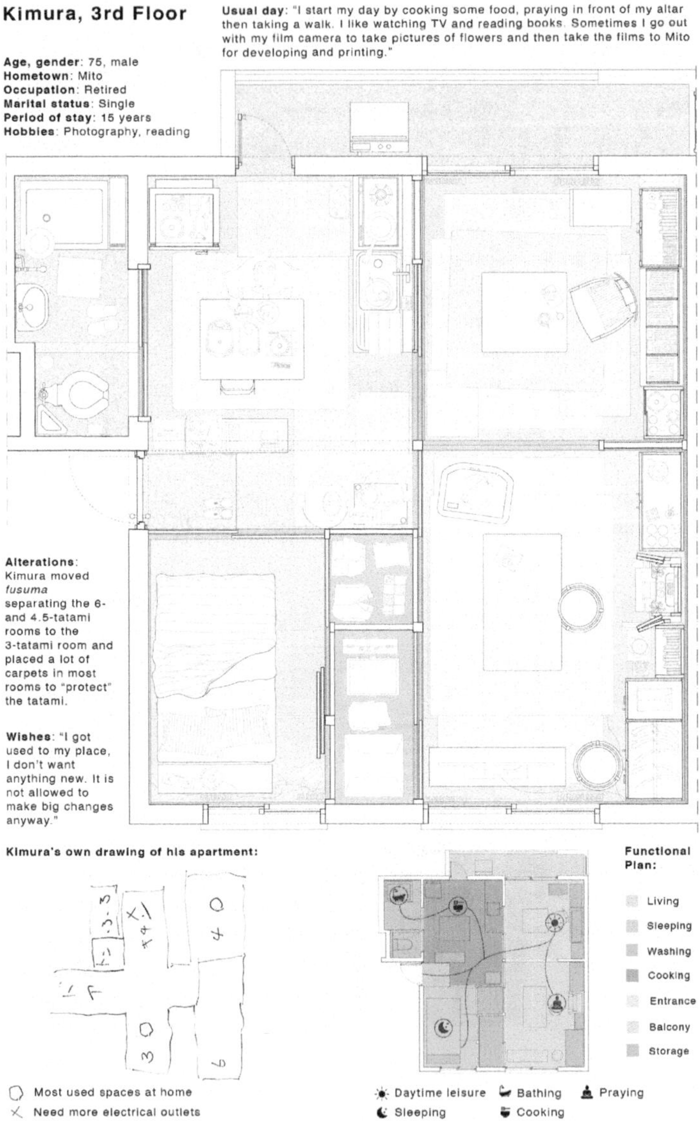

Fig. 3.32 Fieldwork data for Kimura's apartment

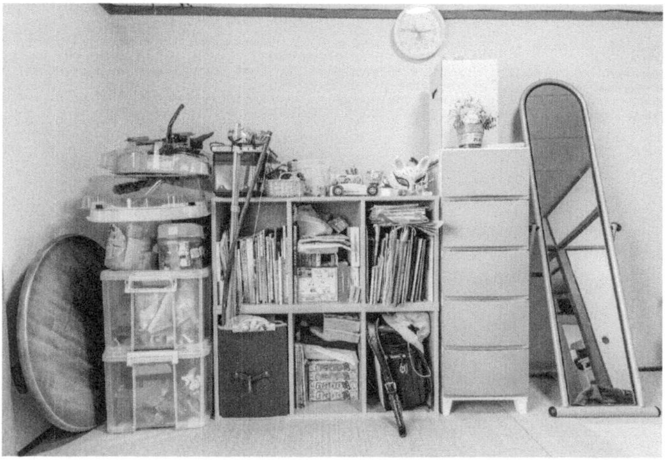

Fig. 3.33 Akane's apartment. Storage area in the six-tatami room, used as a bedroom

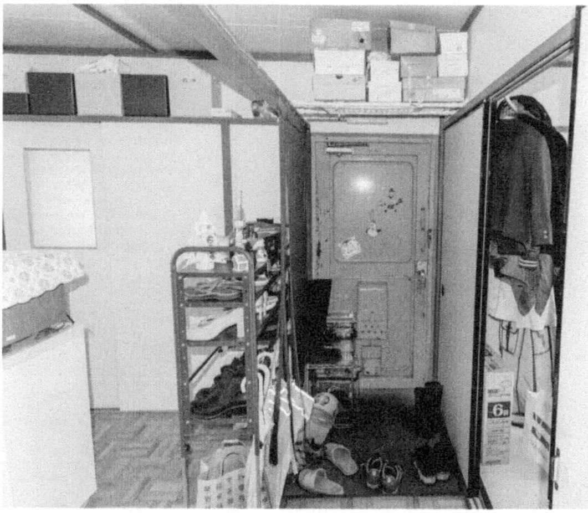

Fig. 3.34 Akane's apartment. Another example of *kamoi*-based overhead storage. Shoe rack together with a string curtain separated *genkan* from the kitchen

Akane + Yusuke (9), 3rd Floor

Age, gender: 34, female
Hometown: Mito
Occupation: Part-time nurse
Marital status: Single
Period of stay: 7 years
Hobbies: Cooking, team sports

Usual day: "I wake up at 7:30, make breakfast, take Yusuke to school and go to work. When I come back at 18:00 I cook dinner, watch TV after eating and help Yusuke with his homework. Then I take a bath and go to bed in the 6-tatami room. Although it is very cold in winter, we still take a bath every evening. We sleep on one big *futon* mattress together to get warmer. On weekends I usually go grocery shopping and take Yusuke to play at my parents' house."

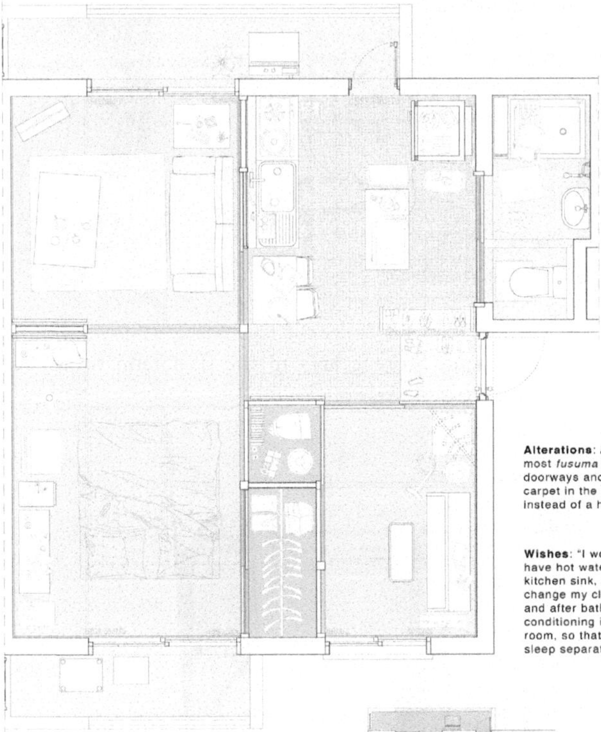

Alterations: Akane moved most *fusuma* out of the doorways and uses electric carpet in the living room instead of a heater.

Wishes: "I would like to have hot water in the kitchen sink, a space to change my clothes before and after bathing and air conditioning in the 3-tatami room, so that my son can sleep separately."

Akane's own drawing of her apartment (rotated):

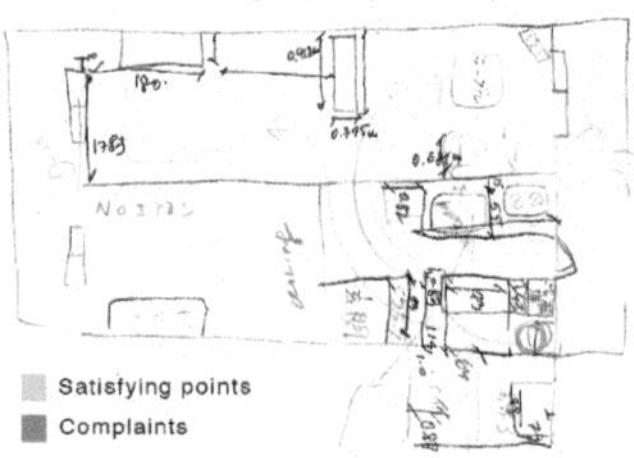

Functional Plan:

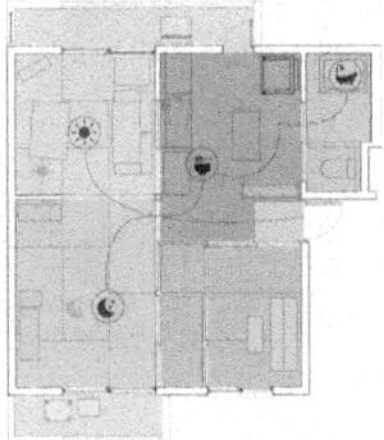

Satisfying points
Complaints

Daytime leisure
Sleeping
Bathing
Cooking
Yusuke (male, 9 y.o.)

Fig. 3.35 Fieldwork data for Akane's apartment

cultural characteristic of *gaman*, which might be translated as "perseverance," much like the British "stiff upper lip."[8] Enduring hardship is a highly regarded virtue in Japanese culture, so the residents transformed negative opinions—especially in the presence of others and in the context of a recorded interview—into replies such as, "I have become used to it" and "Fifteen years ago it was different." Social housing danchi residents knew they had to accept all the difficulties from the beginning. They never see anyone openly complaining about personal living conditions around them, so it gets hard for them to even imagine a better life and even harder to talk about it out loud.

On the Verge Between Ethnography and Architecture

Looking for examples of fieldwork-based literature that deals with dwelling experiences in the Japanese context, Ann Waswo's *Housing in Postwar Japan—A Social History* from 2002 was my first point of reference. While most of the book is centered around the research of archival materials and printed media, the author's detailed interview with a "fairly ordinary urban" Japanese woman, Sasaki, about her past rental housing experiences with plan re-drawings, provides a valuable first-person insight that clarifies and compliments the understanding of the big-picture historical account of Japanese postwar housing. There was no on-site fieldwork, but Waswo's method gave me some inspiration: during all apartment visits, I asked the danchi residents to draw plans of their apartments and point out "problematic" areas, as well as inquired about their previous housing, to see if any anything could be used to extract more data. My interviewees, however, weren't as eager to share their housing histories as Sasaki, given their difficult life paths that led them to seek governmental support in social housing. Their personal interpretation of their living space in drawings, although intriguingly naïve, was not more informative than the verbal comments either.

The search for a new methodology took me to discover another important source: a beautifully illustrated book, *The Japanese House: Material Culture in the Modern Home* by Inge Daniels, published in 2010. Daniels conducted fieldwork with 30 Japanese families in Kansai region and documented their lifestyles with the help of friendly unscripted interviews and

[8] For more about *gaman*, read Moeran, B. (1984). Individual, Group and Seishin: Japan's Internal Cultural Debate. *Man*, *19*(2), 252–266.

interior photography. She analyzed the materials as an anthropologist, connecting her findings with broad cultural frameworks and theories. Anthropologists' main goal is observing and documenting behavior of a selected group of people for long periods; often they decide on the question they want to answer in their research already in the process. In my case where I target the socially disadvantaged, non-mainstream group, the number of participants and time I could spend with them was limited. As an architect I was also more interested in the issues connected to the standard plans and was aiming at researching the best way to approach danchi interior renovations from the start of my project. With so many changed variables, it was difficult for me to rely on classical anthropologic methods alone.

Still, Daniels' approach has one key element that set her work apart from the rest in her area of expertise: an almost excessive realistic photographic surveying of the apartments that did not spare any seemingly mundane corners. Adopting this attitude toward interior photography became one of the main breakthroughs in creating my own method. Moreover, while rereading Daniels' book I encountered, although already long after I finished my project, a less-known study in Japanese, that was so closely connected to my research problem, that I regretted not finding it sooner.

In 2000, an architect Ayaka Yasuda conducted fieldwork in 65 UR-managed rental 2DK units in a high-rise danchi building in central Tokyo (Yasuda, 2002; Yasuda & Nobuaki, 2000). This particular danchi is highly popular people renting in Tokyo, because of its prime location: moving in 2021, one would pay around 100,000 yen for a 2DK apartment. Unlike Wakamiya units, all apartments in Yasuda's study have a single exposure due to a high-rise typology, and with UR rental policies not imposing as many restrictions on interior changes as Publicly Operated danchi, are significantly altered by their inhabitants, who live in more "normal" family compositions, than people I met during my fieldwork. Similar to Daniels' book, Yasuda's research is highly visual and relied on 3000 photographs she took during the short apartment visits. By comparing the images and compiling the floor plans and elevations that included furniture, she developed the concept of "options," that define any change to standard plan or equipment (from a replaced doorknob to a new kitchen cabinet), and the notion "second wall," that describe the tendency of danchi inhabitants to position rows of furniture and objects that often follow the original walls, but sometimes create new walls in-between to improve privacy between the family members. Suggesting that women are the main supervisors of interior furnishing in the family, Yasuda argues that with the decrease in the age of the eldest woman in the household, these "second walls" get lower and more open in an attempt to "display" the belongings, more than to store them away in enclosed chests. While the theory doesn't provide any insight into grade of life quality in every apartment or hints for renovation strategies, it highlights the inherently different modes of living in small-size rental apartments as opposed to permanently owned homes. Although my fieldwork the number of studied apartments is incomparably lower, the social status and composition of families are different, and the constraints for self-renovations are higher, the phenomena of "second wall" was well observed and provided an important reference for the post-analysis.

In European scholarship, there are some more examples of works based on residents' interviews in postwar mass-housing that incorporate detailed interior photography and also provide a historical perspective (Caramellino & De Pieri, 2019), but not many architects engage in fieldworks of the sort as a tool for renovations. As the inhabitants are deeply immersed in their everyday material context and bodily routines, they are unable to notice and assess them (Daniels, 2010; Miller, 1998), so often they cannot supply architects with the verbal information they can rely on directly when designing a project. At the same time, even if these routines and their products can be studied better by an outsider, there is no clear working methodology to analyze large quantities of photographs to get architecturally meaningful results. But what if we could invent one?

Getting Visual: Switching the Fieldwork Focus

The study of the precedents and the understanding of *gaman* cultural code pushed me to reconsider my initial interview-centered approach to processing the fieldwork data; I turned to videos and photographs that I took during the visits to fill in the gaps of the verbal testimonies.

In the beginning, all the images of the cramped interiors, often disconnected from architectural common sense, made me feel completely lost. As Daniels points out in her book, "photographs are subjectively constructed sources of information" (Daniels, 2010), and therefore had been rarely used in academic publications featuring ethnographic methods up until recently. However, she also argues that photographs can attempt to "bridge subjective and objective understanding" and "to stimulate new ways of thinking about social life across cultures" (ibid.). During my photographic surveys, I tried to remain as unselective as possible about what I had in frame and therefore gave preference to wide-angle shots that were the closest to reflecting the rooms in their entirety and made sure to cover all possible corners in different scales.

This method, however, left me with the records of observed reality that turned out to be far more complex than the controlled amount of "clean" data that architects normally study when they perform a preparatory survey for a regeneration project. Following the standard procedure for architectural research, I started with the plans redrawing: by taking the standard Wakamiya plans, I filled them with the details of every case study, constantly cross-checking the photographs I took during the visits. In ordinary circumstances, architects do not include trivial objects like shoe boxes, plastic buckets, or kitchen rugs in their plans because these elements appear to be temporary and are not supposed to influence the design process, but with the existing apartments, they have a bigger role of making up the reality of everyday life of the inhabitants. However, with every trivial detail, it became harder it was to determine to what extent I had to reproduce what I saw. Was it necessary to include shampoo bottles and stacks of newspapers, or should I stop at the level of rice cookers and make-up pouches? While trying to distinguish between the fleeting consumable products and the more permanent objects and structures, some of these apparently useless mundane details started hinting at a way to understand the incompatibility of the original design with the current tenants' lifestyle patterns.

When deciphering the logic behind piles of personal belongings in the photographs to transfer them into the floor plans, I realized that, unlike more spacious commercial apartments, danchi units had a minimum of conventional furniture and many DIY imitations instead. Every surveyed apartment had some unusual structures or systems that could not be described as a single object or a single piece of conventionally used furniture. It could be a combination of several elements of different scales and origins put together by the inhabitant that imitated the functions of a certain store-bought furniture typology. Just in Endo's apartment, there are more than 30 structures of this sort: shelves made from cardboard (Fig. 3.25), bed, and stools put together with pieces of cheap wood (Fig. 3.24), bathroom platform made from concrete blocks and foam boards (Fig. 3.20). Some of these structures partially consist of conventional furniture that was intentionally misused, such as bookshelves repurposed into shoe storage (Kimura, Endo Fig. 3.18), laundry-drying poles used for hanging decorations (Endo Fig. 3.22), and a school desk used as a kitchen surface (Akane).

The process of redrawing and categorizing devices made me remember the research of Wajirō Kon (1888–1973), a professor of architecture at Waseda University in Tokyo and a pioneer of fieldwork in urban studies and architecture, famous for his hand-drawn surveys of the material culture of the 1920s Japan. His career began by documenting Japanese farmhouses, but in 1923 he started redrawing improvised shelters built by people who had lost their homes to the Great Kanto Earthquake. From that moment on, Kon's choice of studied objects became more unusual: he became interested in the process of Japan's transformation into a modern country and started observing ordinary people's lifestyles and behavior (Daniell, 2012). A graphic catalog of all belongings of a newlywed couple, a survey of how many waitresses wear Western clothes as opposed to those who wear kimono and even a list of different crack patterns on ceramic bowls in a number of restaurants in Tokyo—it seemed no aspect of city life could be too trivial for Kon's research (Figs. 3.36 and 3.37). He published most of his sketches and findings in the book *Kōgengaku* (Modernology) in 1930 (Kon & Yoshida, 1930).

Comparing all my plans (see Figs. 3.26, 3.29, 3.32, and 3.36) and photographs, I confirmed that each apartment had intricate systems of impermanent objects that were intuitively assembled by the residents as a solution to some inconsistency between the original planning and their needs. Surprisingly, many similar unconventional structures could be spotted in the published photographs of Yasuda in her study of UR rental units (Yasuda, 2002). Unlike Yasuda's more generic notion of deliberately chosen "options," I felt that these larger systems of objects involved a more complicated composition than a single item but also seemed to be put together by their users in a subconscious manner, sometimes almost accidentally, but their essential trait is the act of solving some inadequacies of the original apartment design.

Reflecting on their functional nature, I tried to develop a method for identifying and categorizing these "devices," similar to Wajirō Kon's studies. In homage, I named my method "devicology"—a taxonomical study of ad hoc solutions invented by the danchi tenants to enhance the standard apartments.

After a few months of studying the plans and the photographs, I decided to revisit Endo and her neighbors to test a more indirect way

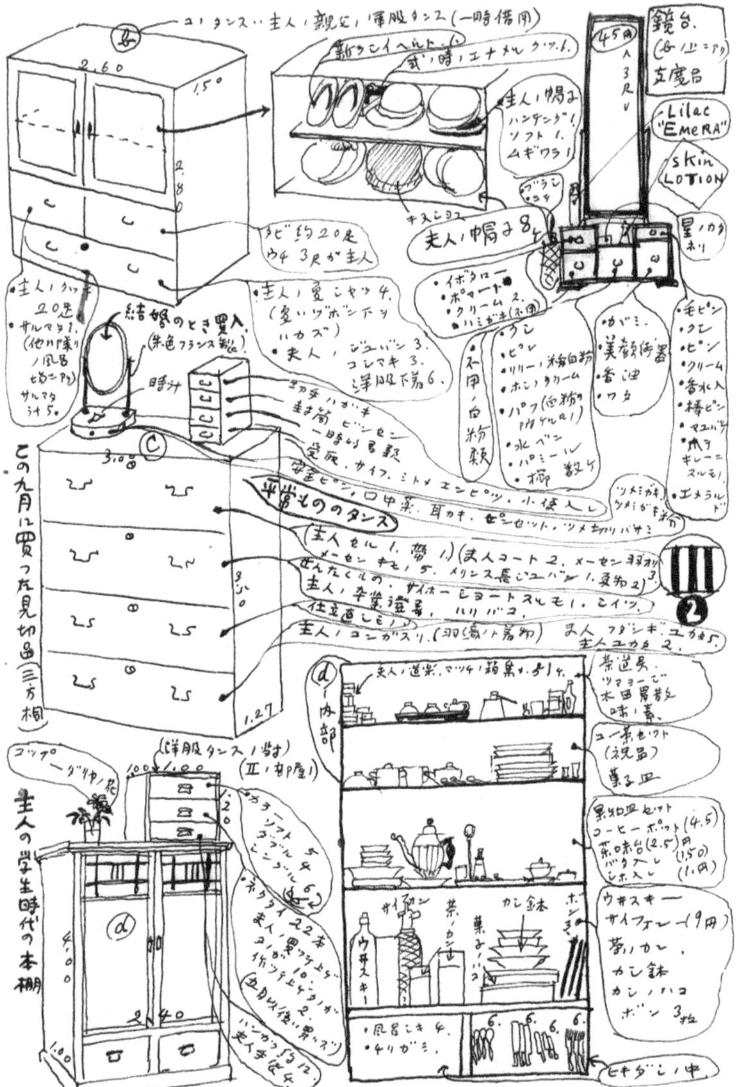

Fig. 3.36 Fieldwork drawing by Wajirō Kon (*Source* Courtesy of Kōgakuin University Wajirō Kon Archive)

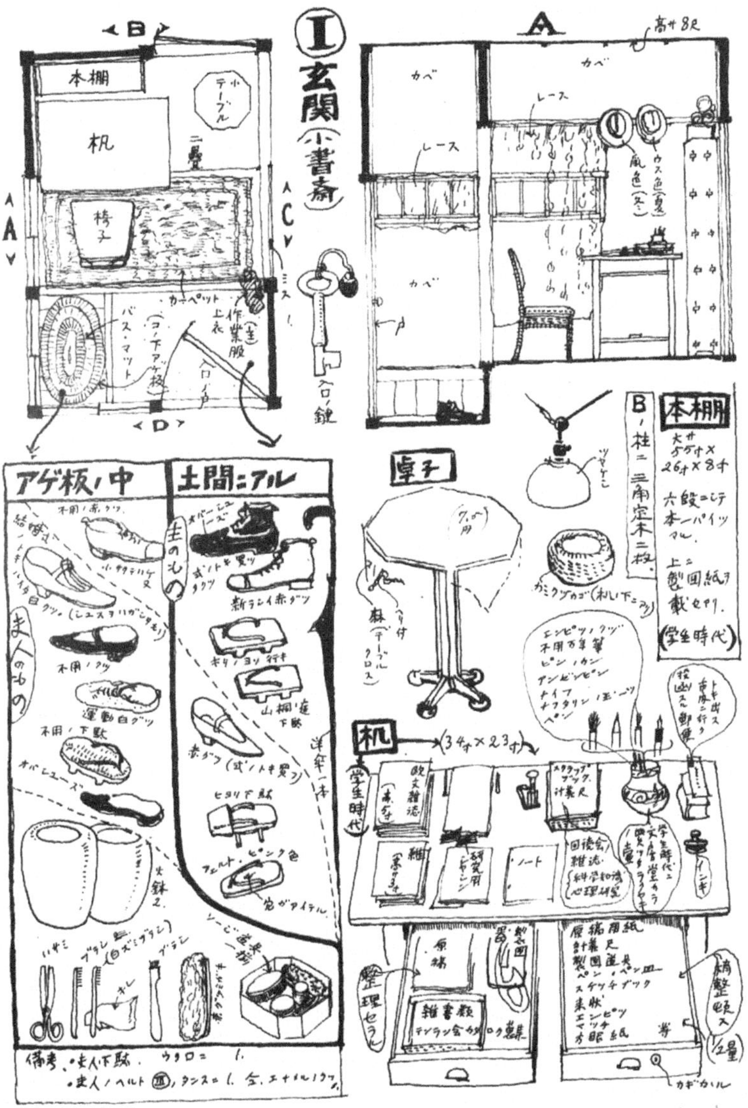

Fig. 3.37 Fieldwork drawing by Wajirō Kon (*Source* Courtesy of Kōgakuin University Wajirō Kon Archive)

of obtaining information by abandoning the sitting interview format and going for an apartment tour instead.

The Devices

We returned in late March. Endo opened the door and smiled at us, holding her dog by the collar to stop him from escaping. "Oh, this person is so happy to see you again!" She looked even more energetic than before, wearing a thin, brightly colored sweater instead of the multi-layered puffy outfit and thick woolen shawl she wore in December. While we were having tea together in the living room, I was less affected by my initial impression of chaos and saw within it a new order. When we finished our tea, I asked Endo to take us on a complete tour of all three rooms and comment on her belongings. The focus on the particular features of her furniture, rather than her personal opinion about living in danchi or complaints, made Endo more enthusiastic and talkative; as she was proudly showcasing her possessions, I became more confident in the hypothesis that I had developed before—discovering the resident's devices and their characteristics might be able to tell us more than words.

Technotowers and Kitchen Islands

> Technotowers—vertical structures containing working appliances, minimizing space occupied by bulky technology, and keeping easy access to all the appliances.
> Type T1—Fridge Towers, fridge-based.
> Type T2—Technoracks, light frame-based.
>
> Kitchen Islands—additional volumes in the kitchen, providing more surfaces for cooking and accommodating kitchen appliances on the same level as the original kitchen surface.
> Type K1—Cupboard Islands, cupboard- or shelf-based.
> Type K2—Cooking Islands, table-based or desk-based.

We started in the DK, where most of the freestanding objects were clustered around the refrigerator in the corner next to the bathroom entrance. There were three vertical stacks: the fridge with a microwave on top, a larger freezer crowned with an electric oven, and a metal rack with another oven specifically for fish on the top shelf, while lower sections contained laundry liquids, bath towels, pet food, old newspapers, and other objects (Fig. 3.22). The rack completely blocked the access to the freezer, and the pet bowls on the floor made it difficult to open the fridge, but Endo had a system. "Easy!" she said, and rolled the wheeled rack into the bathroom entrance, opened the freezer, and lifted the plastic sheet that she put inside to "stop the cold from leaving." Then she put everything back and pushed the pet bowls under the rack with her foot so she could open the fridge. It was hard to argue with the efficiency. These Technotowers developed because the dramatic increase in home cooking appliances since the 1950s created a need for more kitchen surfaces than were provided in the original danchi design. Moreover, as technology developed, the sizes of the kitchen appliances themselves increased, and simply outgrew modest danchi DK spaces. I saw similar fridge-based towers and movable racks containing blenders, mixers, ovens, and rice cookers in Kimura's (Fig. 3.30), Akane's and Hitoshi's units. Kimura and Akane also used horizontal structures together with towers, sort of Kitchen Islands based on cupboards or ordinary tables usually put in the middle of the room, but Endo seemed to prioritize flexibility over accessibility with her compact movable rack. Ironically, none of the tenants used DK for having meals in a way it was originally intended; with all the necessary storage there was so little space, that chairs wouldn't fit it.

Hanging Systems

— Suspended structures of varying shapes, maximizing easy-access storage and space for laundry drying and sometimes achieving porous separation between living spaces.
Type H1—Grids, lattice-based.
Type H2—Pole Systems, stick-base.
Type H3—Hooks, attachment to an existing structure.

Smaller kitchen utensils hung on plastic and metal rods that spanned above our heads in various directions. It was a rather complicated system: some rested on lintels; some had rubber nozzles attached, pressed into the walls; several rods were shorter and were tied to the longer ones for stability (Fig. 3.22). Endo explained that the rods' original use was for drying laundry and kitchen rugs. Most people in Japan use their balconies for such purposes, but here, the balconies are too narrow; there is barely enough space for a tiny washing machine and some potted plants. Another set of rods was used to hang bags and clothes in the three-tatami room.

The rods weren't the only suspended elements in the apartment. Frying pans, plastic buckets, and toilet paper rolls hung onto the gas pipe in the kitchen with wires and cords, and a similar system was used in the bathroom, where there was no space for storage cabinets. In the living room, decorative elements were hanging from the walls, metal rods, and the ceiling. At the entrance, a metal grille hanging from the lintel served as hook-type storage for umbrellas. In front of it was a piece of a wooden fence with bags, fans, decorative masks, and fake plants hooked onto it. When we were discussing this particular accumulation, I asked if Endo had always liked collecting *kawaii* things. She thought for a moment and said, "Well, I have always liked it, but in my childhood years, I only played outside. And after I got married and gave birth … I just couldn't indulge in personal whims when I had a family. Now, I finally have time and money for myself. It feels good to own a lot of different things." Some toys still had their original packaging and even price tags, suggesting that Endo's collections weren't about the objects themselves but the luxury of having them. She displayed her trophies everywhere she could, thereby reducing the space available for everyday necessities, so the Hanging Systems came in handy.

Genkan Shapers

— Shoe-storing devices separating the entrance and the kitchen, providing shoe storage in the context of the small original entrance size, and hiding the uncomfortable proximity of the entrance door to the kitchen.
Type G1—Entrance Blocks, cupboard-based or shelf-based.
Type G2—Entrance Racks, light frame-based.

The repurposed fence was, in fact, the top of an impressive furniture and organizer combination. The base-level consisted of a traditional bookshelf next to a *karabokkusu* unit, both acting as shoe racks. Together, with many small plastic containers on top, they formed a tall screen that helped to hide the proximity of the *genkan*—perceived as a "dirty" area in Japanese houses—to the kitchen and bathroom while providing enough shoe storage. When I visited Kimura, I saw a functionally identical device at precisely the same location: a narrow, old-fashioned cupboard repurposed for shoe storage, combined with a plastic document organizer of a similar height and a lace curtain hanging from the lintel to create a continuous screen. Hitoshi had a tall chest of drawers at the entrance, but Akane preferred to avoid bulky furniture and used an open metal frame shoe rack with a translucent bead curtain hanging from the *kamoi* (Fig. 3.34). Finding a wooden factory-made shoe rack that could fit into such a small space must have been close to impossible, especially one tall enough to function as a screen, but danchi residents overcome the problem through the hybrid Genkan Shaper scheme—cheap, easily modifiable, and open to further additions as necessary.

Sorting Towers

— Vertical structures containing personal belongings, saving tatami from the possibility of damage by heavy Western furniture, maximizing storage, relieving planning stress caused by the absence of apartment ownership, and uncertainty about the future.
Type S1—Sorting Blocks, cupboard- or shelf-based.
Type S2—Sorting Racks, light frame-based.
Type S3—Free Stacks, arranged without base structure.

For storage in the living room, Endo used a mix of conventional *karabokkusu* shelf units, cheap stationery organizers, and her inventions with wood and cardboard. Visiting other apartments revealed two points that set these storage solutions apart from conventional furnishings: tower-like shapes and flexibility, that is to say, the ability to modify, move, or dispose of the objects without much expense. For younger Akane and Hitoshi, these Sorting Towers played the role of the main commodity-containment system in the apartments, while elderly Endo and Kimura tended to combine them with heavy conventional chests, creating "second walls" that Yasuda defined in her research (Yasuda, 2002). Indeed, the height of the "second walls" increased with age of the owner, or maybe simply the number of years the user lived in the apartment. Sorting Towers, as compound elements of "second walls" and as stand-alone phenomena, is a device that populates the highest number of rooms in every studied apartment. Sometimes growing on top of ordinary chests and cupboards, sometimes manifesting in plastic and metal racks or piles of boxes and baskets, Sorting Towers accommodate both decorative objects and everyday items, from books and CDs to cosmetics and Buddhist prayer utensils. Just as with Technotowers, the verticality can be explained by the limited floor areas, while the need for flexibility likely arises from the uncertain status of danchi residents as social housing monthly tenants. The fact that the municipal government doesn't allow self-repairs and that residents can be evicted for breaking the rules contributes to a temporary-stay mentality, which most likely compels Endo and her neighbors to invent storage devices and avoid investing in long-term spatial solutions. This limbo condition induces a fear of "touching" the floors, especially fragile tatami, and the walls with bulky furniture.

Platforms

— Horizontal podium-like structures, solving various shortcomings of the original design, especially connected to elderly tenants' needs.
Type P1—Levelling Platforms, usually based on wooden structures.
Type P2—Stepping Platforms, floor-raising.
Type P3—Sorting Platforms, ceiling lintel-based.

Toward the end of our tour with Endo, I noticed a few platform-shaped devices that didn't fit into any of the preceding categories. These were explicitly horizontal, and rather than providing storage, they adjusted floor or seat levels, going against the dominant logic of space-saving verticality of the other devices. When showing us the bathroom, Endo proudly pointed to a bright green board set on top of eight cinder blocks on the concrete floor (Fig. 3.20) and said, "I made this myself. I am getting old, so this helps me step into the bathtub." This heroic 70-year-old woman could indeed be proud of having carried eight concrete blocks up four flights of stairs. Just like the bathroom stepping Platform, the napping and sleeping beds as well as three tiny stools in the living room, all Endo's skillful creations, provided a comfortable level for her knees, impossible to achieve with store-bought Western furniture. Endo's age is her main reason to negotiate the original design, which didn't take into account elderly needs, but her younger neighbors deal with their share of design incompatibilities, too. Hitoshi put a similar stepping board in the bathroom for his children, and Akane installed a *tsuppari-tana* tension shelf between the *kamoi* over the entrance to gain additional storage for an ever-growing collection of her son's sports shoes that didn't fit into the rack at the entrance anymore (Fig. 3.34).

Quantifying Devicology

The Six Categories and 15 Types

Initially, I categorized the devices I found in the photographs and the second round of apartment visits according to their functional aspects, and six categories were thus formed: Genkan Shapers, Kitchen Islands, Technotowers, Sorting Towers, Hanging Systems, and Platforms. Genkan Shapers and Kitchen Islands are room-specific and could only be found at the entrance and in the DK, respectively, while the other four categories can be located anywhere in the apartments.

Apart from the function, a form was also considered to define the categories. For example, the main function of Hanging Systems and Sorting Towers is storing personal belongings without occupying too much of the floor area, but the formal characteristics of Hanging Systems can allow them to perform as space-dividing screens as well.

However, these categories were too broad to explain some particular individual cases. Examples of Kimura using an ordinary dining table exclusively as a cooking surface and stand for kitchen appliances and Akane setting up a school desk for the same function did not fit into my initial Kitchen Island category, which assumed a cupboard or some other closed volume with storage possibilities as a base. To make the final taxonomy reflect more nuances of Publicly Operated danchi reality, I introduced from two to three types in every category, showing the varying grades of flexibility—the possibility of the devices to be partially transformed or moved to a different place.

Flexibility plays a crucial role in devices. As mentioned above, all of the surveyed apartments were rented under monthly social housing contracts that could be terminated by the government if any rules are broken or financial conditions aren't met, so despite already living in Wakamiya for years, the tenants had a "temporary-stay" mentality and tried to avoid placing bulky furniture in their rooms in case they will be evicted. In the interviews, several people from the community meeting and Kimura mentioned nervously that if they somehow damage the walls or the tatami mats, they will be held responsible by the municipality. This fear drives the residents to make sure that they will be able to transport or dispose of their belongings easily without leaving any visible traces in their unit if they happen to move out someday. Therefore, a major motivation for device creation seems to originate from the user's wish to replace heavier and more expensive conventional furniture with something lighter and cheaper with the same function.

In the resulting Devicology table, the vertical stripes correspond to the six big functional categories, while the horizontal stripes assign subtypes of flexibility levels from one to three (Fig. 3.38). For the first three "bulkier" functional categories (Genkan Shapers, Kitchen Islands, and

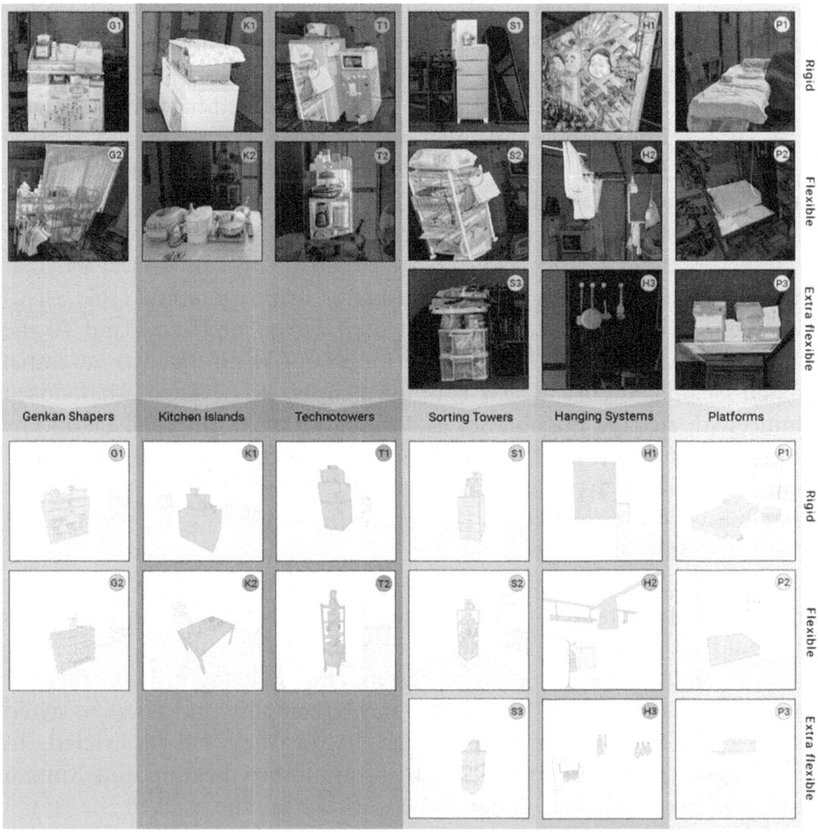

Fig. 3.38 Devices taxonomy table

Technotowers), no examples could be found which fit into the extra flexible (3) type. This relative lack of flexibility is attributed to the size of the devices as well as their particular purposes being defined by their spatial location: Genkan Shapers must be attached to the entrance of the apartment, and Kitchen Islands are in close proximity to the cooking surfaces.

Putting together the six categories and the three groups, 15 types of devices are thus identified. I assigned a letter from the corresponding functional category (G for Genkan Shapers, K for Kitchen Islands, etc.) and a number of the corresponding flexibility level (one for rigid, two for flexible, and three for extra flexible) to add to the name of every type for more efficient use in the graphs later.

Flexibility and Customization Graph

All the devices from the surveyed case studies are categorized now, but it is necessary to understand how they compare to each other and what qualities they have in order to use them in the future evaluation of the living environment in the apartments. At first glance, the most characteristic aspects of the danchi devices that set them apart from conventional furniture are the higher grades of their flexibility and customization.

The amount of effort required to create a fully customized device such as a DIY bed frame (Endo, Type P1) or a cinder block bathroom stepping board (Endo, Type P2) is very high, which highlights the utmost necessity of such interventions on the part of the tenants and thus the severity of the underlying problem they were trying to solve. However, not all the devices require so much labor to set up—some are intentionally misused conventional furniture or partly consist of it or are made of only a couple of stacked elements, if the required adaptation of the original apartment design to the tenant's preferred lifestyle is simple enough to achieve. My interviews showed that the users were not consciously aware of their DIY creations and the functional intentions behind them, so it's safe to assume that in such financially constricting situations, no one would purposefully spend more creative effort, thought, and budget than a design problem would minimally require. Therefore, the higher the customization level of a single device and the resources spent for its assembly, the graver the inconsistency of the original interior to the users' needs in a particular function that the device neutralizes.

To see if there is any relationship between devices' customization and flexibility levels, I decided to make a simple graph with these values on two orthogonal axes. Every device type received my rating for both the customization and the flexibility axes in the interval between −3 and 3 and was marked in the corresponding point on the graph (Fig. 3.39). The rating domain is chosen for the sake of simplicity which would help the methodology be more consistent between observers. Of course, the flexibility and customization values I assigned to each device type depend on my subjective evaluation, but I assume the device types' visual relationship on the graph should look similar for a chosen apartment typology even if other architects assign the values. In any case, it is enough to use the same set values as a starting point for all the graphs for case studies with the same standard plan. The final goal is to see a qualitative pattern for comparison and evaluation, not a precise number on the graph.

The enlargements of the circular area up to three times around every type's point show in how many case studies out of four this device was found. The devices' prevalence in surveyed case studies is added to the graph to check if there are problems that are common for all tenants

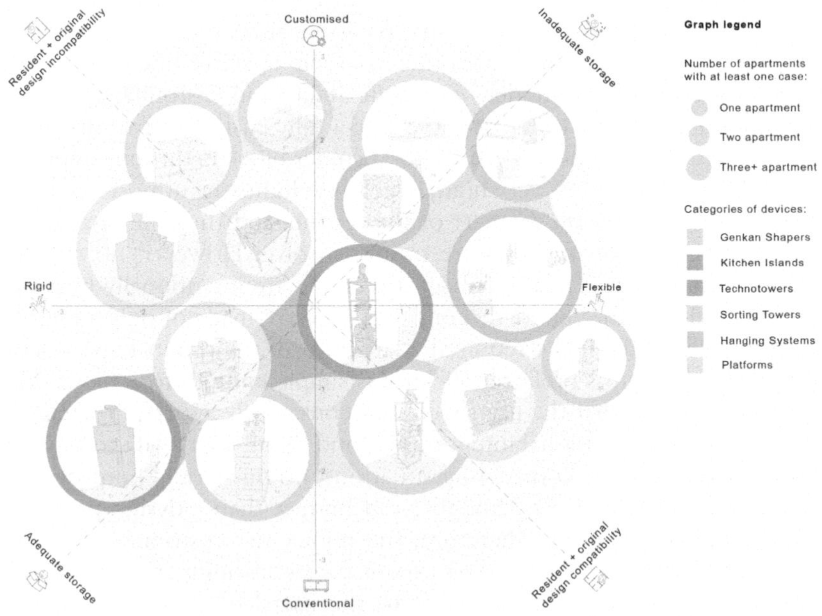

Fig. 3.39 Devicology graph for all 15 device types

regardless of their lifestyle. While my study was limited by four apartment visits and cannot give us any big-scale patterns, but if this methodology is adopted for larger surveys, such as Yasuda's, the prevalence of a particular device can be a useful tool to look for signs of widespread standard plan problems.

The final graph for the four apartments is ready, and we can witness the relationship between customization and flexibility and decipher the meaning of devices' different positions. The below-zero customization areas under the Flexibility axis display fairly "ordinary" devices that can be often encountered in owner-occupied housing in Japan due to floor area limitations coming from high land prices, so they cannot be a clue to any specificity of social housing apartments in danchi.

However, if we look at the upper left quadrant, the types get more and more ingenious. This part of the graph contains devices that are highly inflexible (bulky, requiring physical resources) and very customized (almost fully hand-made, requiring creative thought) at the same time, which means these objects are intended to resolve serious incompatibilities of the user and the original design. Examples of Endo building her own low bed and stools, and a bathroom stepping platform to appropriate the original design that didn't take into account the needs of the elderly, are all found in this quadrant.

The upper right quadrant with more flexibility and an elevated amount of customization has devices that require considerably less physical effort to make than the bulkier types of the left quadrant; devices like Hooks and Pole Systems are cheap and easy to install and can be commonly found in commercial apartments, but their concentration in a certain spot in danchi interiors always indicates a severe lack of storage space with easy everyday access. Endo's cramped DK was filled with Hanging Systems of this sort, sometimes so densely installed and interconnected that it got difficult to identify them as independent devices.

To highlight the patterns of the upper left and right quadrants, we can add two diagonal axes—Design Compatibility and Storage Adequacy, respectively. By projecting points of the devices on these axes, we will be able to see individual indexes of these values per each type of device. The graph gave us a lot of insight into the meaning behind various devices, but our main task is to evaluate the quality of the apartment as a whole, with every device included. Let's test the graph for a selected case study.

Application Method

I chose the apartment of Endo to test the graph method, as it contained the highest number of devices out of all four apartments. Moreover, my personal impression was that it was the least comfortable one to live in. Still, Endo kept telling me she didn't want to change or add anything because she "got used to it a long time ago." As an architect, I wanted to see if Devicology graphing could hint at the necessity of refurbishing or renovating the apartment without relying on verbal sources.

Using the Devicology taxonomy table as a reference, I could find 47 devices of 11 different types in my photographs of Endo's rooms. It was impossible to mark all those devices on the plan: many of them were located above the section height or turned out too small when drawn in projection.

I had to develop a sectioned perspective of the apartment to properly illustrate the situation (Fig. 3.40). Forty-seven is an approximate number of devices, as I could not inspect the three-tatami storage room in its entirety since the entrance was too cramped. Endo's apartment doesn't have any Kitchen Islands, so all the devices fit into the five remaining categories.

Let's take the initial general value graph (Fig. 3.39) and adapt it to this particular case study by removing the types not present in the apartment (Fig. 3.41, step 1). Then, we should add the device prevalence data by enlarging each type point's radius by the number of instances found in the apartment (Fig. 3.41, step 2).

The resulting graph shows that the biggest accumulation of Endo's devices is gathered around the upper right quadrant. However, the device points are too dispersed to determine the precise pattern. We now need to simplify the graph by finding the average data points to get a clearer picture.

To do this, we should calculate the weighted arithmetic mean by standard formula for every functional category having more than one type on the graph—Sorting Towers, Platforms, and Hanging Systems. The ordinary arithmetic mean cannot be used for this graph since some device types contribute more to the final average than others because of the difference in the number of devices found for every type.

Applying the formula to calculate the *x*-coordinate (Flexibility coordinate) of an average point on the graph for Sorting Towers, we sum the products of *x*-coordinates of every point corresponding to every type (S1,

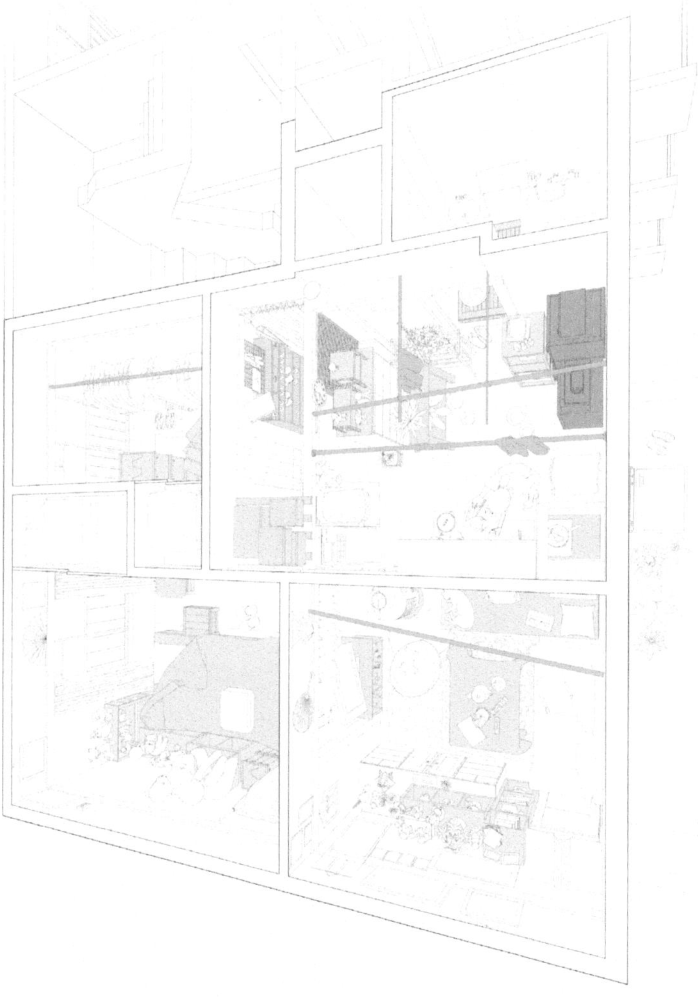

Fig. 3.40 Sectioned perspective of Endo's apartment with devices marked in corresponding colors

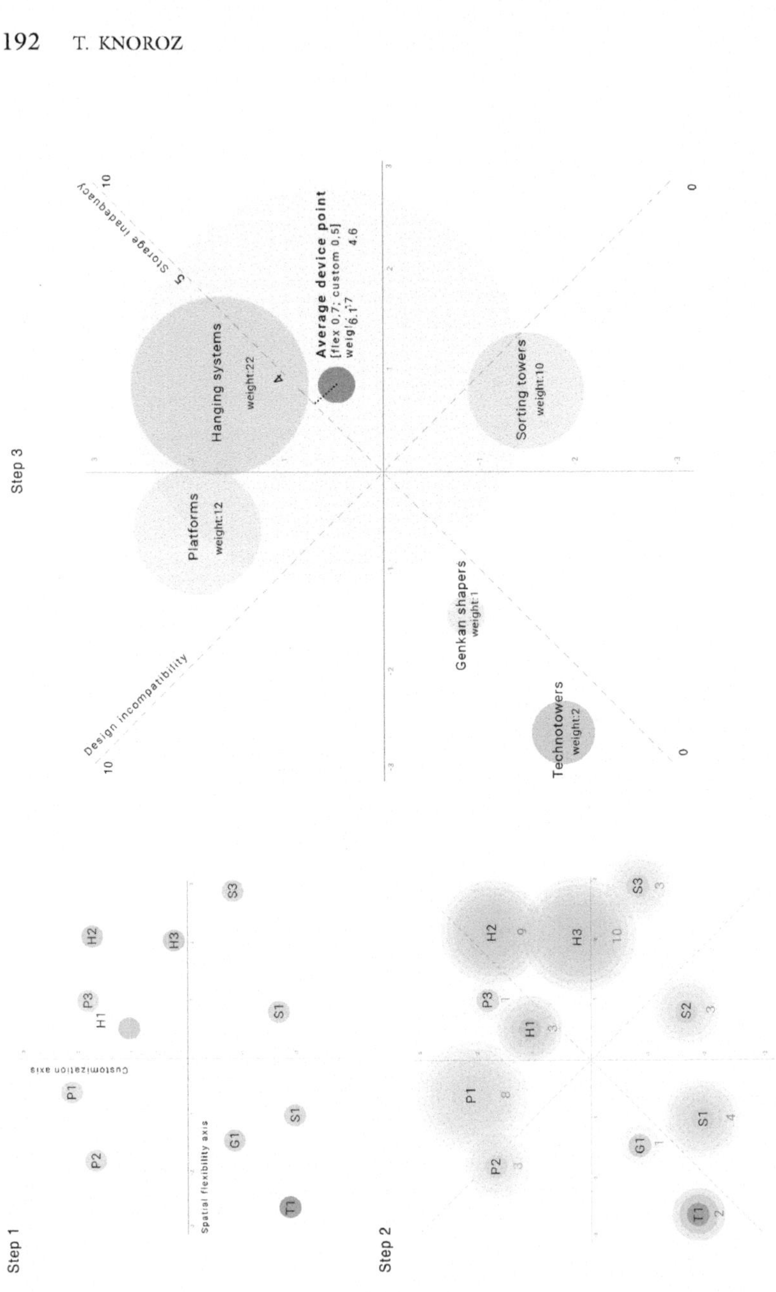

Fig. 3.41 Calculating Devicology graph for Endo's apartment

S2, and S3) and their weight (the number of devices per each type) and divide this sum by the total number of devices in the Sorting Towers category. This procedure will be the same for *y*-coordinates (Customization coordinates) and should be repeated for Platforms and Hanging Systems. Since Technotowers and Genkan Shapers each have only one type-point on the graph, these points are already at their weighted arithmetic mean points.

After the average points for every category are found, we can calculate the weighted arithmetic mean for the entire graph by applying the same formula to the five categories' average points (Fig. 3.41, step 3). The average device point's location is in the upper right quadrant, which shows that Endo tends to have a significant problem with storage space: the projection on the Storage Adequacy axis gives us 6.1 out of 10 total points for storage inadequacy, 10 points being the worst case possible within this grading system.

We got a lower number on the Design Incompatibility axis—4.6 out of 10, but we must keep in mind a big number of Platforms present in this case study (12 in total), that are because of their purposes and bulkiness are a strong sign of the original design and tenant's lifestyle incompatibility, so it is important to have all the categories' weights mapped on the final graph not to lose this information.

Endo might not have enough architectural experience to envision how her apartment could be improved on her own, but the nature and the number of her subconscious device creations tell us that she could benefit from total storage redesign and several compatibility fixes. Moreover, the visual information from the perspective drawing (Fig. 3.40) shows that the kitchen has the biggest accumulation of devices and is also used the most, judging by the daily paths diagram (Fig. 3.26), and thus should be the top priority for renovation.

Summarizing Devicology

I presented Devicology as a method for categorization and analysis of interior photographic data and other field observations, bypassing the at times subjective and inconsistent nature of verbal information collected during interviews with the inhabitants of danchi. Devicology analyses the nature of devices as an observational tool in order to arrive at empirical conclusions regarding the living conditions of the tenants and identify shortfalls of standardized apartment plans in Japanese postwar social housing.

The avoidance of complaints among danchi residents can look like an issue specific to Japan, but interviews in Europe can get similarly difficult because not everyone can objectively valuate their home from a planner's perspective. Ordinary people perceive their living spaces as a given, rarely questioning their architectural potential, and are not used to specific vocabulary and ways of thinking common to professionals dealing with housing. This might be the reason why not many architects engage in fieldwork for mass housing projects: inhabitants cannot provide them with the verbal information they can rely on directly, and there are no existing guidelines on how non-interview-based anthropological research can be effectively used for architectural purposes.

The primary assumption of Devicology is that the motivation for devices' creation seems to originate from the wish to replace heavier and more expensive conventional furniture with lighter and cheaper alternatives in a limiting spatial, temporal, and legal situation, so a high number of devices in a dwelling can be considered symptomatic of the user's disadvantageous housing situation.

The method relies on the categorization of devices into six distinct categories. Individual devices are then plotted against Flexibility and Customization axes. Since the process partly depends on the bias of the architect who places devices on the axes, it is important to be consistent with the values and perform many experimental surveys before implementing the method. Ideally, several independent teams should take a set of the danchi apartments with the same standard plan and assign their own initial values within a chosen domain to all devices before proceeding with the calculations for every case study. Then the teams would compare the results, see whether they show similar patterns or not, and decide on a stabilized set of values to be used in the future.

In order to define which indexes of the two diagonal axes are critical and show the need for renovation, the same research should be repeated on a set of well-designed newer commercial apartments with a higher amount of square meters per person and more freedom to change the environment. However, the strength of this method is that the single data unit is not an individual apartment but a single device. Therefore, the technique is scalable and has the potential for a holistic application: the evaluation can be carried out for one apartment but also for one danchi building or for an entire neighborhood or New Town, showing the extent of a problem and indexes of Design Compatibility and Storage Adequacy on different levels.

Conclusion

Through Chapters 1 and 2, we could trace how the traditional Japanese interiors and living patterns that originally required flexible boundaries and breathable exteriors were transformed and adapted to fit into the rigid limits of solid walls in reinforced-concrete danchi. Thanks to this architectural revolution, the Japanese government, along with the industrial corporations, architects, and social engineers, succeeded in creating the "new middle class" of postwar Japan by designing and mass-producing the danchi housing that served as the main distributor of modern lifestyle with its excessive consumption habits to the entire population in a short period of time. While in the beginning Japanese architectural community was very invested in high-rise apartment building design and the first experiments of the JHC in the late 1950s, they soon became disillusioned and abandoned the mass-housing discourse in the 1960s, engaging with the issues of town planning and public buildings, leaving the matter of danchi entirely up to the government and corporations.

The specificity of postwar Japanese housing policy with its pronounced orientation toward the mass homeownership, required danchi to become a temporary step in the "housing ladder" of an individual family toward its own detached house, so the original plans were never expected to be spacious enough to accommodate families throughout their lifetimes, fit any non-standard family configurations or respond to the needs of elderly tenants.

Since the number of housing units surpassed the number of families in Japan in 1970, the public attention shifted from the quantity toward the quality of residences, and many people started choosing commercial apartments over outdated danchi rental options. However, due to the economic recession that started in 1991, danchi districts were not fully replaced with the new housing, as originally intended, and are still used as either middle-class rental or government-subsidized social housing with a high proportion of elderly residents.

Although there are rarely any structural issues even after the major earthquakes, the buildings are gradually dilapidating, and the new wave of tenants has difficulties using the original plans. There is an evident need to renovate them as valuable housing stock, especially because there haven't been any new social housing built in Japan for many years now, and the land with a large amount of greenery and public spaces, like in most danchi districts, is scarce. While there are emerging renovation projects targeting young couples as potential tenants, there haven't been any attempts at seriously regenerating the already inhabited buildings of the danchi used as social housing due to the lack of available funding.

In an attempt to envision, what a potential interior renovation could use as a design basis, I conducted fieldwork, described in the last chapter. After interviewing several residents from Wakamiya Danchi social housing, I realized they could not tell what kind of improvement they wanted because of psychological barriers. Abandoning the verbal transcripts and using the photographic surveys of their apartments instead, I discovered and defined "devices"—DIY structures consisting of several objects or pieces of furniture in the interior created by the user to "appropriate" the plans and answer their basic living needs which were not met by the original design.

It would be hard to find so much resourcefulness in commercial rental or owner-occupied apartments, even within the same social class, because there are fewer legal and spatial limitations. Beginning as an examination of behavior patterns in several apartments, Devicology has a potential to become a study of the collective unconsciousness of people living in the same conditions with the same set of rules but with different needs. From my videos and photographs, I could count more than 30 devices in Endo's and Kimura's apartments (they both have been living in Wakamiya for 15 years) and between 10 and 15 for Akane and Hitoshi (they moved in around five and eight years ago, respectively). These numbers alone are not enough to precisely evaluate the danchi living conditions, but considering the particulars of the devices, one may go far beyond the verbal data from the interviews and determine if any kind of interior renovations need to be done. The more heavily customized the devices, the more obstacles encountered in the original design. The greater the intended flexibility, the greater the struggle with storage inadequacy and the limbo mentality.

Apart from serving as a tool of standard apartment quality evaluation, Devicology can also inspire architects to consider micro-scale interventions that facilitate and encourage device creation by providing a customizable framework that takes into account qualities of the most common types of devices and helps organize and de-clutter the interiors. In the context of social housing with limited funding, this sort of renovation may be more effective than a full refurbishment.

Perhaps there is another reason that danchi inhabitants, especially the elderly, are willing to invest so much creativity and energy into their interiors: they tend to spend more time than average indoors because of fading community ties and the stigmatization of older apartments. Endo confessed that she worried about her elderly single neighbors staying inside for too long, so she developed the habit of checking the number of newspapers in their mailboxes every day to make sure they weren't piling up. Some elderly tenants are too embarrassed or tired to face the world and refuse to go out for weeks and even months, willingly self-isolating long before the time of pandemic lockdowns. More and more, regional governments and UR are launching outdoor space and community regeneration projects to tackle the problem of residents' alienation.

But isn't this where we are all headed? Ever soaring rental prices in big cities around the world are forcing young people to move into tiny apartments, the absence of long-term employment options and the normalization of nomadic lifestyles are exacerbating the feeling of disconnectedness and temporality of our homes, and pessimistic post-pandemic scenarios describe a future in which we all spend most of our time at home. Soon enough, the catalog of "devices" may be enriched and extended in other apartment types, so we should learn from the danchi dwellers who are already so well adept at dealing with these challenging conditions.

References

Caramellino, G., & De Pieri, F. (2019). The emergence of the micro scale in historical research on modern housing. In A. Kockelkorn & N. Zschocke (Eds.), *Productive universals specific situations* (pp. 295–313). Sternberg Press.

Daniell, T. (2012). Just looking: The origins of the street observation society. In T. Fujimori et al., *Terunobu Fujimori: Architect* (pp. 210–221). Hatje Cantz.

Daniels, I. (2010). *The Japanese house: Material culture in the modern home*. Berg.

Hirayama, Y., & Ronald, R. (Eds.). (2006). *Housing and social transition in Japan* (1st ed.). Routledge.

Izuhara, M. (2000). *Change and housing in post-war Japanese society: The experiences of older women*. Routledge.

Kon, W., & Yoshida, K. (1930). *Modernologio (Kogengaku)*. Shun-yodo.
Miller, D. (1998). *A theory of shopping*. Polity Press.
Moeran, B. (1984). Individual, group and Seishin: Japan's internal cultural debate. *Man, 19*(2), 252–266.
Murakami, S. (2018). Danchi highlight complexity of Japan's interculturalism. *Japan Times*. https://features.japantimes.co.jp/danchi/
Ōnishi, N. (2017). A generation in Japan faces a lonely death. *The New York Times*. https://www.nytimes.com/2017/11/30/world/asia/japan-lonely-deaths-the-end.html
Ozaki, R., & Rees Lewis, J. (2006). Boundaries and the meaning of space: A study of Japanese house plans. *Environment and Planning D, 24*(1), 91–104.
Waswo, A. (2002). *Housing in postwar Japan—A social history*. Routledge.
Yasuda, A. (2002). Kōdan chintai seikatsu. *10+1, 26*, 85–101.
Yasuda, A., & Nobuaki, F. (2000). Kōdan jūtaku kyojū-sha no seikatsu sutairu ni kansuru kenkyū. *Summaries of Technical Papers of Annual Meeting of Architectural Institute of Japan, 2000*, 99–100.

Index

T. Knoroz, *Dissecting the Danchi*,
https://doi.org/10.1007/978-981-16-8460-9

The manufacturer's authorised representative in the EU is Springer Nature Customer Service Centre GmbH, Europaplatz 3, 69115 Heidelberg, Germany. If you have any concerns regarding our products, please contact ProductSafety@springernature.com

Printed and bound by CPI Group (UK) Ltd, Croydon, CR0 4YY

01/10/2026

02226249-0002